An End to
PANIC

Breakthrough Techniques for
Overcoming Panic Disorder

Elke Zuercher-White, Ph.D.

New Harbinger Publications, Inc.

Publisher's Note

This publication is designed to provide accurate and authoritative information in regard to the subject matter covered. It is sold with the understanding that the publisher is not engaged in rendering pyschological, financial, legal, or other professional services. If expert assistance or counseling is needed, the services of a competent professional should be sought.

Copyright © 1995 Elke Zuercher-White
 New Harbinger Publications, Inc.
 5674 Shattuck Avenue
 Oakland, CA 94609

Cover design by SHELBY DESIGNS AND ILLUSTRATES.
Text design by Tracy Marie Powell.

Distributed in the U.S.A. by Publishers Group West; in Canada by Raincoast Books; in Great Britain by Airlift Book Company, Ltd.; in South Africa by Real Books, Ltd.; in Australia by Boobook; in New Zealand by Tandem Press.

Library of Congress Catalog Card Number: 95-69486

ISBN 1-57224-034-2 paperback

New Harbinger Publications' Web site address: www.newharbinger.com.

99   98   97

10   9   8   7   6   5   4   3

Acknowledgments

My deepest gratitude to Matthew McKay, Ph.D., of New Harbinger Publications, who approached me about writing this book at the annual convention of the American Psychological Association, where I was giving a workshop on this subject. I hesitated then and for some time thereafter. How could I find the time for such a complex project? I was ready to say "No." The evening before I was going to do so, I happened to speak with my friend and admired colleague, Geraldine Alpert, Ph.D., who kept me on the phone until she convinced me to accept this challenge. Over the years she has been a most supportive "mentor" and she believed in my ability to bring this book into being.

Later, throughout the writing, Geraldine Alpert and my other dear friend, Gundula Behr, edited chapter after chapter and made many excellent suggestions. I am deeply grateful to both for their interest and for the time they took from their busy schedules. Special thanks also go to another friend, Charles Franklin, who was tireless in helping me learn to use my computer efficiently, which, I must confess, I was not doing before taking on this task. I thank Kayla Sussell for many wonderful comments and suggestions. She was very skillful in editing the manuscript for publication. K.D. Sullivan did an excellent job of proofreading and Tracy Powell did the fine design and typesetting.

The researchers and clinicians who greatly shaped my current knowledge and treatment protocols about panic disorder are Drs. David Barlow, Michelle Craske, and David Clark. Dr. Barlow's book, *Anxiety and Its Disorders: The Nature and Treatment of Anxiety and Panic*, written in 1988, is as relevant today as it was when first published. It provides a most valuable basis for understanding anxiety disorders and panic. His splendid mind and arduous research efforts have contributed enormously to this field.

Much of my psychological training has been influenced by Drs. Albert Bandura, Aaron Beck, Albert Ellis, Gary Emery, Donald Meichenbaum, and Robert Meyer.

Special thanks are owed to the many clients with whom I have worked over the years. They have provided me with the continuous motivation to search for a deeper understanding of panic disorder and for better and more effective ways to treat it. These clients' stories are presented throughout this book, but always in a manner to protect their identities.

This book is dedicated to my dear husband Robert,
who is ever supportive of my enthusiasm in my professional pursuits and other adventures.

Special thanks also to my family and friends, whose loving support is always with me.

Contents

PART I

UNDERSTANDING PANIC ATTACKS AND PHOBIAS

1

Introduction

If you could only run away from these sudden, terrifying attacks: Your heart is pounding heavily or fluttering a mile a minute, you can't seem to get enough air, your hands are numb, your chest is tight, and you feel dizzy and unreal. You fear doing the everyday things that other people normally do: Going to the supermarket, or to a movie, driving a car or crossing a bridge. You are scared. Even if you realize that there is no realistic basis for your fear, you feel that you can't handle it; you just can't cope. You think that you may lose your mind, totally lose control, collapse, or die. Except that . . . you cannot run away from your body.

If this description sounds familiar, you may be one of the many who suffer from panic disorder. And, like so many who have this condition, you may unwittingly hold to certain beliefs that help to maintain the disorder. Some of these beliefs are that anxiety should be avoided at all cost; that anxiety and panic symptoms can last forever and even get worse and worse; and that such symptoms can escalate to physical disaster (heart attack or stroke) or psychological (going crazy) and/or behavioral (losing control) harm. These beliefs, the emotional fear, and the physical symptoms feed on each other. The anxious, *chronic* apprehension that you develop over the possibility of another attack ensures that the cycle will continue.

Must you remain totally trapped in the fear that your disorder creates? Is there no way out? I know there is. I have seen many people overcome panic disorder. It took a great deal of courage and the willingness to persist in the work that they needed to do. But they did it, and I believe you can, too. I strongly encourage you not to settle for a life with the limitations that panic disorder imposes.

Remember, this anxiety disorder is not *all* you are. You are fine, but you have a problem, and problems require solutions. No matter how overwhelmed you may feel, there are solutions. Learn and apply the coping skills. They will teach you that you can cope—that you can master panic, phobias, and anxiety. Then, learn to look beyond the immediate coping skills and to broaden your perspective. Learn all that you can about this disorder and analyze how it fits in with your way of looking at yourself and the world. Question the parts of your view of the world that you think are not helpful. Although you can succumb to fear, you can also discover that *ultimately the only power that fear has over you is the power you give to it.*

Panic Disorder: Biological and Psychological Factors

It is estimated that the incidence of panic disorder in the total population is about 3.5 percent. Many people experience panic who do not have panic disorder. They have a panic in a stressful context, for example, when taking a test or speaking in public. Also, a fair number of people experience occasional "out of the blue" panics, but only a small percentage of them go on to develop panic disorder.

The National Institute of Mental Health (NIMH) has begun a large-scale campaign to educate the public about the disorder and available treatments. The Institute wants to raise public awareness, because early identification and treatment stop or curb the more serious complications of agoraphobia, substance abuse, depression, or suicide that often result from untreated panic disorder.

Panic disorder was formally recognized as a disorder in its own right in 1980 when it was listed for the first time in the third edition of the American Psychiatric Association's *Diagnostic and Statistical Manual of Mental Disorders*. The revised third and fourth editions stress the fear aspect of the disorder. The person suffering from panic disorder has a persistent fear of further panic attacks. This emphasis on fear of further attacks has come about in part from the recognition that many people panic without fearing the attacks; they are the so-called "nonclinical panickers," who do not feel threatened by the attacks.

Panic disorder does not arise from the sudden physical symptoms but from the person's reaction to these symptoms. Psychological treatments are aimed at helping the person experience and believe that these frightening but harmless symptoms are not dangerous. Sounds simple, doesn't it? Unfortunately, it is not. Probably no one knows this as well as you do.

In panic disorder, fear is as important as the panic attacks themselves, and fear is not easily dismissed. In his 1994 book *Panic Disorder: A Critical Analysis*, Dr. Richard McNally poses this question: Why do some people shrug off the physical symptoms of panic as harmless (which they are), and others develop a persistent fear of them? To answer the question Dr. McNally reviews the psychological, biological, and theoretical studies about panic disorder. He finds that it is a complicated "psychobiological" (a term also used by others) condition that incorporates both biological and mental dysfunctions. Studies in the biological basis of panic disorder point to several possible dysfunctions, not just to one. That is, a *number* of different biological conditions may produce panic.

But what about the psychological factors? Why do some people respond so fearfully to unpleasant but harmless surges of physiological arousal and others do not? There is no satisfying answer. There is still a great deal we need to learn about mind-body interactions and how to alter erroneous beliefs. Dr. McNally states that neither psychology nor biology can yet give a full account of the disorder. Most likely, breakthroughs will come from theories that will be developed at the interface of both disciplines.

As research continues, different subtypes of panic attacks may be identified. In that event, it is possible that future treatments will be tailored to the particular type of attack. For example, if a person's panics are primarily produced by hyperventilation, then breathing retraining should be what that person needs. Yet, based on current knowledge about panic disorder, we cannot accurately predict who will respond best to specific kinds of training. That is why this book offers a combination of methods for dealing with the disorder.

Fear—The Core of Panic Disorder

Fear of panics lies at the core of panic disorder. This kind of fear is very closely related to the term "anxiety sensitivity." The term means that, in addition to the unpleasantness of anxiety symptoms, there is the belief that the symptoms themselves are harmful. Dr. McNally, who has studied anxiety sensitivity extensively, says it appears that dysfunction in several biological systems can result in a set of similar symptoms, which, in turn, produce fear in an anxiety-sensitive person. People with high anxiety sensitivity are prone to react with fear to panic attacks, may be prone to having panic attacks, and often become extremely sensitized to such symptoms as they experience more attacks.

I recently asked a member of my Panic/Phobia Group about his *specific fears* in a panic. He said that he feared losing control. Upon further questioning, he said that he was afraid that he would suddenly start running around the neighborhood naked. I asked him which symptom bothered him the most in a panic. He said dizziness sensations. I then asked him if the same held true for headaches. He replied, "No, headaches are normal. Dizziness is not." This typical example illustrates how apprehension about dizziness (a relatively common and usually harmless symptom) can escalate in panic disorder to the fear of losing control and, in his case, of running around naked in the neighborhood.

Methods for Overcoming Panic Disorder

Like most people with panic disorder, you probably wonder, "Why me? Why has this happened to me?" But, as stated above, this is not a simple condition and there are no simple answers. It is much more important to find ways to overcome the panic disorder than to analyze its origin. Trying to find the answer to "Why?" is a theoretical exercise. You could spend a vast amount of energy trying to find the exact cause without ever getting a satisfactory answer. Certainly, you want to look at the circumstances and understand those factors in your past and present that *may have* contributed to this event. But it is of much greater value to ask yourself instead, "What can I do about it?" "How can I change this?"

The goal is to eliminate the *fear* of anxiety symptoms that is at the heart of panic disorder. If you no longer fear the bodily sensations and learn to cope with them, you can master panic attacks and overcome panic disorder. Cognitive-behavioral methods can help alter your thoughts about the catastrophic nature of panics, help you realize in your experiential mind that physical or psychological discomfort does not necessarily equal danger, and that panic sensations do not lead to disaster. Finally, these cognitive-behavioral methods can *produce changes in brain chemistry* that facilitate further improvement. When you alter your thoughts and reactions, eventually you achieve *functional* changes in your brain.

This book does not constitute "treatment" but is a self-help program, which, if learned and practiced diligently, can produce profound changes in you. Because it has been shown that, if panic disorder is not challenged, it tends to become chronic, it is crucial to overcome it. About half the people diagnosed with panic disorder end up clinically depressed, because of how limited their lives have become. In addition, a good number of panickers turn to substance abuse or develop another anxiety disorder as a further complication.

Though my goal is to teach you the cognitive-behavioral methods that have proven effective for panic disorder, medications are another treatment avenue, as well as a combination of the two. It is, however, important to be aware of your motives if you choose the aid of medications. If you simply want to block panic symptoms with medications, the fear of the symptoms will probably continue, rendering you vulnerable to yet another panic. The fact is, when you stop the medications, you are still uncertain about your ability to cope with higher levels of anxiety. Of course, some people's anxiety is so overwhelming they clearly need medications at some periods in their lives. See Chapter 6 for a complete discussion on the pros and cons of medication.

This book is for people suffering from panic disorder, with or without agoraphobia. It is also for people who have had a panic and want to prevent the development of panic disorder, for people diagnosed with "agoraphobia without a history of panic disorder," and for people who have some types of specific phobia such as claustrophobia. Although people in these latter two categories do not have *unexpected* panic attacks (which is the basic requirement for a diagnosis of panic disorder), they often panic in a phobic situation or in anticipation of one. I have found that such people also tend to fear their physical reactions in these situations. Thus, this book is also for them.

Believe that you have the ability to cope. Ultimately, your recovery lies within you, whether you work with a book, a therapist, or medications. No one else can do it for you. No one but you can live your life. As you find your self-strength, you will become empowered and unafraid.

It Takes Courage to Begin Working on Overcoming Panic Disorder.

Read Part I of this book first. It guides you on how to use this manual, explains panic disorder and agoraphobia, and it sets the stage for the work ahead. Parts II and III comprise the main work, including theory and practical guidance to overcome panic disorder (Part II) and phobias (Part III). Finally, Part IV places it all into a larger context and shows you how to gain further mastery.

2

How to Use This Manual

Think of this book as a *manual*, a *working tool*, not just another self-help book to browse through. If you just read it, as if it were a novel, it will not make a dent in helping you overcome your fears. But if you are willing to do the work with me, throughout this manual, then I am certain that you can travel a long way toward recovery. If you decide to put forth a great deal of effort, you will succeed. The hard work is up to you.

How We Learn

According to Dr. Seymour Epstein in his 1993 book, *You're Smarter Than You Think* and in a 1994 article (see References), information is processed in two ways; *experiential* and *rational*. All of our behavior is based on both modes operating and interacting closely together.

1. The *experiential mode* is rooted in early life experiences that were emotionally very important. We develop belief systems and make generalizations about the future based on these experiences. Later in life, this mode helps us to organize our experiences and directs our behavior and feelings. Information processing in the experiential mode takes place automatically, without our being aware of it. It is generally very adaptive and "smart."

2. The *rational mode* is less emotional, more detailed and analytical. It depends more on language and logical thinking, and learning takes place easily with textbooks and lectures. This mode is capable of abstract thought and is more receptive to the concept of delayed gratification than the experiential mode.

Although the experiential mode is intuitive and helpful most of the time, it may contain elements that are not helpful, such as irrational fears. Because they are often based on past experience (it is easy to acquire irrational beliefs in childhood), they are very compelling, even if the person is distressed by them and knows they are irrational. This is where the experiential mind is involved with panic, anxiety, and phobias.

Anxiety and fear, like anger, sadness, and other strong emotions, are experienced as emotional events. They are based less on objective reality than on how we *interpret* the events in our lives. The more emotional the event, the more likely the person is to think about it in the experiential or automatic mode. You cannot simply talk yourself out of your fears. This is because the rational mind has difficulty influencing the thoughts that are based on emotional processing. The good news is that although the task is difficult, it is not impossible. The rational mind *can* be brought in to influence and change the experiential mind.

To overcome panic and phobias you must change the irrational fears in your experiential mode that are set on "automatic." The steps to achieve this are as follows:

1. **Doing cognitive work** (working with your thoughts, as you will be directed to do in Chapter 9), which involves bringing the unsound Automatic Thoughts to awareness, refuting them, and then changing them. Automatic Thoughts do not change by willpower alone or by acquiring new information. Practice is essential; use the indicated worksheets as guides for assistance.

2. **Learning through direct experience**, by behavioral means, especially when they involve *different emotional* responses. This is what you will do in Chapters 10, 11, and 12. When working with those chapters, initially you will experience anxiety—sometimes high anxiety—followed by relief and exhilaration when you realize that what you feared did not happen. With repetitions, this will bring about new learning in the experiential mode.

3. **Using your imagination creatively** to deal with panics and phobias. The directions for this technique are in Chapter 12.

In sum, you will borrow the intelligence and capacity of your rational mind to positively influence your experiential mind. And you will be working *directly* with your experiential mind by confronting fearful sensations and places. Working with these two modes of learning together can bring about change in a very compelling way. However, keep in mind that the experiential mind is *slow* to change, therefore, much practice is needed to produce lasting change.

Setting the Stage

1. *Make a Schedule*
   Naturally, you will work with this material in your own way. However, I strongly recommend that you approach it as a scheduled class or course of treatment. In both, you would have "appointments," and "homework." Similarly, keeping "appointments" and doing "homework" with this manual are essential for success. A schedule makes it easier for you (and your family) to take this work seriously. Set aside specific days and times to read and work with the written practices, and set aside times in between to do the interoceptive exercises (see Chapter 10) and the in vivo exposures (Chapters 11 and 12).

   How many weeks will you need? If you have no phobias, consider spending 6 to 10 weeks. If you suffer from agoraphobia, consider 8 to 16 weeks, depending on the severity of your phobias. Naturally, you may take more time, but if you try to do all the work in less time, it is not likely to work.

2. *Prepare Yourself by Anticipating Barriers*
   Ask yourself, "What will get in the way of my working through this program?" Now list what those barriers might be: Are there time constraints? Do you have difficulty following through? (This book poses a real challenge; it expects you to explore unknown territory.) Prepare yourself as much as you can by thinking ahead about the likely barriers and how you will deal with them.

3. *Programmed Instruction Component*

- **Not everyone must read every page.**
  Sometimes this book will give you a choice to proceed to the specific issue (and page) that pertains to your difficulties. It will provide you with immediate feedback on the issue that is a stumbling block for you. You will move along *your* path and eliminate a few side roads that are not relevant for you. *Resist the temptation to look at the pages that are not relevant for you.*

  Later, if you experience a small setback, you could return to the book and to the work with a fresh outlook. You might have different symptoms and thoughts that would take you along a different path and you might discover things that you overlooked when you worked on it the first time.

4. *"Please Practice NOW (before proceeding further)."*
  Whenever you encounter this request, PLEASE DO SO. You defeat the purpose of the exercise and minimize your learning if you just read on without stopping to practice.

5. *Worksheets*
  All worksheets are numbered. They appear in full page format in the relevant chapters. You can photocopy them, and even enlarge them to work with.

6. *Maximize Your Learning: OVERLEARN*
  It is better to overlearn, rather than to barely learn, especially the working chapters (Chapters 8, 9, 10, 11, and 12).

7. *Plan on Rewarding Yourself!*
  Self-reward is so important that it deserves a whole separate section. See below.

8. *Coping Affirmations*
  Most self-help books and treatment programs have helpful statements or positive affirmations to be used before or during a panic. For example, "I can deal with this very moment," has been very useful to many people. I will ask you to customize your own list. As you work along with this book, jot down on Worksheet 1 any ideas, affirmations, or reminders that you find inspiring or helpful. **Keep a copy of Worksheet 1 handy at all times when working on this book.**

Self-Reward

So long as you are working on your fears, you are succeeding. You fail only when you don't try or when you give up after trying and sink into hopelessness and depression. (Seek professional help before reaching that point.) Building in rewards for yourself leads to greater success. With every small step you take, reward yourself. Do not tell yourself, as some people do, "Oh, this is such a small thing. Everyone else can do it. I should have done it long ago!" If you were not able to do it before, it was a big challenge. If you could not do it previously, and tried now, REWARD YOURSELF! One of my clients said that self-rewards provided her with a "warm, fuzzy feeling."

Reward Each Successful Step
You Take!

Worksheet 1: My Personal Coping Affirmations

1. _____

2. _____

3. _____

4. _____

5. _____

6. _____

7. _____

8. _____

9. _____

10. _____

How to Best Reward Yourself

As you will see in the working chapters in Parts II and III, self-reward is built into the tasks and practices. By far, self-reward works best if you plan it in advance. It will help motivate you to do some dreary tasks and remind you that these are no small feats that you are accomplishing.

There are different kinds of rewards. You can use any you like and even combine them.

1. *Material Rewards*

   These include things that you buy for yourself. For example, some of my clients buy themselves flowers. They like flowers because, while not terribly costly, they are very visible reminders of success and can be enjoyed for several days.

2. *Activities as Rewards*

   You pay for some of these, not for others. Examples are: Going to the movies (assuming you are not afraid of doing so, in which case you may rent a movie and watch it at home); reading a good novel; calling a good friend or a close relative (maybe long-distance); going for a walk on the beach; or visiting a friend.

3. *Acknowledgment from Someone Else*

   Your coach or someone close to you praises you for the steps you have accomplished. This works only if the person has agreed to help you in this way and is dependable in following through with the supportive role.

4. *Your Emotional Self-Reward*

If you use an emotional self-reward, make it more elaborate than a simple "That was good!" statement. Dr. Epstein, in his book *You're Smarter Than You Think* (1993), suggests that you stand very close to a mirror and look deep into your eyes, establishing a profound contact with yourself. Then, say kind things to yourself, for example, "I love you." If you stand at a normal distance, you might look at yourself critically, and defeat the purpose. Tell yourself that you appreciate your efforts, that you did well, that you can count on your support, and give yourself a hug! (I call this a "self-hug.") Dr. Epstein says that this is a great avenue for boosting your self-esteem. Some people may find it very difficult to do, but it can be practiced until it no longer feels odd. What's wonderful about this is it's totally private, and you can be as fuzzy or silly as you want!

Be Kind To Yourself:
Reward Your Accomplishments,
No Matter How Small!

How to Do the Work

I strongly recommend that you read through Part I first, and work with its two worksheets. (Note that you will work with Worksheet 1 throughout the book.) It will give you a solid background and set the stage for the rest of the work in this manual. You will understand that although panic and phobias work together as a unit, they are also somewhat independent. This is because once agoraphobia becomes well-established, it takes on a life of its own. Many people who do not seem to have agoraphobia may, nonetheless, use subtle avoidances or "safety signals." For this reason, when you start working with Part II (at Chapter 7), you should also study Chapter 11 in Part III. It will allow you to advance along both fronts, panic and phobias. You will be able to see the "bigger picture" and use the gains made in one area for the benefit of the other.

The internal references within the chapters can be found in the References Section.

Use the Fear Barometer

Remember your worst panic ever. Use the Subjective Units of Distress Scale (SUDS) to describe how much anxiety and fear you would feel if you had such a panic now.

   0 = Totally calm, no fear or anxiety

  50 = Moderate level of anxiety/fear

100 = Intolerable level of anxiety/fear

Use the number that best reflects your discomfort level.

What Is Your Fear Barometer About a "Bad" Panic Now? Please write it down NOW (before proceeding further). Write in the number: _____ .

At the end of each working chapter I will ask you about your Fear Barometer. If at the end of any given chapter it has not dropped by a number of points, stays the same, or is higher, review and rework the chapter again. The Fear Barometer will be the measure that you will use to assess your progress, step by step.

Now, let's work together and good luck!

Recommended Reading

Epstein, Seymour 1993. *You're Smarter Than You Think.* New York: Simon & Schuster.

3

Recognizing Panic Attacks and Understanding Their Progression

The goal of this chapter is to help you identify panic attacks, and to become knowledgeable about what happens when they progress to panic disorder and beyond. When you have read this chapter, you should then be able to gauge the severity of your panics and panic disorder and how much time and effort to invest in overcoming them.

Anxiety Fluctuates

First let us look at anxiety. You can think of anxiety as a continuum that varies in intensity:

| No anxiety | Moderate anxiety | Extreme anxiety |

All of us move back and forth along this continuum, occasionally touching down at either endpoint. In other words, we are *not* divided into two groups; anxious people and nonanxious people. Everyone experiences some degree of anxiety some of the time. That's just a fact of life.

I often ask my new clients, as I'll ask you: "Is anxiety a good thing or a bad thing?" If you suffer from panic disorder or any kind of distressing or debilitating anxiety condition, you are bound to say "bad." Although *that* kind of anxiety can justifiably be termed "bad," anxiety can also be "good." Without fear and built-in fear mechanisms, we would not survive. Fear helps us to recognize danger and impels us to take steps to protect ourselves. Anxiety motivates us to find solutions, work hard, study for tests, and master new, challenging tasks. However, at the extreme end of the continuum, high levels of anxiety can interfere with basic functioning. In that case, we want to manage anxiety, decrease it, and channel it in constructive ways. The goal will never be to eliminate all anxiety.

Only the Dead Are Never Anxious.

The Three Components of Anxiety

Try to recall an anxious, but not panic, moment from your life; for example, just before taking an important test, or your boss telling you to meet him in half an hour. Do you recall any sensations? Let me guess. You may have felt perspiration breaking out, or nervousness in the pit of your stomach, you may have had a faster heartbeat. Do you recall thoughts like these: "What if I fail?" "Will I do okay?" "Did I make a bad mistake?" "What if I get fired?" While you were waiting, your racing thoughts probably made it difficult to concentrate. What did you do? Did you pace back and forth? Fidget with your pen? Did you share your anxiety with someone who listened and perhaps calmed you down?

- The increased heartbeat, perspiration, and stomach nervousness are the *physical* manifestations of anxiety.

- The questions and worries are the *mental* manifestations or *thoughts* involved in anxiety.

- The pacing and fidgeting are examples of the *behavioral* manifestations of anxiety.

In sum, anxiety and panic both generate physical sensations, cognitions (or thoughts), and behaviors (or overt acts). In the example above, you may have engaged in another, very helpful behavior: If you spoke about your anxiety to someone and that someone was understanding and supportive, that may have helped you to calm down.

Panic Attack: Is It an Extreme Manifestation of Anxiety?

A panic or anxiety attack is a *sudden intense fear or anxiety* or an overwhelming sense of impending doom. The word "attack," by definition, means that the onset is *sudden*. This surge of intense anxiety is called a panic attack if it reaches its peak intensity within ten minutes after starting. But it often reaches its peak within a couple of minutes and sometimes in only a few seconds. It can then continue for a few minutes to half an hour or even longer.

If you have exactly these symptoms, but the build-up is slower (taking longer than ten minutes), this is called high anxiety. It can be extremely uncomfortable, *but it is not an attack.* Although panic attacks can be *seen* as extreme expressions of anxiety, they are also different from other levels of anxiety on the continuum. The sudden onset, the intensity, the number of symptoms involved, and the fear of these symptoms (what the symptoms might mean) make them feel totally different from anything the person has ever felt before.

A panic attack is identified by the presence of at least *four* of the following physical sensations and psychological reactions:

Panic Attack Symptoms*

1. Palpitations, pounding heart, or accelerated heart rate

2. Sweating

3. Trembling or shaking

---

* Reprinted with permission from the *Diagnostic and Statistical Manual of Mental Disorders*, Fourth ed. Washington, D.C.: American Psychiatric Association, 1994.

4. Sensations of shortness of breath or smothering

5. Feeling of choking

6. Chest pain or discomfort

7. Nausea or abdominal distress

8. Feeling dizzy, unsteady, lightheaded, or faint

9. Derealization (feelings of unreality) or depersonalization (being detached from oneself)

10. Fear of losing control or going crazy

11. Fear of dying

12. Paresthesias (numbness or tingling sensations)

13. Chills or hot flushes

A sudden surge of anxiety, with fewer than four of these symptoms, is called a "limited symptom attack." It can be very uncomfortable and it is often experienced periodically by people on their way to recovery from panic attacks. Some people experience other sensations such as sudden diarrhea, instant headaches, intense weakness or stiffness in the legs, or blurred vision. Research on panic symptoms suggests that three symptoms are particularly common; palpitations, dizziness, and suffocation sensations. As the disorder continues over time, and no physical catastrophe occurs, the fear of going crazy or losing control often becomes the chief fear.

It is important to keep the definition of a panic attack clearly in mind. The expression "I panicked" is often used as synonymous for "I got extremely upset," which is clearly not the same as having a panic attack. Remember, high anxiety with several physical symptoms is not a panic attack unless it has a clear, sudden, intense onset.

In a recent Panic/Phobia Group, I asked the members to write down each panic they experienced, with its specific symptoms, during the following week. In the next session, one group member said, "I was so surprised to have had only one panic this week. I realize now that I had been interpreting any high anxiety as panic."

Can the Symptoms Mean Anything Other than Panic Attacks?

Experiencing a surge of these symptoms does not necessarily mean that you are having a panic attack. Some diseases or physical dysfunctions produce sensations similar to those of panic. Hypoglycemia, hyperthyroidism, Cushing's syndrome, pheochromocytoma, caffeine or amphetamine intoxication, temporal lobe epilepsy, cardiac arrhythmias, audiovestibular system dysfunction, and mitral valve prolapse all produce sensations similar to panic. Sometimes a physical ailment can precipitate a panic attack. If you have not had a physical check-up in the last year or since the panics started, you may wish to do so to rule out a medical condition. Remember, sometimes physical ailments mimic panic, and they can also trigger or interact with panic.

If you have been treated for panic disorder, whether psychological (cognitive-behavior therapy) or pharmacological (medication), and you show no improvement, it would be wise to have a medical re-examination. This is important particularly if the following symptoms are present: Clouding of consciousness, actual fainting, or strong feelings of unreality followed by feelings of hostility. If the onset of the panics began with a physical problem, or your panic disorder started after the age of 40, a medical re-examination would be indicated. Note that even if there is a medical condition causing these kinds of symptoms, it does not preclude the presence of an added panic disorder. If you have a diagnosed medical condition, excessive anxiety may make it worse.

In my groups I have worked with people who had cardiac arrhythmias, mitral valve prolapse, and other physical ailments. Such people had to work harder to distinguish between their organically caused symptoms and their apprehension about these symptoms on the one hand, and their *exaggerated* catastrophic thoughts on the other hand.

Panic Disorder

Let us assume that a physician has ruled out a medical condition, and your anxiety episodes fit the panic attack profile. What next? You may already have been diagnosed with panic disorder by a mental health professional or a physician knowledgeable about mental disorders, but if you have not been formally diagnosed, you may wonder if you do indeed have it. I will describe the criteria for the diagnosis of panic disorder but I caution you not to rely on self-diagnosis. The human mind is very complex, and we often see what we want to see and are blind to what we don't want to see. Furthermore, this disorder is not always easy to diagnose because of the wide variety of symptoms associated with it. Only a mental health professional can "tease out" panic disorder from other psychiatric diagnoses.

Panic disorder is diagnosed when at least four of the 13 criteria for panic attacks listed above on pages 14 and 15 have been met. The person must also have experienced *several unexpected or "out of the blue" panic attacks, or have had one attack followed by at least one month of persistent fear and worry over having another.* The interpretation of the symptoms as life threatening, and anxious apprehension (Dr. Barlow's term) over the possibility of future panic attacks are implied in the diagnosis. Behavioral repercussions of even one panic can manifest in *repeated visits to the emergency room or internist.* It can be the *avoidance* of activities or situations where a panic is feared, or the use of safety signals to "save" oneself from harm.

Panic Attacks in Other Anxiety Disorders

Panic attacks can occur in all anxiety disorders. In a *disorder* called *specific phobia,* for instance, if a young woman has a dog phobia, she may panic when confronted with a dog. (Some other very common specific phobias are the fear of heights and claustrophobia.) In *obsessive-compulsive disorder,* a man who washes his hands repeatedly for fear of contamination and death may panic when prevented from washing his hands. In the *disorder* called *social phobia,* a young man may panic when he must make a speech in class. In *posttraumatic stress disorder,* a woman may suddenly panic if she finds herself in an elevator with a man who looks like the man who raped her in the past. In these examples, panic attacks can be expected because they are closely tied to a specific fearful object or situation. Panic attacks can occur in other anxiety conditions. They may accompany depression or the abuse of or withdrawal from alcohol and drugs.

But Why Did I End Up with Panic Disorder?

Many people experiencing their first, or first few, panic(s) go to a hospital's emergency room or a physician's office afraid that they are dying from a heart attack, suffocation, or stroke. An examination showing negative results may lead the physician to suspect emotional factors and to ask if the patient has been under any unusual stress. The patient may wonder why the question is asked since the symptoms are physical, yet answer, "Yes, my mother died five months ago, we moved, and my son is having difficulties in school." The connection is not immediately apparent, because a discrete sudden physical attack seems remote from stress that has lasted for days, weeks, or months. But often a panic attack occurs when the worst is over and life is returning to normal.

Studies have shown and it has also been my experience that for most people their initial panic attack followed a stressful life event. The stresses usually involve a threat to the person's sense of safety and security (divorce, death, start of school, promotion at work, a move to a new home, etc.)

or biological events (surgery, medication effects, being "high" on illegal drugs). I have also found that the precipitating stresses frequently involve interpersonal conflict, especially if the person does not stand up for himself or herself and feels powerless. Sometimes, the person has strong feelings that may be unconscious, repressed, or denied.

Often panic disorder starts in the teens and twenties, that is, when a person is faced with significant changes and challenges. We are becoming increasingly aware of children and seniors having panic attacks. Sometimes hormonal changes, as in menopause, trigger panic attacks during middle age. Furthermore, premenstrual hormonal changes often exacerbate panics.

Does this answer your question, "But why did I end up with panic disorder?" Only indirectly. It is possible that you have

1. an inherited predisposition to anxiety,

2. a specific biological dysfunction,

3. greater anxiety sensitivity,

4. had difficult experiences in your formative years that made you feel out of control, and/or

5. were under significant stress prior to your first panic.

Every person is unique, and in any individual's case we can only make an informed judgment, based in large part on your input.

Agoraphobia and Substance Abuse—Serious Complications of Panic Disorder

I know how terrifying panic attacks can be. Imagine someone having a panic while driving across a bridge or standing in a grocery line. It may have happened to you. Did you think, "But what if I panic again and cause an accident? I better not cross bridges!" "What if I panic while standing in line next time and totally embarrass myself?" It is understandable that you would want to avoid situations that create such worries about safety and embarrassment. Driving, flying, using public transportation, going to movies or restaurants, attending meetings or church, or even staying home alone can all seem potentially too dangerous to risk doing. In its extreme form, the person may become housebound. Once you give in to the urge to avoid situations such as these, you are at risk of developing a second problem on top of the first one: Agoraphobia.

Agoraphobia is the fear of places or situations where in case of a panic: (a) help is not immediately available and/or (b) escape is difficult because of physical or social constraints. The situation can be endured with fear or avoided in order not to feel the fear sensations. If you are able to do all of the anxiety-provoking activities described above, but you need a companion to do so, you also have agoraphobia. The definition also includes the fear of staying home *alone*. Avoidance becomes a coping mechanism which, unfortunately, is not a helpful one. It is not helpful, because it is based on the illusion that panics can be controlled by avoidance. In spite of avoidance, however, panic is always lurking around the corner. An unexpected panic attack will then easily lead to more and more avoidance. The person's world starts to shrink. This condition is called panic disorder with agoraphobia and it is a much more debilitating form than panic disorder without agoraphobia. Agoraphobia can develop immediately after the first panic or days, months, or even years later.

Agoraphobia does not always result from the fear of panic attacks. It occurs in those who have limited symptom attacks and in those who fear losing control over their bodies, for instance people who have sudden, compelling urges to use the bathroom. This often leads to the avoidance of situations where bathrooms are not immediately available. Agoraphobia can also develop in a person who inexplicably or as a result of a trauma starts to fear and avoid places. These people have agoraphobia without a history of unexpected panics, that is, agoraphobia without a history of panic disorder. As phobic fear continues to take its hold (whether or not precipitated by panics), it develops increasingly a life of its own, often separate and different from the fear of panics.

Further consequences of avoidance are lowered self-esteem, exaggerated dependence on others, and loss of confidence in one's ability to cope with fear and panic. Sooner or later, many become depressed in part because their lives are so badly truncated by the agoraphobia.

It appears that twice as many women develop panic disorder than men do, and many more women than men become agoraphobic. Research suggests that this has to do with sex roles in society. Clearly, it is more acceptable for women to be dependent, to stay at home and not to venture out. But how do men cope? For many, using alcohol or drugs is a more "acceptable" way of coping. These substances seemingly help to calm anxiety, *for the moment*, and are another form of avoidance. Unfortunately, when the effect wears off, these men may be even more susceptible to anxiety sensations that they cannot handle, leading to even more drinking or drug use. Such people (men or women) are likely to develop a drug or alcohol dependency.

It sounds quite discouraging, doesn't it? There is hope, however. If you are a new "panicker" (for simplicity, I will continue to use this word to describe a person who has panic attacks), try *not to engage in avoidance behaviors*. Remember, using chemical substances or performing other kinds of avoidances will not cure your panic disorder.

A few years ago I interviewed a young woman who had had panic attacks and probably panic disorder for at least two years prior to my seeing her. I asked her how she had managed not to develop agoraphobia. She told me that from the beginning of her panics she had seen the college physician who had prescribed tranquilizers. She found a brochure about panic disorder in his office, and read that avoidance, a complication of panic disorder, would easily lead to agoraphobia. From that moment on, whenever her natural tendency was to avoid, fearing panics, she pushed herself to confront the situation.

New panickers are helped by this knowledge about the development of agoraphobia. Many people practice avoidance out of ignorance, believing that they are helping their panic condition. Unfortunately, the exact opposite is true. Avoidance of fearful situations aggravates the condition. If you leave a situation when your anxiety is rising or at its peak, the relief you feel teaches your body that the way to feel better is to avoid. Thus, avoidance reinforces fear. Generally, if you are in a phobic situation, it is helpful to keep pushing forward before considering retreating. (See Part III of the book for more information on this subject.)

Deep-seated agoraphobia cannot be simply pushed away. It requires hard work. However, I have seen many people overcome it and I am therefore optimistic and hope that you are too. If you have agoraphobia, Part III will instruct you on how to overcome it.

Panic Disorder Increases General Anxiety

After developing a fear of panics, most panickers become anxious anticipating the next attack and fearful (phobic) situations. A number of panickers also start to worry and obsess about many other things as well. They start to sound like hypochondriacs, worrying about every little ailment. They begin to worry much more than they used to about the safety and health of family members. They become tense and stressed for no apparent reason. Is this happening to you? Anxiety may have become a part of your life, as never before. If that is the case, first and foremost, you want to get rid of your panics. But you must also open your mind to more far-reaching goals: You must want to overcome your *fear* of panics, anticipatory anxiety, phobias, excessive general anxiety, worry, and depression. If that's what your goals are, let's work through this book together. If you decide to work hard on your panic problems, your rewards will be increased self-esteem, increased ability to cope with fearful situations, and better functioning at work, with your family, and in your social life.

Working on the First Step: Recording Your Panic Attacks

Clinical research has shown that the mere act of recording each panic *immediately after it has passed* helps in the mastery of and recovery from panic disorder. After you look at the following worksheet, before you actually start writing, I would like you to go back to the beginning of this chapter and review the criteria for identifying panic attacks. Review the symptoms and the discussion about the suddenness of the onset of an attack. Many people who develop panic disorder become so anxious and fearful that they start to label any slight increase in anxiety as panic. This is *not helpful*. Labeling every anxiety experience as "panic" makes you believe that your problem is much worse than it is. Learn to distinguish between high anxiety and panic!

Your first assignment will be to "meet" your panics face to face. Take a step back from your emotions and make the observations you need to record the details on the worksheet. Become a *participant-observer*—it will help you to begin healing yourself.

How to Use Worksheet 2 to Record Your Panic Attacks

1. *Date.* Always record the date. This gives you an excellent way to assess your progress over time.

2. *Time.* Always record the time. This will help you to observe patterns.

3. *Situation Where Panic Occurred.* Recording the situation will also help you to observe patterns.

4. *Panic Symptoms.* State all the symptoms you had during this particular panic episode. Although, technically, fewer than four symptoms do not constitute full-blown panic attacks, also record sudden episodes of fear accompanied by three symptoms or less. The reason for this is that on the way to recovery, you are likely to have limited symptom attacks. Observing your attacks as less severe will help you to be optimistic about your progress.

5. *Symptoms Peaked Within 10 Minutes?* This is a reminder to be accurate. If the symptoms did not reach their peak (= highest point) within 10 minutes of their onset, you experienced very uncomfortable high anxiety, but not a panic attack. Do not label the slower building high anxiety episodes as "panic attacks."

6. *Maximum SUDS.* SUDS = Subjective Units of Distress Scale. 0 = totally calm, no anxiety or fear; 50 = moderate level of anxiety/fear; 100 = intolerable level of anxiety/fear. Use the number from 0 to 100 that best describes your highest level of anxiety/fear during the panic.

7. *Time in Minutes: From Start of Panic Till Able to Function Again.* This measure of time will also help you observe your progress. Instead of the panic controlling you, you can see how you are learning to control the panic experience over time, and thus go on with your activity.

Copy Worksheet 2. Start to *record every single panic* you have from now on. Carry your copy with you at all times. Record *immediately* after the panic episode is over. There is no other way to record your panics that will allow you to remember the details as accurately.

Record Each Panic Immediately After It Has Passed.

Worksheet 2: Recording My Panic Attacks

1	2	3	4	5	6	7
Date	Time	Situation Where Panic Occurred	Panic Symptoms	Symptoms Peaked Within 10 minutes? Check if Yes	Max SUDS	Time in Minutes: From Start of Panic Till Able to Function Again

4

A Human Dilemma:
Uncertainty About the Future

Diana came to see me at age 12. Her parents had brought her in for treatment because her fearfulness had recently worsened. She had been worrying about the future for years. Hers were not the average, everyday kind of fears, but rather a kind of philosophical angst that illustrates humanity's profound dilemma. Diana worried about life 1,000 years from now. When she thought about that far off future, she felt nothingness, empty black space, and experienced intense anxiety. She also realized that she is helpless over the events of the distant future. She worried about catastrophies all over the world; earthquakes, floods, hurricanes, and the sufferings of the people involved. Sometimes her fears came a little closer. She worried about finding herself at age 70, near death, and not wanting to die. She said to me, "There's no point, if it will end anyway."

My work with her began by acknowledging the truth: There is an infinite number of situations that are not under her, her parents', or my control. She proved to be an exceptionally bright youngster, willing to debate many psychological and philosophical dilemmas with me. And her disorder was healed when she finally realized that while she worried about events outside of her control, her life could pass her by; along with all the things that she *could* control.

Trying to Control an Uncertain Future

All my clients with panic disorder have one thing in common; an obsession with *control*. They want, at all cost, to control their internal emotional and physical reactions as well as worrisome and frightening external events. They say: "What if I panic? I just need control." "I feel that I have no control." "I can't stand being in a situation where I have no control."

Anxiety is a future-oriented state. Of course, it can also be felt in the present, in the here-and-now; as when a person with public-speaking phobia is just about to make a speech, a woman apprehensive about dating is out with a new date, or a man with a bridge phobia is crossing a bridge. Yet even in these examples, there is a strong orientation toward the future, even if the feared future is only minutes away. Let me illustrate with a few of the self-doubting questions that plague my clients' minds.

- "What if I start stammering or forget my material?"

- "What if they notice how much I'm sweating?"

- "What if he thinks I'm a boring date and never asks me out again?"

- "What if I have a full-blown panic, lose control of the car and crash, killing some people?"

"What if . . . ?" questions are, by definition, future-oriented and they are central in the tendency to catastrophize.

> ## Anxious People Obsess About What They Cannot Control, Instead of Paying Attention to What They *Can* Control.

The Need for Control

Control has to do with uncertainty. We cannot change the past, so we usually do not try to control it. In contrast, humanity has always tried to control its future; to make the future more certain, more predictable. I believe that every single being wants to exercise some kind of control—animals as well as humans. Even newborn babies want to be fed when *they* are hungry, to sleep when *they* are sleepy, and to be held when *they* want to be cuddled. My own attempts to exercise some kind of control over the future include praying for myself and my loved ones, buying insurance, and setting aside money for my retirement.

Wanting to control the future is not unique to modern life. Along with our modern ability to control many actual events, there is also the illusion that we can control even more things than we actually can. In other times, there were other ways to channel humanity's fear of an uncertain future. For instance, many cultures made offerings to the gods; some even made human sacrifices to appease these gods in their appeals for future rain, fertility, or successful combat. Were these not attempts to exercise control over the future?

You say, "No, that's not the kind of control I need! I just want control over my emotions like everyone else has, that's all."

So, I must ask you an important question here: Do you believe that most humans turn their emotions on and off at will? I do not believe that the majority of people do. Rather, to fully experience ourselves as human, we need to accept the richness of our emotional lives—be they pleasant emotions or not.

Before proceeding, let me make a distinction between feelings and actions. Although I can feel a variety of negative feelings and accept those feelings, how I act on those feelings is a different matter. Just because I feel so angry with someone that I want to wring his neck does not mean that I will literally try to strangle him. I have other, more acceptable, choices—like *telling* him that I am angry with him. But before we can explore choices about how to act on our feelings, i.e., how to *behave*, we first need to acknowledge and accept the feelings.

Losing Control

You may worry more about how you will react to an event than about the event itself. In our culture, many people think of crying as "losing control." Undeniably, there are instances where it is better not to cry. Being familiar with other cultures, however, I am always perplexed when I hear this judgment applied to crying. The most extreme example is when people say that they absolutely don't want to cry at a funeral they are going to attend. They don't want to "lose control." Isn't a funeral the one social institution where it is acceptable—even expected—to cry? How far do we want to move away from our human ability to experience a wide range of emotions? Why is crying less acceptable than laughing or smiling?

Let's stop for a moment and play with an image. Envision a world where everyone had full control over their emotions. No one would show signs of anxiety, fear, anger, sadness, irritation, excitement, joy, amusement, or happiness. What would the world be like? I think that many negative and destructive reactions might be kept at bay, but so would many warm and constructive feelings that bring people together.

Control Issues and Worrying About Panic Attacks

You could be a panicker who worries about the possibility of having a heart attack. You've been told that your heart is fine, and you've had a number of panic attacks without ever having a heart attack, but you reject your own evidence and keep on worrying. After all, you reason, it *could* happen. Next, you begin to avoid freeways because you could panic then, and panic could lead to the feared heart attack. Once we surrender to these fears, there is no end to the extent they can spread to other places and situations. We can always find reasons to fear all that *could* happen.

Jennifer was in one of my groups. She told us her story. One day she was driving with her best friend along as a passenger. Suddenly, her friend, a woman in her late 30s, slumped forward, dying instantly of a heart attack. Jennifer became phobic about driving. What had happened to her dear friend, totally unexpectedly, could, after all, happen to her. Over time she became increasingly phobic, panicking in many situations. Despite medications, she became essentially housebound. One day she could no longer stand being housebound and decided to go out for a drive. She expected to die, but decided that leading her life in self-imposed imprisonment was not much better than death. She went on her drive and of course did not die. Sometime thereafter Jennifer joined my group. Every time she chose to confront her fears, she developed more courage. Many times she thought that she was going to die. She realized that not driving and not leaving the house did not necessarily assure her of a longer life. Her example became an inspiration to the other group members.

Even if you overcome your panics now, there is no guarantee that you will never have another panic attack again. But, if you overcome your *fear* of panic attacks, future panics will most likely be occasional, isolated events.

Becoming a Chronic Worrier

In Chapter 3 I said that people who develop panic disorder often start worrying about many things in life that they have not worried about before. They worry about finances, children, health, and work, in addition to worrying about panic attacks. They may start to worry constantly. Fear over the uncertain future can turn worry into an obsessional habit.

But worrying can also take another form: It can become a means to attempt to *control* the future. Of course you know that this is irrational. Nonetheless, you may develop the hidden belief that if you worry enough, the dreaded event will not happen. This is magical thinking, but it employs a powerful circular logic. In other words, how can I prove to you that the bad event would not have happened even if you hadn't worried? You worried and the bad event did not happen. *Is* there cause and effect? (See Chapter 9 for a complete discussion on this type of magical thinking.)

Another kind of magical thinking is premised on the belief that if you are not apprehensive, if you dare to relax, let down your worry guards, and be happy—something bad will happen. Yet here is the ebb and flow of life: Good things happen and bad things happen. A bad event can follow another bad event *or* a good one. A good event can follow another good *or* bad event. The future is always uncertain. Why not enjoy the good times while they are happening?

Other clients say to me, "I have been a worry wart all my life." Dolores comes to mind. Dolores was in my New Panickers Group. She had overcome her fear of panics but she stayed in the group to try and modify her life-long tendency to worry. While in the group, she sent her children to Virginia to spend part of the summer with close relatives. This was extremely hard for Dolores. She had never been separated from her children for long periods before and she worried and worried. She called them daily. When she was out, she rushed home looking for the blinking light on the answering machine and dreading bad news. She could not relax or enjoy the time alone with her husband.

Her worry culminated on July 4 when her relatives and children went to a party and were not home by 10 p.m. She called repeatedly until she finally reached them after midnight. They had had a wonderful time and Dolores was relieved. In group she expressed disbelief that anyone would not have children home by 10 p.m. Her assumptions had to be challenged: "Is there an absolute "right" or "wrong" about how late to allow youngsters to stay at special events with proper supervision?" "If one of your children had drowned in the pool, do you think that you would not have been notified?" Finally she drew some new conclusions herself: "Well, my children were having a good time. They loved it. They are on vacation after all. My relatives are very responsible, or I would not have entrusted my children to them to begin with. If something bad had happened, they would surely have called me right away."

Dolores got a good perspective on that event but she continued to worry. She was often tempted to have them return from their trip earlier than scheduled. The group continued to work with her. Someone asked, "Your children are the most important part of your life and having something terrible happen to one or both would be very painful and tragic. Has anything bad happened to them while at home?" She described a couple of dangerous events. Someone else asked, "What if you had your children sent home earlier, and a terrible accident happened at home? Do you supervise your children 24 hours a day? Do you have full and total control over their lives?" Again, she was able to draw her own conclusions, "If they came home earlier than scheduled because of my fears, and something bad happened here, I would feel even worse. I cannot fully control their lives; I can only hope for the best. I have tried to teach them to be careful and hope they remember what I taught them. I can try to plan well and take precautions; that is all I can do. The rest is not up to me."

It was not surprising that Dolores had learned to worry since she was a child. Her mother was a constant worrier, often predicting doomsday scenarios. When Dolores discovered in group that she was not doomed to a life of chronic worry and that there were other alternatives, even for her, there was a dramatic turnaround. She told her relatives that she would no longer call daily. Incoming calls and messages stopped frightening her. She started to relax and began to enjoy the time alone with her husband. The test of her newly acquired confidence came when she received a call from her sister-in-law one evening: Dolores' son was quite ill; and perhaps he needed a physician. Dolores asked about his symptoms. These were familiar to her, so she gave her sister-in-law exact instructions on how to care for him and told her to wait till the morning to see if he still needed a doctor. Dolores told her sister-in-law not to worry so much! She slept well that night. The next morning she learned that he was greatly improved.

Dolores realized that worrying did not provide security. Her coping ability had been greatly enhanced. She saw how much constant worrying drained her enjoyment of life. She did not want to pass this affliction on to her children. After terminating with the group, some major adversities took place in her life, but she faced them without catastrophizing.

Making Peace with an Uncertain Future

You may say that you want certainty and control. Yet if you could predict and control everything in the future, what would life be like? Nothing would be a surprise. What could you strive for? You may say that you realize you cannot control the future, but still you want certainty. You want to be absolutely sure that the plane you will fly with will not crash, that the elevator will not get stuck, that you won't have a panic on the freeway. Isn't this really the same as wanting control over the future?

One client of mine worried about dying of a heart attack during a panic. Her worry escalated after her closest friend died in a car accident. She kept repeating how her friend had not known what was going to happen, and she became obsessed with the possibility that she might also die unexpectedly. Because her panics were accompanied by extreme fright, she now directed most of her worry to the panics. I asked her if her friend would have benefited from knowing ten years prior to dying that this was going to happen. She replied, "Of course not." Such knowledge would have brought much grief to her friend's life for ten years.

The wisdom of uncertainty is that we are spared much grief. If tragedy strikes, then we *must* feel pain and suffering. We are spared grief if no tragedy strikes, and it is not wise to seek grief unnecessarily.

Each one of us must grapple with the uncertainties in life. It is never a given to be absolutely safe or certain. Thus, there is no way to eliminate uncertainty and the anxiety that accompanies it. We need to find healthier ways to cope with this anxiety; because fear feeds upon itself. The more you surrender to fear, the more fear you will experience.

The Worst Fear Is the Fear of Fear.
You Must Face and Embrace Your Fears,
Anxieties, and Uncertainties,
and By So Doing,
Develop Self-Confidence and Mastery.

5

Motivation and Self-Defeat

If I asked you, "Do you want to overcome your panic attacks and phobias?" most likely you would reply, "Of course!" But, if I ask, "Are you willing to work hard on overcoming your fears? Are you willing to spend quite a few hours over the span of several weeks on this, even when experiencing great discomfort?" How do you answer these two questions?

Everyone would like to overcome his or her fears, but there are often formidable emotional or cognitive blocks that get in the way. Here are eight of the most common kinds of blocks.

1. *It scares me to think and talk about fears let alone to read about them!*

   You may feel that you are very suggestible and think that, if you hear or read about other people's symptoms and phobias you will "catch" them. This is rarely a problem. Many of my clients have expressed the same concern when I offered them group treatment. And, although some were very preoccupied initially, this always vanished by the second or third session. Not wanting to hear or read about others' fears is a form of avoidance. In this book the first step is to think and read about fears.

2. *I don't have time.*

   Sometimes this is true, other times it's an excuse. If you are truly in the middle of a major upheaval (e.g., a child custody battle) or project (e.g., final exams), you will have to wait until you can find the time required to do the work. But often, lack of time is an excuse. Many people live day to day, feeling overwhelmed because they haven't set priorities or organized their lives in a more manageable way.

   Don't undertake this project without making a firm commitment. If you do it halfheartedly, you won't gain much. To be successful at this, you must invest time and energy.

   Keep in mind, however, that your fears frequently take a great deal of your time, because they, rather than you, are in charge. They prevent you from being able to do what you need and want to do.

3. *I have tried before, but nothing helps.*
   This argument can take many forms:
   —If medications didn't help me, how will a book? Who's this writer anyway? I never heard of her! Self-help books never helped me!
   —A book cannot help solve an emotional problem.
   —There's no hope for me. I'm so anxious, I'll never get better.
   —I'd rather go to a therapist. If that doesn't help, nothing will.
   —People don't change.

"Giving Up" is an Unhelpful, Maladaptive Thought, as you will learn in Chapter 9. What lies behind this Unhelpful Thought? You may have had many setbacks over the years and, consequently, have developed a pessimistic outlook. It is likely that you have been struggling with very high anxiety for a long time now, and it is hard to imagine living without it. The thoughts in an anxious state of mind tend to be catastrophic and self-defeating. If you feel like giving up, talk to loved ones, and see if you can find some ray of hope deep within you. I believe that people want to strive toward healing. Believe that there is life beyond anxiety.

4. *It's too hard. I'm not sure I'm up to it.*
   It is true that you have a tremendous task ahead of you.
   Justine, a client of mine, attended a conference of the Anxiety Disorders Association of America. (At these conferences, all events can be attended by professionals and lay people alike.) A therapist in the audience asked the presenters, "What do you do when you have tried everything, including the best treatments, and nothing works?" The presenters' answer, "The client also has to *want* to get well," made a strong impact on Justine. She came back to the New Panickers Group from the conference somewhat changed. She had realized that ultimately it was up to her, not to anyone else, to move ahead. She saw that she was confronted with the same choice again and again: "I can continue to obsess about all the serious hardships I have with my family and worry about my future, or I can go on with my life and start to put my energy into action." That was how she interpreted "wanting to" get well. She made dramatic progress after that, even though it was not easy.

5. *What else can happen if I give up my fears?*
   This may have to do with Disaster Expectation, another Unhelpful, Maladaptive Thought (see Chapter 9). In other words, if I rid myself of my fears, other "bad" things will happen. It can also mean that you are afraid of what may happen if you were to change your life. For example, if you are in a bad marriage and do not want to face making the choice to leave (or stay), getting rid of your phobias could give you the psychic space you need to consider such a difficult choice. (It's like hiding behind the phobias, isn't it?)
   Your fears are predictable and familiar, you might feel lost without them. How would you deal with the unknown? If the "imaginary" fears that stood in your way were gone, then you would face real life with its unlimited unknowns. Remember that real life brings many rewards as well.

6. *My family life is functioning well now. If I change, all the balances will shift and I'll have to contribute more!*
   This may not apply to you, but for some people it is very relevant. Panic disorder and phobias can release the person from the necessity of doing mundane, everyday tasks, such as grocery shopping or going to the bank. In other people, fear gets in the way of holding down a job, with all the stress and challenge that work and having a boss implies. Although living your life with fear is hard, living a life without fear is also hard, in different ways.

7. *I need someone to help me.*

   As humans, we are interdependent and all need assistance from each other. However, no one can change your thoughts and behaviors except *you, yourself*. If you are in therapy, trust in a therapist can help you confront severe fears. Yet a therapist cannot do magic, you still need to do all the work—the mental and behavioral tasks required to overcome your fears. Furthermore, there is one significant advantage to doing the work with a book such as this: There is no illusion that someone else can somehow change you. You *know* that it is up to you. And the reward, too, is all yours!

8. *I don't deserve to get well.*

   When this feeling exists, it is usually unconscious. I recently worked with a client, who was the worst hyperventilator I have ever seen. He visibly hyperventilated all the time. Naturally, he was obsessed with feelings of suffocation and had deep-seated fears about dying for lack of air. Yet he also said, "I don't deserve to breathe. I don't deserve to live because of what I have done." (His "crime" was standing up to an elderly woman, who had taken advantage of him! Nevertheless, he felt very guilty.)

Is Your Body Your Enemy?

Historically, the body and the mind were viewed as separate entities. Luckily this view is changing. But, even today, a high percentage of those who visit physicians with complaints of physical ailments have nothing wrong with their *bodies*. Their physiological functioning is being adversely affected by stress or emotional problems, like anxiety and depression. Most often the person is unaware of this. A large number of my clients with panic disorder make sharp distinctions between their minds and their bodies. They do so in very specific ways.

For example, when John had a relapse, he came back to me complaining that this time his panics were much worse than they had ever been before. He said they were worse because now he was waking up from sleep in a panic, and his symptoms were different from those in previous panics.

At the height of his distress, he sat in my office and said: "Just look at my body. Look at how it is shaking! It shouldn't do it! I cannot go outside and be seen this way. It's terrible! I try so hard to stop it, but I can't. Look at this. It's disgraceful!" Yet I found it noteworthy that he did not hold the same judgmental attitude towards headaches or flus; he considered these to be "physically" caused, and therefore not "blameworthy."

John helped me to see that many people with panic disorder feel this way about their symptoms. I am not referring to the extreme discomfort or the fear feelings. I am talking about the *anger* and *disdain* that they feel toward their bodies' anxiety symptoms. They feel deep "shame" about any visible symptoms of anxiety (like John's trembling—or blushing, sweating, or "looking lost"). How *dare* their bodies express anxiety like that? They feel their bodies have betrayed them. So, they view their bodies as their enemies, deserving merciless judgment. Do you relate to this?

This can reflect a deep-rooted lack of acceptance of the wide array of feelings that we are capable of experiencing. In this view, only a narrow set of feelings of the "right" kind and in the "right" place are acceptable.

John had a lot of stress in his life. His boss had promoted a junior employee, whom John had trained, to the position that John had hoped to get. But he continued to try hard to please his boss and never mentioned how unfairly he felt he had been treated. At the same time, his elderly mother was becoming very demanding of his time, refusing to do anything for herself.

There is not always such a clear connection between such stresses (caused in large part because of a lack of assertiveness) and panic. John's example, however, clearly shows how tolerating a "toxic" interpersonal environment, while trying to go about one's business as usual can wreak emotional havoc. While his mind was trying to ignore the stress, fortunately, his body was telling him that the situation *was not okay*. I say "fortunately" because if the panics had not alerted him to stop and think, he might have ended up later with some stress-related physical disease.

After my experience with John, I began asking clients in all my groups about this judgmental anger toward their bodies. Almost all of my clients indicated experiencing it. These thoughts and feelings are very private and many people will not share them openly, unless asked directly. Yet most panickers *do* carry this additional burden of self-blame and suffering within themselves.

Now I turn to you, and ask you to examine your beliefs. Are they similar? Do you view your body as an enemy? This kind of stance will not help in your recovery. It is to your advantage to see yourself as one whole being composed of body and mind. Both are so intertwined that they cannot be separated. In sum, the more you view your body as your "friend" deserving your compassion and alliance, the better. Think of working with, rather than against, your body. The more you fight your body, the worse your symptoms tend to be.

Your Body Is Your Friend— Work With Rather Than Against It.

Moving from Fear to Action

Fear can consume you and devastate your life. If you spend your time worrying about your fears, they tend to worsen. As long as anxiety is vague and formless, you cannot do anything about it. It helps to "clothe" the fear in a specific thought or image. It is also very helpful if you always try to move from fear to specific action.

Let me give you an example of what I mean. Rita was extremely frightened by the 1989 Loma Prieta earthquake. Afterwards, she became obsessed with the idea of another one. She came to see me two years later. She was anticipating the next earthquake with increasing dread. She worried about it most of the time. She would watch closely for anything that might indicate earth movements. For instance, if her plants swayed a bit in a breeze she would think immediately that it was an earthquake. I suggested that she should become *an expert in earthquake preparedness*. She followed my advice and read up on any materials she could find. She made sure that she had all kinds of the necessary provisions. She rehearsed a plan of action with her family every six months. As she got into it more and more, her anxiety began to dissipate. She had to acknowledge to herself that she had done everything she could, and that it was not in her control. This is a way of channeling anxiety into very constructive action.

Drs. Robert Ornstein and David Sobel in a 1994 article made a statement about this that is very much to the point. "Move from worry to action, and the action will absorb the anxiety." Keep this saying in mind as a motto for dealing with general anxiety.

Move From Worry to Action, and the Action Will Absorb the Anxiety.

Recommended Reading

Beckfield, D.F. 1994. *Master Your Panic and Take Back Your Life!* San Luis Obispo: Impact Publishers.

Ross, J. 1994. *Triumph Over Fear*. New York: Bantam Books.

6

When to Consider Medications

Elke Zuercher-White, Ph.D. and Dennis J. Munjack, M.D.[*]

Medications, to take them or not, that is the question. It may seem like a simple question, but the answer can be quite complex. Once, an elderly client of mine became terrified after falling down inside a moving bus. She was treated with cognitive-behavioral methods, similar to those you will learn in this book. But, after extensive work, she was still having a hard time with her anxiety and, at that point she was offered a medication evaluation. As she seldom even took aspirin, she did not like the idea. She asked, plaintively, "Besides pills and trying to work on this myself, is there no miracle?"

Unfortunately, there are no miracles. Although some people may think of medications as "miracle" drugs, remember, "There Is No Free Lunch."

The Widespread Use of Medications

Although psychological treatments for phobias have been available for many years, *panic disorder* was not identified as a distinct and separate diagnosis until about 15 years ago. Consequently, the development of psychological treatments for panic attacks and panic disorder is relatively recent. Medications were used long before that, however, to alleviate clients' discomfort from panic *attacks*.

The first report of imipramine's effects on panic attacks was published in the early 60s by Dr. Donald Klein. Therefore, it is not surprising that psychiatrists traditionally have treated this condition with medications. In addition, psychotherapists from various disciplines are often unfamiliar with the cognitive-behavioral treatment methods that have proved effective to treat panic disorder.

---

[*] Dr. Munjack is an Associate Professor of Psychiatry and Director of the Anxiety Disorders Clinic at the University of Southern California-Los Angeles County Medical Center. He is in private practice in Beverly Hills.

That is why many clinicians prescribe medications or make a referral for a medication evaluation when people go to them for the treatment of panic disorder. Furthermore, many people suffering from panic attacks go to internists, family, or general practitioners, and these physicians are also likely to prescribe medications. Unfortunately, not many of these doctors and therapists are well-informed about the alternatives to medication.

We would like you to become a well-informed consumer; understanding the many factors involved and the variety of treatments available so that you can make the best possible decision for yourself. Keep in mind, however, that the information on psychopharmacological treatments provided here is very general. *You must seek the advice of a physician.* If you do see a physician for medications, ask lots of questions so you have a good understanding of what to expect. Don't take a drug blindly without knowing anything about it. A psychopharmacologist (a physician trained to use these types of medications) has a great deal of information about the appropriate medications for panic disorder. Work with your physician to maximize a positive benefit.

Biological and Psychological Considerations

You may have already taken medications and been helped by them. On medication, you may not have intense anxiety symptoms, or even any panic attacks at all! And, you may take this as proof that your problem with anxiety is biological, not psychological. However, this is not necessarily (or even logically) the case. Biological treatments help psychological disorders, and psychological treatments positively affect physiologically based problems. Even if there is a strong biological component to your panic disorder, and medication would be considered, that does not mean that medication is the only route open to you. *As a rule, medications do not permanently eliminate fear and they do not teach coping skills.* For instance, whatever the basis for phobias, phobias are not usually cured by medication, but by exposure to the feared situation.

Biological functions, cognitions (thoughts), feelings, and behaviors are all closely linked, and changes in one area can produce changes in all other areas. Remember, using psychological methods to confront anxiety can eventually produce changes in brain chemistry.

Placebos

When research on medications is being conducted, a group of people on medications is often compared with a group taking only placebos. A placebo is a pill that does not have any active chemical ingredients in it. Clients always know that they will be assigned to either group, but they do not know which. Frequently, one-fourth to one-third of all clients in a placebo group improve. What does this tell us? That although active medication treatments are generally twice as effective as the placebo "treatments," part of the beneficial effect is psychological! In other words, people respond to the *belief* that they are getting effective treatment, or to their brief visits with the nurse or physician for medication. Likewise, cognitive-behavioral treatments for panic are compared to other "placebo" treatments, e.g., relaxation, support, and education about anxiety and panic. The latter seem convincing on the surface but do not contain the critical treatment components.

Cost/Benefit Ratio

Years ago, Dr. Zuercher-White chaired a research committee in a hospital. Researchers who submitted proposals had to list all the potential risks and benefits that could apply to their subjects. The ratio of risk vs. benefit helped the committee to determine whether to approve a proposal or not. The ideal situation was, of course, to have as low a risk (or "cost") and as high a benefit as possible. This is a good approach to take if you are considering taking medications. Ask yourself: "What are the possible risks and costs and what are the possible benefits?"

Potential Benefits of Medications

- You may benefit if you are feeling so terrified of the panic attacks and possible phobias that you cannot function, that is, you feel that you cannot work or do other everyday tasks. We firmly believe that it is better to be able to function on medications than not function at all. Staying away from situations where you feel overwhelmed by high levels of anticipatory anxiety and fear of having a panic can lead very rapidly to the development of agoraphobia, sometimes in a severe form. (The more you avoid situations out of fear, the more this fear tends to grow.)

- You may benefit if you are having such a hard time with anxiety, panic, and phobias that you cannot concentrate on doing the work required, either in this book or in a psychological treatment regimen.

- You may benefit if you are feeling very depressed and thinking about suicide.

- You may benefit if, in addition to suffering from panic disorder, you have other emotional or personality problems that make it very hard for you to cope.

- You may benefit if you are in the midst of a major life crisis that makes it impossible for you to concentrate on the tasks involved in overcoming panic and phobias.

- You may benefit if you go through this book and/or treatment with a therapist and find that you have not been helped sufficiently.

- You may benefit if you don't have any access to cognitive-behavioral treatments for panic.

- You may benefit if you have a strong preference for medications, and lack the desire to try other methods and treatments.

In sum, you may benefit from taking medications if your biological make-up or psychological problems are so compelling that you cannot concentrate or follow through with the work set forth in this book, or with professional psychological treatment, or if such treatment is not available. If the benefit you may obtain from taking medications seems to outweigh the risk or cost of taking them, for whatever reason, honor that decision.

Potential Risks of Medications

- You may risk spending quite a bit of money over time. Drug therapy can be very costly, depending on the particular medication.

- You may risk bothersome side effects. Some people are more affected than others.

- You may risk psychological and/or physiological dependence. It is easy to attribute gains to medications rather than to your own efforts. Also, physical dependence can be a factor with longer term use of some tranquilizers.

- You may risk relapse, withdrawal, and rebound effects. See more on these under the "High-Potency Benzodiazepines (BZs)" section in this chapter. Discontinuation from *any* drug *can* lead to relapse.

- You may risk the interference of benzodiazepines with cognitive-behavioral learning because of its effect on short-term memory (especially with high doses or prolonged use).

In sum, your risks in taking medications are such that they could outweigh the possible benefits.

Medications Commonly Used in Panic Disorder

A few years ago, based on extensive research, the National Institute of Mental Health proposed three main classes of medications for panic disorder: Tricyclic antidepressants, monoamine oxidase inhibitors, and high-potency benzodiazepines. More recently, selective serotonin re-uptake inhibitors became available and today they are gaining rapidly in popularity.

Tricyclic Antidepressants (TCAs)

Imipramine (Tofranil™) is the best studied of these medications. Clomipramine (Anafranil™) is also clearly effective. Other medications in this class that may be effective (although systematic studies have not been done) are desipramine (Norpramin™), nortriptyline (Pamelor™), and amitriptyline (Elavil™).

Advantages: The TCAs do not lead to physical dependence. They have beneficial effects on mood, anxiety, and panic symptoms. They have a direct antipanic effect without necessarily affecting anticipatory or chronic pervasive anxiety. This class of medications helps with anxiety or panic whether or not the person is depressed, although sooner or later many people with panic disorder do become depressed.

Disadvantages: Symptom relief with the TCAs is not immediate. It may take from 3 to 6 weeks for the effect to take place; although sometimes this occurs sooner. There are a number of possible side effects, although not everyone will experience them or be troubled by these. The side effects include "anticholinergic" effects: dry mouth, constipation, and blurred vision. Low blood pressure (when standing up suddenly), weight gain and sexual dysfunction can also occur. There may be increased stimulation and/or sedation: sensations such as tremors, jitteriness, lightheadedness, or low energy, especially early in the treatment. Most, but not all, side effects decrease or disappear over days or weeks. All of them disappear when the drug is discontinued.

Dosing: It is recommended that TCA medications be started at a low dose and increased slowly. This may help to minimize or eliminate initial side effects. Tofranil, Anafranil, and Norpramin should be started at doses of 10 mg. a day to avoid the "jitteriness syndrome," as it has been called, as well as a possible temporary worsening of panic symptoms. The usual effective dose for imipramine is 25 to 300 mg. a day. The daily dose is often taken all at one time.

Monoamine Oxidase Inhibitors (MAOIs)

This is another class of antidepressants. The most commonly studied is phenelzine (Nardil™). It may be one of the most effective medications for panic disorder. However, it is used primarily when other treatments have failed.

Advantages: Nardil is a potent antidepressant and antianxiety agent and does not lead to physical dependence. It is very energizing for many people. It may be particularly effective for individuals who have panic disorder and accompanying social phobia, or depressive symptoms that are not typical.

Disadvantages: Symptom relief may take 3 to 6 weeks. The main disadvantage of the MAOIs is that they require a strict diet, one that is low in "tyramine." Interactions with the wrong foods (e.g., aged cheeses) and certain medications can be serious. Problems can be minimized when the psychiatrist and the patient work closely on following the recommended guidelines. There may also be anticholinergic-like side effects, but they tend to be lower than for the TCAs. There also might be hypotension (low blood pressure), weight gain, sexual dysfunction, and difficulty falling asleep. These side effects are often most pronounced during the third and fourth weeks of treatment.

Dosing: The starting dose of Nardil is 15 mg. three times a day. It is then kept at that level, or increased up to 90 mg. a day over a period of several weeks, depending on the patient's body weight and response.

Reversible Inhibitors of Monoamine Oxidase (RIMAs)

Newer versions of MAOIs may be available, the so-called Reversible Inhibitors of Monoamine Oxidase, Subtype A, e.g., brofaromine and meclobemide. These may not require the special diet alluded to above, and are likely to be more easily tolerated. Unfortunately these drugs have hit a snag in their development, and it is not clear at this point when they will become available.

High-Potency Benzodiazepines (BZs)

The most extensively studied BZ has been alprazolam (Xanax™). Although Xanax is the only drug approved by the Food and Drug Administration (FDA) for the treatment of panic disorder, other medications of this class are also widely and effectively used. Examples include lorazepam (Ativan™) and clonazepam (Klonopin™). Because Xanax and Ativan are eliminated from the body relatively rapidly, they require 3 to 4 daily dosages. Klonopin is longer-acting and usually requires only 2 or 3 daily dosages.

Advantages: The onset of symptom relief is fast. Although BZs can be taken *as needed* (not necessarily following a set dosage schedule), many psychiatrists prescribe them to *prevent* panic attacks; and not to be taken after a panic attack has occurred. The above-named three BZs (unlike the TCAs) have the added advantage of being effective against both panic anxiety and anticipatory anxiety. The BZs also tend to have fewer side effects than the TCAs.

Disadvantages: Patients sometimes complain of sedation effects. Symptoms such as lack of coordination, spaciness, dizziness, and loss of memory occur, but are seen more among the elderly. These medications should *not* be combined with alcohol. Furthermore, there is a risk of becoming physiologically dependent, if higher doses are taken for several weeks. When attempting to get off BZs, any or all of the following effects may occur. The first may be a return of the original symptoms. This is called *relapse* and is the most common consequence of discontinuing a BZ. For patients treated with BZs alone, this will usually, sooner or later, occur. Second, a *withdrawal* syndrome may occur within hours to days of the last dose of a BZ *that has been tapered too quickly*. Examples of withdrawal symptoms include muscle tension, headache, jitteriness, and an inability to sleep, symptoms that may not have been present as panic symptoms originally. Finally, *rebound* symptoms can occur. During rebound, panic symptoms intensify for a brief time when the drug is discontinued. All of the above are less likely to be so problematic if tapering is done very slowly. Some patients develop "pseudowithdrawal" symptoms that are unrelated to the medication they are taking. (This has been observed also upon abrupt discontinuation of a placebo!)

Dosing: The dose is often started low to minimize or eliminate side effects, and is then increased to the level needed. If doses are spaced too widely during the day, patients may experience "between dose" anxiety. This is the reason that short-acting drugs such as Xanax and Ativan require multiple daily doses and the reason that many physicians favor longer acting ones such as Klonopin. The effective dose for Xanax, Ativan, and Klonopin is between 1 to 10 mg. a day. The average effective dose is between 3 to 6 mg. a day.

Selective Serotonin Re-Uptake Inhibitors (SSRIs)

These newer antidepressants have not been studied as much as the previously mentioned medications for panic disorder, but a number of large-scale investigations are presently underway. Many clinicians are finding them very helpful. The best known is fluoxetine (Prozac™). Other popular SSRIs are sertraline (Zoloft™), paroxetene (Paxil™), and more recently fluvoxamine (Luvox™).

Advantages: These drugs are usually tolerated more easily than the TCAs. Because of their improved side effect profile, the SSRIs have become very popular.

Disadvantages: Side effects may involve jitteriness, tremors, agitation, and insomnia. A significant proportion of patients complain of a loss of sexual drive or an inability to experience orgasm. Although this side effect occasionally disappears with time, or more commonly as a result of lowering the dose, some patients find this to be unacceptable and insist on discontinuing the drug.

Dosing: To treat panic disorder and to avoid a temporary increase in the number or severity of panic attacks, it is necessary to start an SSRI at an extremely low dose. This requires, for example, beginning with Prozac at 5 to 10 mg. a day or Zoloft at 12.5 to 25 mg. a day for a week. The effective therapeutic dose is usually in the range of 20 to 40 mg. a day for Prozac and 50 to 100 mg. a day for Zoloft. Paxil is less well-studied, and therefore Prozac and Zoloft should be considered first.

Other Medications

The most commonly used medications for treating panic disorder are discussed above. A few other medications should be mentioned. The medications that are *not* effective for panic include buspirone (Buspar™), buproprion (Wellbutrin™), maprotiline (Ludiomil™), and trazodone (Desyrel™). Propranolol (Inderal™) is often used for a variety of medical conditions, including high blood pressure. Many internists and cardiologists prescribe it for panic attacks, particularly if the patient has the accompanying (usually harmless) cardiac condition—mitral valve prolapse. This condition does not *cause* panic disorder and Inderal does not help panic disorder. It is probably not much more effective than a sugar pill. Remember, 30 percent of patients with panic disorder respond, at least for a while, to pills or capsules with nothing in them except sugar!

How Medications Might Be Prescribed

Medications work by blocking panics and/or lowering the anxiety level; with lowered anxiety panic attacks seem less likely to occur. In spite of few or no panic attacks, some patients still experience high levels of anticipatory anxiety or even panic when confronting a fearful agoraphobic situation.

Some psychiatrists no longer prescribe the short-acting, high-potency BZs (Xanax and Ativan) for panic disorder on a long-term basis as readily as they did a few years ago, because of increased concern about their effects. If you have an urgent need for medications, you may be started on a benzodiazepine and an antidepressant at the same time. Once the antidepressant takes effect, the benzodiazepine can be tapered off. The risk for physical dependence is then significantly diminished. On the other hand, some patients need to take antidepressants such as the TCAs, MAOIs, or SSRIs along with a high-potency BZ for prolonged periods. Many have done this successfully for many months or years and report feeling quite well.

A frequent approach to prescribing the BZs is to have the client take them as needed. This has advantages and disadvantages: The main advantage is that the person is much less likely to develop a *physical* dependence. However, there is a significant disadvantage in that a *psychological* dependence may develop. People take the pill when feeling high anxiety or an attack coming on. They also take it in the middle of an attack, or just after one. Since the medication makes them feel less anxious, this feeds the notion that only the medications can "save" the person who then trusts his or her own resources less and less. Sometimes the psychological dependence is less pronounced when the person takes the medications on a schedule rather than in response to the feeling of anxiety.

For some people, medications are a lifesaver. If their lives are too constricted by their phobias, or they are experiencing extreme discomfort due to frequent panics, high anxiety, or depression, medication can give them room to breathe. They may then choose to concentrate and work on the cognitive-behavioral techniques. It is unfortunate that some patients feel as if they are "weak" or a "failure" if they take medications. Yet we have had clients come in with recent recurrences of panics, who had very positive results in the past with medications. When taking their histories, we learned that they had a few panics years ago, were given medications for a short time, the attacks stopped, and they were fine afterwards. Although some of these returning clients wanted medications again, others preferred to try cognitive-behavior therapy, which was less widely available a few years ago.

Medications are often administered for long periods of time. Concerning anxiety disorders, it is well-known that for many clients, their symptoms will return when they end drug treatment. It is important for panic patients to taper off extremely slowly, especially from BZs, and from the various antidepressants, as well. Even with slow tapering, it is difficult for some to give up medications. When you get quick relief from high anxiety states and panic, you become less tolerant of the sensations, and the temptation to stay on medications is high. But from a psychological perspective, feeling and confronting the sensations of anxiety are essential to overcome the fear (see Chapter 10). Overcoming panic disorder without medications is desirable and quite possible for many people if they obtain specialized psychological therapy.

Should Psychological Treatments and Medications Be Combined?

Many studies suggest that medications alone do not produce long-lasting changes, that is, gains are frequently not maintained after all medications have been discontinued. The addition of cognitive-behavioral methods to medication, however, can increase the effects of medications and can be used to help the person taper off. Thus, a combination is better than medications alone.

In some cases the reverse is also true, that is, medications can increase the effects of cognitive-behavioral approaches. But this is not always the case for the following reasons: First, there is a phenomenon called state-dependent learning. This means that learning and change take place within a specific context, in this case under drug sedation. When medications are discontinued, what has been learned may not transfer to a nonmedicated state. Second, the person may believe that the medications helped, not his or her own efforts. This may reduce feelings of self-efficacy (see Chapter 9). On the other hand, the more you believe that *you* brought about the changes, the higher your self-efficacy will be. Third, BZs may adversely affect your short-term memory and recall and thus *interfere with the new learning* that you are attempting to achieve with cognitive-behavioral work. Finally, by *blocking bodily* sensations and fluctuations of anxiety and panic, you *cannot benefit fully* from the cognitive and interoceptive work. (See Chapters 9 and 10.) To achieve the maximum benefit, you need to work on the sensations and related thoughts when they are at their highest levels. This will prepare you better for occasional setbacks later.

Recommendations Regarding Medications

- If you are a "new panicker" and can function, even if it is difficult, you may first want to try and do the work without medications. Panic attacks in themselves are not life-threatening emergencies; the less you consider them as such, the better off you are.

- Use medications if you are very troubled and feel that you cannot function without additional help. It is better to work and lead a normal life than to develop avoidance behaviors.

- Use medications if your life is in turmoil, preventing you from concentrating on the psychological work.

- Use medications if you have tried the state-of-the-art psychological methods and are not satisfied with the results.

- Consider medications if psychological treatments are not available.

- Use medications if your doctor suggests that because of your history you need them on a long-term basis.

- If you are on medications and plan to withdraw from them, taper off very slowly under your doctor's supervision. If you have a hard time, try to combine medications with cognitive-behavioral methods.

- If you have a strong preference for medications over other treatments, see a doctor about medication treatment.

Do not get started on medications without doing a cost/benefit analysis. Weigh the pros and cons. Remember that although your symptoms may improve (sometimes totally) during the time you take the medicines and possibly for some time afterwards, medications can create new problems. They are not a *cure* for panic disorder. As you can see, there is no single answer. Every person is unique. Your therapist and/or doctor will be able to assist you in making the best decision.

If you are on medications now, depending on your and your physician's plans, you may follow the program in this book, and later, if you taper off medications, rework Parts II and III, especially Chapters 9, 10, 11, and 12.

Before concluding this chapter, we should say that cognitive-behavioral methods have their advantages and *disadvantages* as well. While often extremely helpful, they do not work for everyone, and they do require a firm commitment and a lot of time from you. The results will not be immediate. But if you choose to *work* your way through this program, you will very likely gain mastery over panic attacks and phobias.

PART II

WORKING THROUGH YOUR FEAR TO CONQUER PANIC

7

The Physiology of Fear and Panic

This chapter is fairly technical, and it is very important for this information to really "sink in." I encourage you to read it thoroughly because it lays the groundwork for the work that you will be doing in subsequent chapters.

In Chapter 3, I listed the panic symptoms and conditions that must be met for the diagnoses of panic disorder and agoraphobia. I also stated that, in normal amounts, anxiety is healthy, adaptive, crucial for survival, and often leads to greater productivity and enhanced performance. When daily anxiety is excessively high, however, it can interfere with functioning.

You may have some idea of how *your* panic attacks developed, and also understand what they represent to you. Yet see if you can answer this question: *How are panic attacks produced physiologically?* In other words, what is happening in your body when you have a panic attack? You know your *symptoms* and how you feel, but *what produces the symptoms*? Take a few minutes now and jot down your answers on a piece of paper to compare later with the information in this chapter. PLEASE DO SO NOW (before proceeding further).

Looking for the Components of Panic Attacks

As stated in Part I, the three components of anxiety and panic are the *physiological* (physical symptoms, e.g., sweating, rapid heart beat, numbness, choking sensations), *cognitive* (pertaining to thoughts, like "What if I die?" "I cannot stand this heat." "I'm going to faint."), and *behavioral* (e.g., tensing the body to prevent fainting, pacing, avoidance). A panic attack is thus a *reaction,* a *response.* You might view your panic as an "entity" with an almost separate existence, that suddenly comes over you, completely outside of your control. But it is important to view panic attacks from a vantage point that includes all three components. When you begin dissecting the panic attack into its three components, you will understand the steps that panics take—the sequence that panics follow.

I like to use the image of an accordion. Think first of viewing the panic as a compressed accordion. Then, you start pulling it apart, as if opening it. This image also allows you to view the panic in a different time frame. Instead of being a single, sudden event, it is spread out over time, the way an accordion takes some time to open. Like each fold in the accordion, each step in the panic process provides another opportunity for intervention. As you do the work, you can increasingly look for those opportunities and make an impact at various points along the panic continuum. You will find that you have more and more control. However, as I stated earlier, control is very tricky, and you cannot expect to have total control over whether or not you panic. The goal we are seeking is a combination of gaining control and yielding control.

Let me give you an example. After learning how to identify the three components, a client described the following panic attack.

Client: "I was at a party last Friday and I had a panic."

Therapist: "Can you describe the exact process?"

Client: "I arrived at the party. Soon after I got there I started to feel hot and dizzy. I began to worry that I might faint. My heart started beating faster and my breathing became more labored. I felt like I could faint. I had to find a way to leave the party. First, I sat down so I would not faint. Then I couldn't stand it anymore and I left."

In looking at the above description, think about the three components of a panic. To make it easier, I will put each sentence on a separate line and number them. There is a short line to the right of each sentence. Write down which panic component the statement represents. You can use *P* for physiological, *C* for cognitive, and *B* for behavioral.

PLEASE DO SO NOW (before proceeding further).

1. I started to feel hot and dizzy.   _____

2. I began to worry that I might faint.   _____

3. My heart started beating faster and my breathing became more labored.   _____

4. I felt like I could faint.   _____

5. I had to find a way to leave the party.   _____

6. First, I sat down so I would not faint.   _____

7. Then I couldn't stand it anymore and I left.   _____

The correct designations are: Sentence No. 1 is P, 2 is C, 3 is P, 4 is C, 5 is C, 6 is B and C, and 7 is B. P thus stands for physical symptoms/sensations. C stands for thoughts (in this case including statements like "I feel . . ."); in the description above, the feeling of fainting is a thought, because the client is not actually fainting but is worrying that she may faint. B stands for any action, like sitting down or leaving. "I sat down so I would not faint" includes the action of sitting down and the thought that it would prevent her from fainting.

To help yourself effectively, you need to become a very good participant-observer, observing the events that are taking place within yourself. You will greatly benefit from learning to observe your body, thoughts, and behaviors with fresh eyes, as if you were outside yourself (an observer). You observe the participant, which is you. The interaction of the components is *unique to you*. Someone

---

Become a Participant-Observer
and Study Your Own Panics.

---

else may feel, think, and behave very differently under the same circumstances. Each of us sees the world through our own lens. This is a *different way of observing* than helplessly succumbing to strong emotions and catastrophic thoughts, such as, "I can't stand this panic. It'll get worse and worse till I collapse."

As a valuable learning exercise, you should begin dissecting every single panic attack from now on. (Take their different components apart and examine them.) Identify each part as a P, C, or B component. You may say that you have no panics at this time. Then there are two other ways to approach this task. If you have any phobias, approach one (for instance, if you fear going to the supermarket, go as closely to it as you can possible tolerate) and see what happens with your antici-patory anxiety, which is the anxiety experienced *before* approaching a feared situation. If you are a panicker without phobias, and currently you have no panic attacks, you can do this task when you next experience high anxiety. Although high anxiety is not the same as a panic attack, it will help you to practice separating the various components and see how they interact with each other. Try to dissect 5 to 10 panics over the coming days/weeks.

I'm providing a worksheet with 10 lines to use when you dissect panics. Use as few or as many lines as you need to list all the components. Make 5 to 10 copies of this worksheet so you have one for each panic you dissect. At this point you might say, "Okay, I've started to do this task, but what *are* panic attacks?" As you know, panic has to do with fear. In fact, the dictionary defines panic as "a sudden overpowering fright, especially a sudden unreasoning terror . . . ," so I will first describe the physiology of fear, and then I'll draw some connections between panics and this physiology.

Fear: The Normal Reaction When Threatened

For survival, all organisms able to sense and move must be able to anticipate threats and react quickly when threatened. This reaction is variously called the *stress response, alarm response,* or *fight/flight re-sponse.* Although this response is an ancient survival strategy, it is just as relevant today. If I were attacked while walking down the street, I would try very quickly to mobilize a great amount of energy to save myself. Or if I were in a building that caught fire, I would need to assess the situation very quickly and determine how to save myself. These are the kinds of threats that mobilize the fight/flight response.

When the threat registers in the brain, fear activates the hypothalamus, and a signal is sent to the autonomic nervous system. (This is the part of the nervous system that usually functions "auto-matically" or outside of awareness. It is responsible for the regulation of respiration, circulation, di-gestion, body temperature, etc.) The autonomic nervous system consists of two main parts: The sympathetic nervous system (SNS) and the parasympathetic nervous system (PNS). In essence, the SNS is responsible for mobilizing the body and preparing it for the fight/flight response. The PNS relaxes the body and brings it back to normal. The two systems help to maintain the body's balance.

In the fight/flight response, many changes take place in the body. Fear activates the SNS as an entire unit producing a *mass discharge*. The ensuing reaction, the SNS-adrenal-medullary arousal (so named because of the SNS stimulation *and* the release of the adrenaline and noradrenaline hormones from the adrenal medulla), results in the following changes:

- *Cardiovascular:* The heart's output is increased with the heart beating faster and harder, to redistribute the blood volume to help deliver oxygen and glucose where it is needed. There is increased blood flow to the big muscles and decreased flow to the skin, hands and feet, gastrointestinal tract, and kidneys. The increased blood flow with added amounts of oxygen and glucose going to the arms and legs result in the greater muscle strength, needed to fight or flee. The resulting symptoms include tachycardia (rapid heart beat), and numbness and tingling in the extremities (because of decreased blood flow). Think of the symptoms you

Worksheet 3: The Components of Panic (or Anxiety)

State Event/Situation: _____ Put each panic (or anxiety) component on a separate line.	State if: Physiological, Cognitive, or Behavioral
1. _____	
2. _____	
3. _____	
4. _____	
5. _____	
6. _____	
7. _____	
8. _____	
9. _____	
10. _____	

experience in a panic and you will begin to see the connections between panic attacks and the physiology of the fight/flight response.

- *Pulmonary:* The lungs respond to the danger signals by greatly increased breathing (heavier and faster) to bring in the extra oxygen needed for the muscle tissues (as explained above).

- *Skin and Sweat Glands:* Because of decreased blood volume from the skin, there is vascular constriction in and under the skin, which produces symptoms such as numbness and tingling. Sweating helps regulate the body temperature and prevents it from rising to dangerous levels.

- *Mental/Behavioral:* Adrenaline increases concentration. When you are extremely alert to threat signals, you do not worry about irrelevant matters, such as whether you left dirty dishes in the sink. Your behavior will require either aggression to fight off the attacker, or fleeing for fear of your life.

- *Other effects include:* Dilation of the pupils to increase the visual field, accelerated blood coagulation to protect against hemorrhage, and increased blood pressure to improve circulation. The hypothalamus helps to coordinate the SNS effects with those of other neuroendocrine systems. Thus, certain hormones (catecholamine and corticotropic hormones) are secreted in larger amounts and are responsible for some of the physiological changes occurring in the fight/flight response. You may wonder what would happen if the SNS maintained this arousal state indefinitely. This would be very dangerous, indeed, but in fact, it does not happen. The reason it does not happen is that before adrenaline and noradrenaline can reach potentially harmful levels, they are destroyed by other chemicals; and the PNS automatically "kicks in" to restore balance in the body.

The Fight/Flight Response Is Designed to Protect, Not to Harm the Organism.

Now you might be thinking, "While this makes sense, what does it have to do with panic attacks? When I panic, I *know* there is no real danger."

The Connection Between Fear and Panic

For a number of years, researchers have been aware of the connection between the physiology of the fight/flight response and panic attacks. The first panic can be seen as a misfiring of the fight/flight response, or a "false alarm." In 1988, Dr. David Barlow, in his book *Anxiety and Its Disorders: The Nature and Treatment of Anxiety and Panic,* emphasized this connection in the treatment of panic disorder. Since then, many panic disorder sufferers have found this information invaluable in their struggle to understand their panics.

The SNS is stimulated in a number of situations. Stressors other than fear can also activate the SNS. Physical stresses might include surgery, injury, or certain illnesses. Mental stresses might include rage, facing dilemmas with no easy solutions, or other emotional upheavals. A variety of different situations can all elicit the same stress reaction. Emotional stressors are among the more common precipitants of the stress response.

Panic disorder seems to occur more in people with a psychological vulnerability and/or a biological predisposition. The first panic attack often occurs in a stressful context. When asked about conditions preceding their first panic, people often describe stressful circumstances such as divorce, death, illness within self or family, bankruptcy, interpersonal conflict, and illegal drug usage. Frequently, the stresses involve new, demanding situations and experiences. But often people do not make the connection, because the panic doesn't necessarily take place right in the middle of a particularly stressful event but when things have calmed down. Stressful life experiences activate the SNS, sometimes in its entirety, producing the fight/flight or alarm response.

Panic Attacks Act Like Fear Responses— but Are Triggered in the Absence of Life-Threatening Danger.

In panic, the physical reactions are the same as in true danger—but there is no outlet. If you panic when you are in a traffic jam on a bridge, you do not have someone to fight and you cannot very well leave your car and flee. Yet your body prepared itself for such action. There is now too much oxygen coming in compared to your body's need. This leads to diminished oxygen release to the tissues (see Chapter 8). As a result of less oxygen to the tissues, including the brain, you may have feelings of lightheadedness or dizziness, or feelings of unreality, or blurred vision. You may try to compensate by breathing harder, perhaps causing yourself discomfort and chest pains. So here is the paradox: You may feel as if you are not breathing enough air, when in fact you are *taking in more oxygen than you need!* (When experiencing the above-described sensations, intervening by slowing your breathing is very helpful.) This constitutes the *physiological* component of panic.

In many people the single panic attack remains a rare event. The panicker may say to him/herself, "I had a fight with my wife/husband," or "The pressure I'm under is getting to me; I must calm down." Because the first panic attack can be such an overwhelming experience, however, some people seriously start to worry about the experience. This may have happened to you. You may have said, "This must be a sign that something is drastically wrong with me." "What if I have a heart attack and die?" "I may go totally insane." "I could faint." Some people don't even dare to tell others what has happened for fear of being judged as crazy.

As human beings we are constantly evaluating and trying to understand the world, our reactions, and events outside of us. When we have no explanation for an event, we still want to label it and give it meaning. If you interpret the sensations in your body as indicating a disease or loss of functioning, and you expect disaster, fear results. Similarly, you may develop an alertness to situations easily perceived as entrapping, resulting in thoughts of flight. These negative thoughts or interpretations represent the *cognitive* component of panic.

The *behavioral* component of panic, naturally, is composed of behavioral changes, or overt acts. You may feel restless during a panic and pace back and forth, become easily angered, and later avoid situations where you might feel trapped. Escaping from situations when a panic seems imminent is common, e.g., from a restaurant, a meeting, a freeway. You may go to an emergency room repeatedly, seeking reassurance. After all, the sense of danger and the impulse to escape are built into the fight/flight response, so it is understandable how all this happens.

It is worth stating again that the *fight/flight response*, whether to *true danger*, or as a *panic attack* (in the absence of danger) *is not dangerous.* Nature is very smart. It would hardly have developed a protective mechanism that killed the organism in the process of protecting it! Therefore, panic attacks do not lead to heart attack, stroke, psychosis, and rarely do they even lead to fainting.

Fainting

Although theoretically, a person *could* faint during the fight/flight response, it is extremely rare. This is due, in part, to the elevated SNS arousal which does anything but lead to fainting. However, I have had clients who reported fainting on rare occasions. But it was always in a context in which there were other mitigating factors. One woman was pregnant; another woman was severely anemic.

Blood-injection-injury phobia is a separate condition that occasionally causes fainting. This is a phobia unlike others as far as the physiological response is concerned. Although the very first reaction may involve SNS arousal, it soon gives way to a drastic *decrease* in physiological arousal, with PNS activation. Heart rate and blood pressure are *lowered*, which can lead to fainting. In other words, the reaction is not the sustained SNS response of people with panic and agoraphobia. (Blood-injection-injury phobia is believed to be inherited. But even if there is a genetic component, such people can be taught to overcome their fear and tendency to faint with behavioral treatments.)

Nocturnal Panics

Nocturnal panics are panics that occur during sleep stages other than the dreaming stage. If you have a nightmare in which someone is trying to kill you, you may wake up with your heart pounding. This is a fear reaction, not a panic, because in the dream the threat to your life seems real, just as it might be if you were awake. But nocturnal panics occur at those times when you are not dreaming.

Some people claim that night panics prove that there is a biological abnormality involved in panic disorder. After all, the person is unaware of any thoughts that could have triggered the panic. Yet, the mind works at some level whether awake or asleep. The same happens with hearing. Hearing developed to receive danger signals. The ears cannot be "turned off" during sleep, and sound is registered during sleep. If the brain interprets a sound as dangerous, the person is most likely to wake up. We can develop extreme sensitivity toward certain sounds, for example, a mother is easily awakened from deep sleep by the sounds her newborn baby makes.

Likewise, people can develop extreme sensitivity or vigilance to their own somatic sensations. The body goes through some normal sleep stages where the heart beats faster and breathing is significantly slowed down. If you suffer from panic disorder and you believe that a rapid heart beat signals an impending heart attack or that extremely slow breathing signals a lack of oxygen and impending suffocation, then that belief operates at some level even during sleep; and may wake you up with a full-blown panic. The good news is that as you overcome your fear of panics, eventually you can learn to sleep through those sleep stages characterized by rapid heart beat and slower breathing.

The Same Psychological Mechanisms Operate Whether You Are Awake or Asleep.

It is also possible that a sudden physical arousal or a sense of suffocating due to hyperventilation (Ley, 1988) is triggered during sleep and awakens the person, who *then* reacts with immediate fear to this arousal. Furthermore, for some people "letting go," whether in deep sleep or deep relaxation, is also frightening. They fear unfamiliar sensations and thoughts.

Other Biological Dysfunctions

Today, a great deal of research is being conducted on the biological underpinnings of panic. Studies indicate that some people are more vulnerable to anxiety than others because of a more excitable, easily aroused nervous system. In some, but not all panickers, the fight/flight response may be inappropriately triggered. Other investigations suggest very specific dysfunctions (e.g., in the serotonin, noradrenergic, audiovestibular, or hyperventilatory systems; or there may be a carbon dioxide sensitivity that gives rise to sensations of suffocation). For more details, consult Richard McNally's *Panic Disorder: A Critical Analysis* (1994, N.Y.: The Guilford Press). But none of these findings have been shown to cause panic consistently. Thus, there are many ways to arrive at panic disorder biologically. A biological predisposition can make the person more vulnerable to panic disorder at any time in his or her life, especially if the person becomes anxious (has high anxiety sensitivity) over the symptoms.

Some interesting studies with children suggest that infants who are inhibited in their behavior (showing more difficulty with new situations, more distress when separated from parents, and exhibiting greater dependency) may be predisposed toward later anxiety disorders. Stressful events seem to activate a biologically vulnerable system, which may result in a panic. People who have had difficult childhoods, an alcoholic parent, or suffered early abuse or trauma, are likewise psychologically at risk.

Emotions and Chemistry

Although there is often a strong connection between our physical reactions and the emotions we feel, emotions are not just determined by chemistry. Studies with panickers have shown that feedback from their bodies, e.g., the rate of their heart beat, even if false (*not their own* heart beat), can determine whether or not they react with anxiety.

It is interesting to note here that about 40 percent of panic attacks are *not* accompanied by any physiological arousal! You might believe that you were aroused when in fact you were not. If asked whether you had any physical symptoms, you might respond that your heart was beating fast, you were not getting enough oxygen, or that other such events were occurring. Hence, your body's stress reactions and your emotional responses may have little in common. This suggests how complex the association between physiological symptoms, emotions, thoughts, and behaviors are.

As you develop a fear of panics, *the fear itself feeds the panic cycle,* and it may become easier and easier to panic. For instance, many panickers say, "I just think that I might panic, and I end up with a panic attack!" "I start feeling hot, and suddenly I panic." The first stage in the initial panics may have been a physical sensation, but later *thoughts can also trigger panics.* Look at Worksheet 3, where you dissected your own panics. Has thinking about panic triggered any panics?

The two diagrams on page 51 illustrate this interaction.

Let me give you an example of this process that is not panic-related. It is an excellent illustration of how the mind and body interact. A colleague of mine told me this story. He had been painting a

---

The Panic Cycle Is Fed by Fear.

Diagram 1

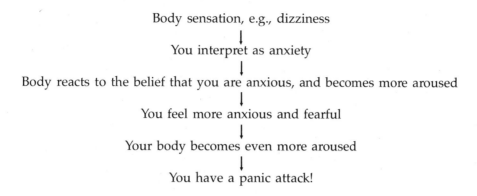

Body sensation, e.g., dizziness
↓
You interpret as anxiety
↓
Body reacts to the belief that you are anxious, and becomes more aroused
↓
You feel more anxious and fearful
↓
Your body becomes even more aroused
↓
You have a panic attack!

Diagram 2

You enter a meeting and ask yourself, "What if I panic?"
↓
Body responds with alarm (your mind is telling it to do so)
↓
You take your body's reaction as more evidence of an imminent panic
↓
Body senses more danger and becomes more aroused
↓
You panic!

room very late at night and didn't quit until about 3:00 a.m. Since he had paint on his right arm, he removed it with turpentine, washed his arm off, and went to sleep. He was too tired to shower. The next morning he woke up and noticed that his right arm was quite red. He immediately got scared and asked himself, "What is happening to my arm?" He was alarmed, started to sweat, and loosened his pajamas top, feeling that he could not breathe very well. His arm *visibly became redder and redder.* Then, he suddenly remembered that the redness must have been caused by the turpentine. As soon as he realized this, his fear subsided rapidly, and, more interestingly, right in front of his eyes, the red color started to dissipate! The entire episode took less than five minutes. I cannot think of a better example to illustrate how fear influences our symptoms. Thoughts often precede emotion. The good news is that if you change your interpretation, your emotion will change. You will work much more on this in Chapter 9.

Your Alarm Response Is Influenced by Your Perceived Ability to Cope

Let me introduce this section with an analogy. Imagine a young boy playing a team sport. He "goofs" and his teammates give him a very hard time. The boy may feel terrible, cower, and decide never again to take the risk of playing on a team. He might even give up sports altogether. In a different scenario, the boy might feel bad but say to himself, "I'll show them!" and start to practice diligently to become a better player. In the first example, the experience threatened his self-esteem, and he felt emotionally injured. He responded with a stance that was not at all adaptive. In the second example, the event was perceived as a challenge, in spite of how badly he felt.

When confronted with a stressor or threat, we assess whether it is potentially harmful (stress perceived as a negative) or provides a challenge (stress perceived as a positive). Although for many years, *any* kind of stress was seen as negative, it is now believed that stress can also be very positive and adaptive. For instance, a surge of adrenaline has been shown to have a positive correlation with superior performance on many different tasks.

Experts generally agree that a situation is judged as negatively stressful as opposed to positively stressful depending on how *predictable* the stressor is and how much *control* the person feels that he or she can exert over it. The more obsessed you are with control, the more you will pay attention to those aspects of a situation that you cannot control, with the result that you will feel less able to cope with uncertainty. Which hormonal and other chemical responses take place depend to a large extent on how effectively you cope or think you can cope with the situation.

The SNS produces a set of responses that may lead to feelings of anxiety, exhilaration, a sense of power, and so forth. *How you feel about the physiological arousal depends on how you perceive the situation.* The perception is influenced by temperamental and cognitive styles, for example, whether or not you like to be challenged, to work hard, or to speak your mind. If you interpret stress as a challenge, the neuroendocrine events are likely to be more positive than in a negatively perceived stress situation. These positive neuroendocrine events, which, by the way, are measurable, may lead to "toughening up," so that you are better able to deal with stressful events in the future. (See Chapter 14 for more about "toughening up," and Richard Dienstbier, 1989 and 1991.)

If, on the other hand, the person feels that he or she has no control, gives up, and resigns himself or herself to the negative stress, a "learned helplessness" style may develop, which in itself can become a stressor, rendering the person even more anxious and depressed.

How does "toughening up" apply to panic disorder? It appears that finding more positive and healthy ways to respond to panic and phobias is crucial. Can *you* learn to look at panics and phobias as challenges to be mastered? You will succeed if you work hard on developing a new mind set about panics. You must be willing to take risks in approaching frightening internal (see Chapter 10) and external (see Chapters 11 and 12) situations.

This book provides one avenue to overcome panic disorder. If working with the book does not help you, find other avenues. You could investigate psychotherapy with a therapist knowledgeable about anxiety disorders, medication treatment, and/or support groups in your community. The most important thing is not to give up.

Has your fear decreased at all based on what you learned in this chapter? You may want to review this chapter a few times to be sure that you understand the basic concepts that have been presented.

Did you find any particularly useful thoughts, ideas, or actions to take in this chapter to add to Worksheet 1: "My Personal Coping Affirmations"?

What is your Fear Barometer doing now? If you had a bad panic right now, how much fear would it evoke in you? What is the number, using the 0 to 100% scale? Determine what the number is NOW. Write in the number: _____.

Recommended Reading

Barlow, D.H., and Craske, M.G. 1994. *Mastery of Your Anxiety and Panic II.* Albany, N.Y.: Graywind Publications Inc.

8

Breathing Retraining:
Severing the Connection Between
Panic and Hyperventilation

Section 1: Hyperventilation and Panic

Chronic hyperventilation is a condition that can last for months or even years. As in panic, the symptoms often are very anxiety-provoking and can devastate a person's life. In a dizziness clinic at a university, studies showed that almost one-fourth of all patients experienced hyperventilation as the major or only cause of their dizziness.

Hyperventilation, like panic, can mimic many organic diseases and can also complicate conditions such as asthma, which is another good reason for a medical check-up: All possible diseases should be ruled out. Most people, however, will not show any organic cause. Hyperventilation is not a disease, but it is not "all in your head" either. If unidentified, the person may undergo numerous tests and possible hospitalizations. The patient may worry about having contracted a mysterious disease and be seen more and more as a hypochondriac. Where there is chronic hyperventilation, something is *definitely* wrong, even if it is not organic in nature.

In our culture, there is a strong tendency to view the mind and the body as separate entities. Most physicians look only for the "disease" and, failing to find it, tell you, "You are fine." Some patients do not want to accept that their physical symptoms, which are so real, might be due "merely" to hyperventilation, or the fight/flight response, and insist that their symptoms are caused by "illness." Most people are unaware that anxiety, depression, obsession, or internal conflict can manifest as an array of physical symptoms. Furthermore, mental health professionals may see the symptoms merely as by-products of anxiety and depression and if they treat only the anxiety and depression, a possible hyperventilation condition may go undetected.

*Panic and Hyperventilation Can Cause
Identical Symptoms*

Let's begin by describing a situation in which you might experience a variety of physical symptoms. Imagine yourself in a very crowded store or sitting in the back seat of a two-door car.

You start to feel weak in the knees, lightheaded, and dizzy; your hands tingle or they are numb; you have heart palpitations and a lump in your throat; and you feel that the ground beneath you is shifting. More than feeling breathless, you have this need to take a deep, satisfying breath. But no matter how hard you strain for air, you can't seem to get enough. You are hungry for air, but there's just not enough. Now you fear that you may embarrass yourself, faint, or die, and you want to scream out loud, "Let me out of here!" Yet there does not seem to be enough air for even those few words, and you're now desperate to step outside and get fresh air. Once outside, you finally feel that you can breathe again.

What caused these symptoms? Anxiety, panic, or hyperventilation, or any combination of the three can produce those sensations.

Overbreathing Test

Before proceeding further, let us do a test that may help determine how much you can benefit from breathing retraining. The overbreathing test is *not* dangerous and it is very unlikely to trigger a panic. Nevertheless, *people with certain conditions should not take this test*, unless permitted by their physicians.

CAUTION: You can do this test *unless* you fall in any of the following categories: If you have epilepsy or a history of seizures, serious asthma, chronic arrythmia, heart or lung problems, a history of fainting and/or *very low* blood pressure, or are pregnant. (If you have any doubts, consult your physician.) If you cannot do this test for any of the reasons above, proceed to page 58 "Recognizing Hyperventilation."

What You Need

1. A timer or a watch or clock with a second hand.

2. Pad and pen.

3. A brown 6"x10" paper bag (lunch-size bag). (**Do NOT use a plastic bag.**)

Practicing Before Taking the Real Test

The overbreathing test is sort of like panting, but a little slower. You need to breathe deeply, in and out through your *mouth*. Make your breath audible, i.e., produce a sound, loud enough so that it can be heard across the room. Now, stand up and while *standing*, practice by taking four to six breaths like that. When you have finished, return to this page.

PLEASE PRACTICE NOW.

Did you feel strong symptoms? Then it was probably done correctly. For the real test, below, make sure that you blow out a lot of air each time you breathe out.

Test Instructions

1. Overbreathe as described for 1.5 minutes while standing.

2. While doing the exercise, pay attention to any sensations that you feel and remember them.

3. If you find the sensations intolerable, naturally, you can stop, but if at all possible, try to complete the 1.5 minutes.

4. After the test, place the paper bag over your mouth and nose, not allowing much air to escape from the edge of the bag. Now breathe normally in and out. See how quickly you can stop the symptoms that were activated by the overbreathing.

5. Write down all the sensations that you had during the test.

PLEASE DO THE TEST NOW (before continuing reading).

Question

Did the symptoms produced in this test resemble some of the symptoms you have in a panic?

Answer

§   I felt just a little lightheaded, but nothing like the sensations in a panic. Turn to the next page.

§   I was too scared to do the test. Turn to page 57.

§   The symptoms were very similar to what I experienced in a panic. Turn to page 58.

⚕ You felt just a little lightheaded but nothing like the sensations in a panic.

I'm glad that you tried! It is possible that hyperventilation does not play a major part in your panics. However, we know that about 60 percent of all panic attacks are accompanied by acute hyperventilation. Possibly you have not given it your best shot. You may have been apprehensive and not done it quite right, or you may not have done it long enough.

This test is an attempt to produce hyperventilation by overbreathing. We are deliberately trying to induce what is called hypocapnic respiratory alkalosis, which is a set of physical events associated with a whole series of sensations. The advantages of taking this test are as follows:

- First, if your symptoms are similar to those in panic attacks, we can assume that hyperventilation is a likely component in your panics. Consequently, the breathing retraining will be an important step in your recovery.

- Second, if we find out that hyperventilation, acute or chronic, is not relevant in your case, you may still want to learn to apply deep, diaphragmatic breathing during panics. Rapid heart beat, sweating, tingling, feelings of unreality, chest pain, and many other symptoms of the autonomic nervous system cannot be controlled directly. Although breathing is also a function of the autonomic nervous system, it *can* be brought under direct, voluntary control.

When you are in a panic, once you calm down your breathing, other physical events eventually normalize.

Now, let us review how to do this test. Imagine a dog that just stopped running and is now standing still and panting. You want to pant like that, but slower. Try to take deep, loud breaths through your open mouth. You want to take about 40 breaths per minute. A minute and a half may have been too short a time to produce symptoms in you. In that case extend your time up to three minutes. Have your timer or watch, pad, pen, and paper bag ready. Set the timer for three minutes. Should you get strong sensations before the time is up, pay attention to them and stop.

PLEASE DO THE TEST NOW.

Did you have stronger sensations this time and did they remind you of panic attacks? Whether you did or not, proceed to page 58, "Recognizing Hyperventilation."

§ **You were too scared to do the test.**

It is good that you are honest with yourself and with me. Let us review. If you do not fall into any of the medical-exclusion categories, there should not be any risk involved in doing this exercise, but I can understand that being very sensitive to panic symptoms, this test might scare you.

At this point, a coach may be essential to you. (I always take this test along with my clients, so they will feel more comfortable. You can imagine how many times I have done this!) If you are too frightened, you may ask your coach to do it alone first. Then the coach can share with you what it was like. You will know better what to expect and will be able to discuss your apprehensions. A truly helpful coach will encourage you and be there for you. Then you can do it along with your coach. Remember, the more you understand what contributes to your panic, the easier it will be to learn the skills necessary to overcome them. Understanding increases hope and motivation.

If you are not ready to proceed yet, I suggest that you set this book aside for a while. Just reading through it without doing the exercises will not be very helpful. Talk to someone you trust, and discuss your concerns.

I hope, though, that reading this page may have helped you overcome your resistance, and you are now ready to try. If you plan to do it with a coach, get an additional pad, pen, and paper bag for your coach. Make sure that he or she knows about the medical-exclusion criteria. Compare notes after the test.

If ready to take the test, turn back to pages 54–55, "Test Instructions."

§ The symptoms were very similar to those in panic.

This is good news! "How can she say that?" you might ask. "This is extremely uncomfortable! It's an awful experience!"

My reaction may seem strange at first, and believe me, I know how uncomfortable this test is! However, we are moving closer to understanding your panic symptoms and how they are produced. This is *not* to say that hyperventilation alone *causes* panics. Panic attacks are quite complex. Yet open your mind to the possibility of a connection. I rejoice with you every step of the way toward your increased knowledge and recovery.

If you found many similarities between the hyperventilation and your panic symptoms, you stand to gain a great deal from breathing retraining. Often, the symptoms can be effectively and directly diminished, which will lower the intensity of your anxiety and fear.

Now read "Recognizing Hyperventilation" below.

Recognizing Hyperventilation

Symptoms of Hyperventilation

The major components of this syndrome are as follows:

- Lightheadedness

- Giddiness

- Dizziness

- Shortness of breath with a sense of impending suffocation (called dyspnea)

- Heart palpitations

Other common symptoms are:

- Numbness and/or tingling sensations (paresthesias)

- Chest pain

- Dry mouth and throat

- Clammy hands

- Swallowing difficulty

- Tremors

- Sweating

- Weakness and fatigue

As mentioned earlier, hyperventilation can be brought on by some organic causes due to injury or disease. It is more often brought on by drug effects and withdrawal from drugs, emotional reactions to stress, and just plain faulty breathing habits. Breathing retraining is then the preferred course to bring hyperventilation under control.

How Does Overbreathing Produce Symptoms?

When you breathe in (inhale) the hemoglobin in the blood carries the oxygen from the lungs to the tissues, where it is used by the cells in their various functions, and, in turn, carbon dioxide is produced as a by-product of metabolism. The carbon dioxide is carried by the blood back to the lungs, where it is breathed out (exhaled). Breathing *in excess* of metabolic needs (i.e., more than is needed) is called overbreathing. When hemoglobin is saturated with oxygen, the excess oxygen is exhaled along with any available carbon dioxide from the arteries. This results in an excessive loss of carbon dioxide, creating an imbalance. If continued, this drop in carbon dioxide leads to hypocapnic alkalosis (alkalosis here pertains to the blood becoming less acidic, or a rise in the blood pH level). This indirectly causes the symptoms of *hyperventilation*.

Secondary changes also result. For example, oxygen is bound more tightly to the hemoglobin so that *less* oxygen is released to the tissues. Another change is vascular constriction, resulting in diminished blood flow to the brain and other parts of the body. Eventually, if continued over a longer period of time, renal compensation (involving the kidneys) takes place to help lower the pH level. The symptoms may diminish through this compensation, but the person remains in precarious balance. Minimal exertion or very mild stressors make the person easily symptomatic. A few deep breaths or sighs per hour may do the same. For more information on hyperventilation see Ronald Ley, 1985 and B.H. Timmons and R. Ley, 1994.

How Can I Know if I Am an Overbreather?

There are two kinds of hyperventilation—acute and chronic. If our overbreathing test brought on distinct symptoms in you (as it *always* does in me), we successfully produced *acute* hyperventilation. Normally, people do not pant like that. You probably do not pant even in a panic. Acute hyperventilation is more easily recognized than the chronic, in that frequently there is a clear symptom such as gasping for air; but in chronic hyperventilation the symptoms are far more subtle. Because of the ability to overbreathe without a visibly increased respiratory rate, chronic hyperventilators often go unrecognized. In other words, overbreathing can occur in a person who *seems* to be breathing normally. So, you might ask yourself "How do I know if I am hyperventilating?"

Many people breathe with short and shallow breaths from the upper chest or thorax. They often take 18 to 22 breaths per minute. Also, mouth breathers are more prone to hyperventilation. Once hyperventilation is established, the person is easily vulnerable to more extreme symptoms. It takes very small variations in breathing to produce very uncomfortable sensations. Up to 80 percent of those who hyperventilate tend to sigh and yawn frequently. When they take a deep breath to get that "satisfying" amount of air, it may instead trigger the hyperventilation process again or aggravate hyperventilation symptoms even further. It is estimated that 6 to 10 percent of all patients who visit internists and 30 percent of panickers chronically hyperventilate. Some people start to hyperventilate as children or adolescents.

Breathing through the nose may seem to take more effort than through the mouth. When resting, however, breathing through the nose is more efficient. Yet, some people take what feels like the path of least resistance and continue to breathe through the mouth, even at rest. This is often the beginning of the learned habit of overbreathing.

To assess hyperventilation, look for the following signs: Upper chest (thoracic) breathing, breathing through the mouth rather than the nose, 18 or more breaths per minute while relaxed, frequent sighing, gasps (sudden, fast inhalations), yawning, coughing or clearing of the throat, moistening of the lips, and outwardly apparent, "heavy" breathing.

A young woman in my New Panickers Group had been asking one of her parents to come home from work to stay with her every time she panicked. Her panics had started three months before she came to see me. Her father had tried to help her. He told her that she should breathe in through the nose and out through the mouth, and once in a while take a deep breath, sigh, or yawn. She tried it but complained to him that it made her feel dizzy. He told her not to worry about the symptom but to keep doing it; feeling dizzy was part of life. This is what *he* did to calm his own anxiety! We quickly corrected this situation in our breathing session by teaching her about breathing physiology and by practicing diaphragmatic breathing.

Are Dizziness and Lightheadedness Signs of Imminent Fainting?

Dizziness, lightheadedness, and blurred vision in panic or hyperventilation are not signs of imminent fainting. These three symptoms can result from overbreathing. Remember, when you are *overbreathing* (taking in more oxygen than you need), less oxygen is released to the brain and other tissues. The decreased oxygen in the brain also can produce sensations of unreality or depersonalization.

Many panickers have the belief that these symptoms invariably lead to fainting. This is, in fact, extremely rare. How often have you *thought* that you were about to faint in a panic, and how often have you actually fainted?

A great majority of panickers report dizziness, but that is not always the result of hyperventilation. Some people report a combination of marked dizziness, lightheadedness, unsteadiness, and veering toward one side while walking or driving. A balance system dysfunction could be causing these symptoms. However, most people with balance and visuospatial disorders do not have panic attacks. (Visuospatial means the ability to comprehend and conceptualize visual representations and spatial relationships.) This shows again the complex interaction between the physiological, cognitive (relating to thoughts and beliefs), and behavioral components of panic disorder. The belief that these symptoms will make you faint is a cognitive error that leads to anxiety, further bodily symptoms, and still more anxiety in an increasing spiral, culminating in panic. (Note that one study does report an increased rate of visuospatial dysfunction in panickers; Hoffman, O'Leary, & Munjack, 1994.)

Why Do I Feel Chest Pain During a Panic When I Have Been Told My Heart Is Okay?

Chest pain, even sharp chest pain, can result from hyperventilation. It can last from minutes to hours, be sharp or dull, be located in different places, and may be confused with heart disease. (Let me say again, a physical exam is essential precisely because a serious health condition must not be overlooked.) Also, when the muscles in the chest become strained due to prolonged upper chest breathing, dull chest aches lasting from hours to days may result.

Chest pain is also the most difficult symptom to reproduce with only a few minutes of hyperventilation. This is unfortunate, because it would be helpful if we could easily demonstrate to you that this type of chest pain occurs and is *harmless*. However, when diaphragmatic breathing is learned and applied, much of the pain is eliminated.

How It All Fits Together: Panic, Hyperventilation, Biology, and Habit

Hyperventilation can be the opening phase in the panic process. Symptoms like shortness of breath, chest pain, heart palpitations, and dizziness can frighten vulnerable individuals who fear suffocation, heart attack, or stroke. These kinds of catastrophic thoughts may elicit acute fear, which activates the sympathetic nervous system (pupils will be dilated, salivary glands inhibited, heart rate increased, etc.), which in turn increases the rate of breathing (the number of breaths taken per minute) even further. This cycle produces more intense hyperventilation symptoms, which can increase the fearfulness. A panic state can be reached within seconds. The catastrophic thoughts and underlying beliefs may become so deeply rooted and automatic, that they operate outside of one's consciousness. The same interplay can occur if hyperventilation *follows* the onset of panic.

Acute hyperventilation is not *generally* sufficient to produce panic (remember, most people don't panic during the voluntary hyperventilation test), and the anxiety symptoms in panic disorder are not necessarily secondary to overbreathing. However, they can be closely related. Anxiety (like other emotions) can easily lead to a faster breathing rate; and hyperventilation may result. Hyperventilation, in turn, can affect your emotions, especially if you fear the sensations. Panickers who chronically hyperventilate are physically more aroused, and psychologically they may also be more intensely affected.

Let me illustrate this with an example: A few years ago, a man in my Panic/Phobia Group discovered during the overbreathing test and subsequent breathing retraining that he was an extreme chronic hyperventilator. He had frequent symptoms of breathlessness and feelings of suffocation, especially in hot, crowded places, such as elevators. He described feeling a combination of strong anger ("Why are these people pushing themselves into this already crowded elevator?") and anxiety. At the end of the treatment, he said that the breathing exercises had been the most useful part of therapy for him. He had made the connection himself: His body was always in a state of high arousal and any added strong emotion (including anger) would bring on difficulty in breathing, which would then intensify his anxiety in a cyclical fashion.

Why do many people with panic disorder hyperventilate? Some researchers think that there might be a biological basis for respiratory abnormalities. Others suggest that the mechanism controlling panickers' breathing fluctuates more than in the average person. Put simply, some people may hyperventilate more easily or be less tolerant of the symptoms. In such individuals a bad breathing habit could make them feel less in control of their bodies without their understanding why (as described in the example above).

How to Stop Hyperventilation

There are four ways to stop hyperventilation:

1. *Hold your breath*
   Holding your breath for as long as you comfortably can will prevent the dissipation of carbon dioxide. DO NOT hold your breath until you are close to passing out. I suggest you hold your breath for no more than 10 to 15 seconds, a few times successively. This sounds paradoxical, because in a panic you may feel as if you are not getting enough air, and may think you are suffocating. Remember, you are most likely breathing in *more* air than you need—and that is creating the problem.

2. *Breathe in and out of a paper bag*
   This is what we did in the test, as a way to stop hyperventilation symptoms quickly. Why does it work? You are inhaling the carbon dioxide that you exhale (it is in the bag). This will restore the normal blood pH level. Of course, this method has clear limitations. If you were driving, you would not be safe while trying to hold a paper bag to your nose and mouth. You are not likely to use a paper bag in a classroom, in a meeting, or on the grocery line. Furthermore, carrying a paper bag with you at all times turns the bag into a "safety signal" (like a talisman). You will not feel confident that you can function without it, so a panic will always be lurking around the corner.

   One of my clients (diagnosed with long-term panic disorder with agoraphobia) carried a carefully folded small white plastic bag in his wallet for years, just in case. Although he knew that no one *ever* recommends using a plastic bag, he figured that it was the only thing that fit into his wallet. He never used it, but it had become his "safety net." (Actually, it was very strange that he thought of it as a safety net, when he could have suffocated if he had ever used it!) The whole Panic/Phobia Group celebrated with him the day he announced that he got rid of it. And he saw that he survived.

3. *Vigorous exercise*
Examples are running, brisk walking, going up and down stairs very quickly, several times, aerobics, while breathing *in and out* through your nose or open mouth. You may breathe out a lot, even through an open mouth, but you will take in a great deal of air as well, in order to produce the energy you need for the vigorous exercise. Here, you are *increasing* your metabolism, thereby *producing larger amounts* of carbon dioxide, and thus lowering the blood pH.

NOTE: In vigorous exercise, since breathing lags behind the metabolic demand, wind down the exercise *slowly*.

4. *Deep diaphragmatic breathing*
This is the best of all methods, so the next section is devoted entirely to this procedure.

Section 2: Breathing Retraining

If you are a chronic hyperventilator, this retraining is *crucial* to normalize the chemistry in your body and to make you less vulnerable to minor changes in breathing. Whether or not you hyperventilate acutely in a panic, diaphragmatic breathing can be an extremely useful coping skill for you.

Take a Deep Breath
Before proceeding, let us check your current breathing.

What You Need

1. A mirror.

2. Pad and pen.

Instructions

1. Watch yourself in the mirror, and immediately afterward write down in detail what you did.

2. Take one or two deep breaths in and out.

PLEASE DO THE TEST NOW (before continuing reading).

- Now that your responses have been written down, look for the following:

- What did your chest do?

- What did your mouth do?

- What did your shoulders do?

- Was there a pause anywhere?

- How fast did you breathe?

Keep your notes for later reference.

Stage 1: Compare Your Regular Breathing with Diaphragmatic Breathing

The goal of breathing retraining is to bring about balance in the oxygen/carbon dioxide levels. This is accomplished by slow, diaphragmatic breathing *through the nose*. It can help reduce the severity of symptoms during acute panic. The more you can slow down the physical sensations during periods of high anxiety, the more you can use your rational mind to assess what is going on.

Slow, Deep Breathing—
Your *Natural* Relaxant.

Why is it important to breathe in and out through the nose? The nose's primary function is to control our breathing. It reduces the volume of air going in and out. You are much less likely to hyperventilate while breathing in and out only through your nose.

Of course, if you have a bad cold, allergies, or something else blocking the passage of air through your nose you will not be able to do this. In that case, keep your mouth open just a little and try to let the same amount of air go slowly in and out through your mouth. Other autonomic (involuntary) functions are very difficult to control directly, but breathing—which is also automatic—can be brought under voluntary control. You can learn to control your breathing under relaxed *and stressful* conditions, even in the midst of a panic.

What You Need

1. Your notes from "Taking a Deep Breath" (at the beginning of this Section), to compare what you did previously with what we will do now.

2. A mirror.

Instructions

1. Standing up, place one hand on your diaphragm/stomach area so that at least your little finger (and maybe your ring finger) is positioned over your navel.

2. Take in a deep breath through your nose while pushing the diaphragm/stomach *out* against your hand. When you slowly *exhale through your nose*, the diaphragm/stomach area should be pulled back in. Here is an easy way to remember it: When you take a deep breath you need to make room for the extra air that you are inhaling. You don't want to direct that air just to your chest (you remember why) but to take it all the way down to your diaphragm, so naturally, your diaphragm must expand. With that expansion your lungs get pushed downward and can utilize the oxygen to the fullest. Conversely, when you exhale and release the used air, your diaphragm should naturally pull back in.

3. Try not to lift your chest or shoulders. Your shoulders should not move. Keep your mouth closed throughout the breathing cycle. Breathe as slowly as you can without making it feel artificial.

PLEASE PRACTICE NOW. Try it several times.

It may not feel natural at all, especially if you have been a chronic chest (thoracic) breather. It may be exactly the opposite of what you are used to doing. Get feedback from the mirror. Is it difficult? If yes, then you are conforming to the norm. Take heart: There is an almost foolproof way of learning to breathe diaphragmatically.

Stage 2: Learning Diaphragmatic Breathing

I will provide *very* detailed instructions for you to learn this well.

What You Need

- One or two bed pillows.

Instructions

1. We will proceed from the easiest to the more difficult steps. Practice all the steps. Practice without fail at least five minutes, twice a day, every day, until you master all the steps. *Do not proceed to the next step until you have mastered the previous one.* Remember to breathe in and out through your nose, *keeping your mouth closed at all times*. Breathe slowly rather than

quickly. Take about one week to practice before proceeding to Stage 3. If you run into problems, proceed to the question and answers at the end of this section.

2. Lie down on your *stomach* on a bed or carpeted floor. Bend your arms so that your hands are resting alongside your head. Breathe diaphragmatically in and out through your nose slowly and deeply. Feel what is happening. It is very difficult to expand your chest in this position. Since your stomach is flat against a surface, you will feel your back (around the waist) expand upward. Do this until you have a good feel for it, for as long as you need.

3. With your arms at your sides, lie down on your *back* on a bed or carpeted floor, without a pillow under your head. Instead, place one or two pillows on your diaphragm/stomach. You should be able to observe the top of the pillow from the corner of your eyes. (If it strains your neck, make sure you use two pillows.) When you breathe in, expand your diaphragm/stomach so the *pillow moves up*. When you breathe out, the pillow should go down again. I want you to exaggerate the movements, so the pillow clearly moves up and down. Inhale *slowly*, and when ready, exhale *slowly*.

   If you have studied yoga, do not follow the instructions that suggest you should take in a deep breath, hold for a few seconds, and breathe out. Instead, pause only at the *end* of the breathing cycle. Either breathe out slower than you breathe in (e.g., 1, 2, 3 seconds breathing in; 1, 2, 3, 4, 5 seconds breathing out) or breathe in and out at the same rate and hold after the exhalation (e.g., 1, 2, 3, 4 seconds in; 1, 2, 3, 4 seconds out—and then hold). Hold only for as long as is comfortable before you take in your next breath. Practice this for as long as you need until you have a good feel for it. I usually do not instruct people to count seconds, but you may do so if you find it helpful. The *ideal* rate of breathing at rest is 8 to 10 breaths per minute. The exact number of breaths per minute is not crucial, however. What is important is to practice breathing increasingly *slowly*.

4. Once you can do the exercise above with a pillow, put it aside and practice the same way, only with your hand resting on your diaphragm/stomach rather than the pillow.

5. When you can do the exercise well with your hand, lie with your arms at your sides while looking at the ceiling. Or close your eyes. Now put your mind in your diaphragm/stomach and *feel* it. The way I view this, it is like "becoming one with my breathing," as if my mind were not located in my head but in my diaphragm/stomach area. The goal is to *feel* your diaphragm/stomach area without looking at or touching it.

6. Lie on your *side* on a bed or carpeted floor. Place a pillow under your head and your hands somewhere near your head or holding the pillow. Breathe diaphragmatically. Feel your diaphragm/stomach area move out (breathing in) and move in (breathing out).

7. Sit on a sofa *leaning back* and watch your stomach move out and in. Your shoulders should be perfectly still.

8. Sit *erect* in a straight-backed chair and practice the same exercise as in number 7, above.

9. *Stand* and practice as we did in Stage 1, Instructions on page 64.

10. Remember, breathe *as slowly as you can*.

Question

How did the breathing practice go?

Answers

§ It feels good when I do it, and I can feel satisfaction when I breathe this way. Turn to page 67.

§   I feel lightheaded and can't seem to get enough air. It feels uncomfortable when I do it. Turn to page 69.

§   I understand it now, but cannot get a rhythm going, or I can't breathe slowly enough. Turn to page 70.

§   I can breathe diaphragmatically when lying down or sitting, but not when standing. Turn to page 71.

§   I have not taken the time to practice. Turn to page 72.

It felt good when you did it, and you feel satisfaction when you breathe this way.

Congratulations! This is great! By taking the time to practice you have shown that you are committed to mastering panic attacks. We can now proceed.

Stage 3: Apply Diaphragmatic Breathing When Anxious

Instructions

1. Now that you know how to do diaphragmatic breathing, start paying attention to your breathing during the day. Plan on doing a "check-in" with your breathing at least five times a day. Spend two or more minutes on it each time. Don't do less. Ask yourself, "How is my breathing this very moment?" Then breathe slowly diaphragmatically, for at least two minutes. Try to get used to breathing this way. (It is much healthier, anyway.) Do it while at work, in the car, watching TV, waiting in line. Do this for a week, while you are proceeding with the next chapter in this book. If you forget, place reminders in different places; on a bathroom mirror, on the refrigerator, on your desk at work, and so forth.

2. Next, pay attention to your breathing in situations where you are tense and anxious (nonpanic situations), for example, working on a project with a tight deadline, watching a suspenseful movie or ballgame, or visiting a relative with whom there are tensions.

3. Start to "check-in" with your breathing in situations of strong emotion, where people often tend to overbreathe (we all do). Good situations to do this in would be when you are frustrated, angry, or upset, or when someone is yelling.

4. If you reach the point of successfully checking in and controlling your breathing in situations such as those described under number 3, above, you are well on the road to learning the calming breath! You are now ready to try diaphragmatic breathing when very anxious, experiencing anticipatory anxiety (anxiety before a fearful situation) in a phobic situation, when you feel a panic coming on, or even in the middle of a panic. This latter suggestion may seem incomprehensible right now. Many individuals *feel as if* they *lose control totally* during a panic, but trust me, it can be done, and you can do it.

5. Practice diaphragmatic breathing next time you actually have a panic. If the panic has already started, try to observe it. Do two things: Breathe diaphragmatically and pay attention to your thoughts, *listen to them* (you will need them in the work we will do in the next chapter). Flow with and through your panic. Some people think of it as "riding a wave." The wave continues under you and passes you, as in surfing. Instead of thinking of the panic as an overwhelming entity, learn how to *manipulate* it. Pull it apart like the accordion I mentioned in Chapter 7, and observe the pleats or folds as it opens. Think of these pleats as the thoughts, sensations, and behaviors that constitute the panic response.

You are now learning how to manipulate your physical sensations through your breathing. In Chapters 9 and 10 you will learn how to manipulate your thoughts and behaviors. Now, proceed to the next page, Section 3: "Breathing Can Help You in Many Ways."

Section 3: Breathing Can Help You in Many Ways

In addition to helping with panic, diaphragmatic breathing is also helpful in other ways. I, personally, use it in two situations. Occasionally, I have difficulty falling asleep because my mind is too active, either preoccupied or excited. Then, I usually lie on my side and decide to do the deep breathing. I place all my attention on the feeling of my diaphragm/stomach moving out and in as I breathe slowly through my nose, and I "become one with my breathing." I cannot fully pay attention to that feeling *and* think of other things at the same time. It is the closest that I can get to blanking out my mind, because I am not thinking in words but just *feeling* the breathing. Of course, before I know it, my mind takes off again, and I forget to focus on my breathing. That is why I need a prior conscious commitment to do so. As soon as I become aware that my mind is wandering off, I shut down my thoughts and return my attention to my breathing. I may need to go through this over and over again. (Without making a commitment, I won't stay with it.) But, I am seldom awake five to ten minutes after I begin.

The other situation is when I feel very anxious and worried about something. At some point, I think of doing diaphragmatic breathing, and I stop all thoughts and spend two to three minutes doing it. When I return to the problem or worry, it is still there, but I seem to get a different perspective on it. More than once I have then thought, "Was *that* what I was so worried about?" I think that the physical sensations of anxiety and the anxious thoughts get carried away, interacting with each other. If I can slow down my body, it is as if my mind can collect itself and get a fresh look at the worrisome issue. I seem better able to concentrate and to find "solutions" or different approaches.

I would not mention these personal experiences if they applied only to me. But I have had quite a number of clients who, after merely a few weeks of breathing practice, attempted the same usage and succeeded. Not infrequently, a client comes into the group and says, "Guess what? I can now put myself to sleep with the breathing!" I believe that many of you, my readers, are capable of performing the same action. The KEY: FREQUENT PRACTICE.

(One caveat: I would not expect heavy-duty insomnia to necessarily be controllable this way.)

One last caution about this breathing technique. If you use it just to avoid the physical sensations of panic while still remaining terrified of those sensations, you are doing yourself a disservice. Whether you use medication, diaphragmatic breathing, or distraction, if your underlying fear and catastrophic beliefs remain intact, you always remain vulnerable to more panics. If you use the breathing to calm your body and to get a better look at the situation rather than "run away" from the panic sensation, then you are receiving the full therapeutic benefit of the technique. Chapters 9 and 10 (targeting your thoughts and beliefs, and exposing yourself to the fearful physical symptoms in order to conquer them) are designed to eliminate the feelings of terror.

Did you find any particularly useful thoughts, ideas, or actions to take in this chapter to add to Worksheet 1: "My Personal Coping Affirmations"? Proceed now to Chapter 9.

What is your Fear Barometer doing now? If you had a bad panic right now, how much fear would you feel? What is the number, using the 0 to 100% scale? Determine the number NOW. Please write it in: ____.

§   **You felt lightheaded and couldn't seem to get enough air when you breathed this way.**

Let's go back to the breathing physiology. I would venture to say that you have a tendency to chronically and subtly overbreathe. By doing that your symptoms may come and go. Through renal compensation, the symptoms can be partially suppressed. You would, however, find yourself in such a precarious balance that any change in respiration pattern, brought on by minimal exertion or mild daily stress, might activate the hypocapnea, and with it the symptoms would present themselves in full force.

This could make it more difficult for you to stay motivated to continue the practice. Why should you do it if it makes you feel worse? On the other hand, if you have been a chronic hyperventilator, the pay-off will be greater for you. Keep practicing. As you master the technique and start to apply it through the day, you will be able to change your breathing habits. Remember you are not alone. Many people in my groups discover that they have been breathing incorrectly. Not only panickers do this. In fact, we all tend to overbreathe when anxious and upset. It is just that other people may be less sensitive to the symptoms.

A woman recently told my New Panickers Group: "I'm 35 years old and I was taught since I was a young girl to keep my chest high and my stomach in. I have been breathing through my upper chest all these years. And no doctor has ever explained to me that my undefined chest pains could be related to my breathing." Another group member, an older woman who was frequently light-headed, said that since she learned to do diaphragmatic breathing, she seldom feels lightheaded anymore. If she does, then applying the deep breathing technique stops the lightheadedness immediately.

In your case, it is very helpful to have a coach who also wants to learn how to do diaphragmatic breathing. Whether you have a coach or not, be sure that you first learn it and practice it under normal circumstances. Do not apply it when anxious or in a panic unless you have practiced it under nonpanic circumstances.

Now Let Us Try Again

1. Whenever you start a practice, *first exhale* (before inhaling) through your nose. Breathe in and out through your nose. Breathe *slowly*.

2. Lie down on your back with the pillow on your diaphragm. Exhale. Now lift the pillow while inhaling. Let it go back down while exhaling.

3. Practice with your hand on your diaphragm/stomach.

4. Practice with your arms at your sides; send your mind into your diaphragm and try to feel it there.

5. Practice this routine while sitting and standing.

PLEASE PRACTICE NOW.

How did the practices with diaphragmatic breathing go? If you now feel good doing it, proceed to Stage 3: "Apply Diaphragmatic Breathing When Anxious," on page 67. If you are still having difficulties, return to Stage 2: "Learning Diaphragmatic Breathing" on page 64 for the fully detailed instructions. For other difficulties, check out pages 65–66.

You understand it now, but you cannot get a rhythm going, or you can't breathe slowly enough.

It is true that in yoga and other disciplines that work with breath control there is an emphasis on a different kind of breathing: For example, inhale for four seconds, hold your breath for four seconds, and breathe out for four seconds. Try this once. PLEASE DO SO NOW.

How did it feel? Natural or unnatural? I bet unnatural! Today, we have quite a bit of information about the physiology of breathing. Remember what you learned in Chapter 7 about the sympathetic (SNS) and the parasympathetic (PNS) nervous systems? The SNS, as you may recall, is responsible for activating and mobilizing the body. The PNS is responsible for calming down the body. How does this relate to breathing? Inhalation is an activity of the SNS and exhalation an activity of the PNS. If you inhale a deep breath and hold it for a few seconds, you are extending the SNS activity, which is *not* what you want to do. Conversely, if you exhale and pause before your next breath, you are extending the PNS activity, which is very desirable.

If counting helps you find your way toward breathing in a slow rhythm, by all means, try it out. You need to find what works for *you*.

Instructions

1. Count 1, 2, 3 seconds breathing in; 1, 2, 3, 4 seconds breathing out. Practice this a number of times.

2. Ready to slow down further? Count 1, 2, 3, 4 seconds breathing in; 1, 2, 3, 4 seconds breathing out—and hold; 1, 2, 3, 4 breathing in, 1, 2, 3, 4 breathing out—and hold. Hold for as long as it feels comfortable.

3. You can use words to help, for example, you could say subliminally "In" while you are breathing in, and "Relax" while you are breathing out.

Practice the exercise above for a while, perhaps for several days.

PLEASE PRACTICE.

How did you do? If it helped, turn to Stage 3: "Apply Diapragmatic Breathing When Anxious" on page 67. If you are still having difficulties, return to Stage 2: "Learning Diaphragmatic Breathing" on page 64 for the fully detailed instructions. For other difficulties, check out pages 65–66.

You can breathe diaphragmatically when lying down or sitting, but not standing.

You are on your way! Take heart! It does seem as if standing is a particularly difficult position to push out your stomach while you inhale. If placing your hand on your diaphragm/stomach does not seem to bring about results, try this version.

Instructions

Place your hands on the sides of your waist, thumbs to the back, sort of resting on your hips. Now when you breathe in, see if your hands are pushed *out*. Imagine holding a balloon by its sides while someone else is blowing it up. Can you visualize how your hands would move outward, following the contour of the balloon? It's the same with your diaphragm. Feel it pushed out. Now, for comparison, take in a breath from your upper chest, really lifting your chest and shoulders as you breathe in. Now, feel how your diaphragm becomes elongated and your hands move in toward your torso. Now, go back to the diaphragmatic breathing and try to expand your diaphragm/stomach while breathing in; feel it contract while you breathe out.

PLEASE PRACTICE NOW.

Did this help your breathing training?

If it helped, turn to Stage 3: "Apply Diaphragmatic Breathing When Anxious" on page 67. If you are still having difficulties, return to Stage 2: "Learning Diaphragmatic Breathing" on page 64 for the fully detailed instructions. For other difficulties, check out pages 65–66.

§ **You have not taken the time to practice.**

It is true that this kind of program requires quite a bit of your time and commitment. You may want to backtrack a bit and ask yourself what stands in the way.

- Is your time limited, and do you feel pressured?

  Maybe you can reevaluate your routine and schedule, and see if it allows for any changes. If you have a family, ask them for help. Perhaps they can take on specific chores to help free up your time a bit. *If* you tend to be a perfectionist, want to be in control of everything, or feel uncomfortable asking for help, you may not find the time for all the work required to overcome panic disorder. However, your panics, anxieties, and phobias most likely take a lot of your time and attention. You may need to make some sacrifices to fit this work in.

- "I should be able to control my panics without all this."

  You have probably already tried other ways. Give this program a try.

- "This won't help my panics."

  It is true that breathing retraining will not make your panics go away. This is a coping skill, for many it is a very useful one. If you are a chronic hyperventilator, then it is essential. For your fear to go away, there is work ahead.

If you are not ready to proceed with the practices, take a break from this book. Return to it when you can make the time for it.

If you are ready to do the practices, turn to Stage 2: "Learning Diaphragmatic Breathing" on page 64.

9

Targeting Your Thoughts and Beliefs About Panic and Anxiety

Section 1: Identifying the Cognitive Component of Panic

As I briefly mentioned earlier, many people with panic disorder are overly sensitive to anxiety. "Anxiety sensitivity" means that they fear the symptoms of anxiety more than other people do. They believe that anxiety symptoms are physically harmful to them. They also believe that they can't cope with anxiety or stress, or that their nerves are "shot" or otherwise damaged. It seems that people with higher anxiety sensitivity are more likely to develop panic disorder. Therefore learning new ways of thinking about and reacting to uncomfortable physical sensations is an essential step for recovery.

Chapter 7 describes the physiology of panic. You were encouraged to read the chapter more than once so that you would become thoroughly familiar with that information because it provides the foundation for the work that we will be doing now. From the reading and the work you have done thus far, you may now understand what panics are and how they are produced, yet you continue to feel fearful of panics and to avoid feared situations.

Perhaps some new panickers may need only the information already given, especially if their fears have not had time to take hold. Most people, however, need more training to overcome their panics. Panics do not disappear just by talking about them or understanding them.

Identifying Specific Thoughts During a Panic

In initial interviews with my clients I always ask, "When you are in the middle of an attack, what specific *thoughts* go through your mind?" Now, imagine that you are being interviewed. I have just asked you that question: Thinking back about a typical, "bad" attack that you have had, how do you answer me?

Please write down your thoughts (*not* your feelings or physical sensations) in the space below. Be as brief as possible. PLEASE DO SO NOW, before proceeding further.

Thoughts I Have During a Panic Attack

1. _____

2. _____

3. _____

4. _____

5. _____

When you read what you wrote down, are your thoughts specific or general? By "specific" I mean, would a listener or reader know exactly what the fear is? Compare your thoughts with those of some of the people I have worked with:

- I'm losing control and I won't be able to function.

- I want to run, I feel trapped and caged. Something bad will happen to me.

- I have to run to look for help. I'm going to die; I'll go crazy.

- I want it to be over. This time it may be more severe, and I won't be able to stand it.

- I'm going to die.

What do you think? Are these thoughts stated in specific or general terms? They are rather *general*. "Losing control," "Not being able to function," "Something bad will happen to me," "I'll go crazy," or "I won't be able to stand it" can mean many different things. Even "I'm going to die" is a general statement, because there are no specifics given about how or why death will occur. The more vague your thoughts and feelings associated with anxiety are, the harder it is to reduce your anxiety.

Let's go back to your list of thoughts while you are in a panic. Maybe your thoughts were not like the examples I listed but instead were highly specific. Perhaps you found it hard to write down any thoughts at all. Did you say to yourself when confronted with the task something like this: "I'm just afraid. I have this awful feeling . . . I can't think of anything." If you had a hard time coming up with any thoughts, or your thoughts were very general in nature, you can try another approach. Thoughts must be pursued until they become very specific and precise. Remember, you need an *awareness* of highly specific thoughts before you can start to work with them. Write down your thoughts as they come, even if they seem irrational. Try not to censor them.

1. Close your eyes. Imagine yourself in the middle of a "bad" panic. Why is it bad? There is a reason. The reason has to do not only with the sensations produced but with the thoughts around them. What are you thinking when you imagine yourself approaching a very fearful

situation, driving over a bridge, on the freeway, having to go to a meeting at work, or standing in a grocery line? Then "listen" to the reasons why you do not want to enter or remain in the situation right at that moment. Please write down your specific thoughts in the space provided in Worksheet 4: "Specific Thoughts I have During a Panic Attack." PLEASE DO SO NOW before proceeding further. If this does not work, try 2, below.

2. If no thoughts come to you, take a break from this book and approach a real-life situation that frightens you. For instance, prepare to go for a drive over a bridge, or shopping at a crowded supermarket. Move as close as you can to it and pay attention to your thoughts. Then return to Worksheet 4 in this chapter and write those thoughts down.

Good, you did it! These thoughts that you have just identified perpetuate your fear of panics. As long as that fear persists, you are vulnerable to continued panics, now or later. We will return to the thoughts you wrote down at various points throughout this chapter. From now on, please keep a pen and pad handy when you are out and about or when reading or working with this book. As we cover the following material and work on it, you will become aware of assumptions, beliefs, and other thoughts about anxiety and panic. Jot them down onto Worksheet 4 as soon as they occur. This will make your task easier later on. Remember, it doesn't matter whether your thoughts make sense or not. Even if they seem illogical, they need to be worked on.

The More Specific Your Anxious Thoughts Are, the Easier It Will Be to Challenge Them Successfully.

Decreasing Anxiety Through Cognitive Work

Cognitions pertain to *thoughts*. Cognitions is a more inclusive word than thoughts, because cognitions also include images and fantasies; therefore it is more useful to us here. For a long time it was believed that insight alone could produce changes in people. Recently, however, the evidence has mounted showing that cognitive and behavioral change often produces emotional change. Feelings, thoughts, and behaviors are all interrelated; therefore changes in any one can produce changes in the others.

The cognitive work described in this chapter is derived from work by D.H. Barlow and M.G. Craske (1994), A.T. Beck and G. Emery with R.L. Greenburg (1985), D.D. Burns (1989), D.M. Clark (1989), A. Freeman, J. Pretzer, B. Fleming, and K.M. Simon (1990), and J.B. Persons (1989).

Automatic Thoughts and Perceived Danger

Automatic Thoughts govern many of our reactions. They can be either positive or negative. Examples of some positive Automatic Thoughts are:

- My needs are just as important as anyone else's.

- No matter how tough things get, there's always a solution.

- Because I respect myself, others are likely to respect me.

Here, we will be working on Automatic Thoughts related to fears.

Worksheet 4: Specific Thoughts I Have During a Panic Attack

1. _____

2. _____

3. _____

4. _____

5. _____

6. _____

7. _____

8. _____

9. _____

10. _____

11. _____

12. _____

When a person develops the fear of panic attacks, his or her mind becomes dominated by thoughts of danger. These thoughts often become repetitive and even obsessional. The person starts scanning for danger, looking for it, and fearing it more and more. This heightened vigilance results in the attention focusing on signs of danger. If you were facing imminent danger to your life, such vigilance would have positive survival value. However, because there is no actual threat during a panic, this vigilance is not helpful.

We know from research on how pain functions, that the more a person focuses on his or her pain, the worse it feels. In a panic, focused, *fearful attention* on the physical sensations makes them more frightening. The physical symptoms of anxiety are also made worse by further anxiety. If your heart is beating fast, the more you focus on it *with worry*, the faster it is likely to beat. Thoughts of a heart attack, dying, or losing control can make it beat even faster! The physical sensations are real, they are not imaginary, but they are *produced by anxiety rather than by physical abnormality*. Your fears are further worsened by the thought that you cannot cope. Your anxiety and sense of danger can become overwhelming.

My goal for you is twofold: I want you to learn (1) that you can cope and (2) by changing your Automatic Thoughts that you will not think of the symptoms as being dangerous any longer.

Automatic Thoughts are well-rehearsed; they occur easily and spontaneously, without effort. No matter how irrational they seem when exposed to the light of day, they are believed. They are often associated with strong emotion (e.g., feeling terrified of the panic sensations), and are therefore resistant to change. Your rational mind cannot control them easily. Hence, they aren't challenged or put to a test. You may not have realized that you can *learn* to control and change them. In this chapter, you will be asked to challenge your Automatic Thoughts and in Chapter 10 to put your thoughts to behavioral tests.

Automatic Thoughts Are *Learned* and Can Be *Unlearned!*

Often, people have limited awareness of their Automatic Thoughts. For instance, when I ask clients, "What thoughts came into your mind just *before* the panic?" some clients can remember those thoughts, others cannot. They haven't a clue.

It is very different with thoughts that arise in the middle of a panic; most people can easily describe those. Even in the "no clue" unexpected panics, by paying attention and trying to remember what the thoughts were just before the panic set in, people often can discover the Automatic Thought that flashed through their minds. For example, one client had occasional panics while he was watching TV or lying down relaxing. After some therapeutic work he realized that while he was relaxing, his mind was subtly scanning for skipped heart beats, because of his fear that he had a heart problem.

Obviously, because Automatic Thoughts are "automatic" they are very difficult to pinpoint, and hard to articulate. Remember the task earlier in this chapter about recording your thoughts while in a panic? I told you that if you drew a blank or came up with thoughts that were too general, to take a break from this book and approach a real-life situation that you find frightening. There is another approach to become aware of thoughts when you are anxious and they are not easily apparent: Stay with your feelings and describe all of them and all of your sensations in great detail. "What exactly was I feeling then?" "And, after that, what did I feel?" and so on. Thoughts often surface this way. Also, some people relate better to images than to words. One client pictured himself running screaming out of a restaurant. This was an image only, not something he had previously articulated. But when encouraged to stay with the image, he eventually was able to describe it in words.

NOTE: If this section has helped you to identify more specific panic-related thoughts, remember to jot them down on Worksheet 4.

Distinguishing Between Feelings and Thoughts

Many people have difficulty separating their feelings from their thoughts. Feelings can be expressed in *one word* as in: I feel sad, angry, hopeless, disappointed, furious, happy, content, frustrated, depressed, anxious, or jittery. If someone starts a sentence saying, "I feel that. . . . ," the word "that" indicates not a feeling but a thought will follow; as in, "I feel that I don't deserve to have these attacks." "I feel that he should accept his pain." "I feel that my boss is unfair to me." "I feel that I am to blame for what happened."

When you look at these sentences, you can see that they are actually thoughts, not feelings. Clearly, there are feelings *related* to the thoughts. "I feel angry because my boss is unfair to me." Do you see the difference? Keep this distinction in mind when you and others talk: A feeling can be expressed in *one* word. If more words are used, or if the words "I feel" are followed by "that," we are most likely dealing with a thought rather than a feeling.

Many negative Automatic Thoughts can be categorized as irrational thoughts (also called cognitive distortions) or unhelpful thoughts (also called maladaptive thoughts), or both. For instance, people who are sensitive to social evaluation don't say, "Gee, if I walk into that gathering, people will admire how I look and think that I must be a great person." Instead they think, "I can't walk into that crowd. They'll think badly of me." While not irrational, this is an unhelpful thought. If you consistently believe that people evaluate you negatively, it lowers your self-esteem. The belief of a positive evaluation, even if a bit unrealistic, tends to feed a more positive self-image. In neither case can we read people's minds, but what do our beliefs and thoughts do to *us*?

Irrational Thoughts or Cognitive Distortions

Researchers and clinicians have made lists of a number of Cognitive Distortions. The following is a short list that I have found helpful for people with panics and phobias. The first two are particularly emphasized by Drs. Barlow and Craske in their book, *Mastery of Your Anxiety and Panic II*. If you wish to learn more about Cognitive Distortions, I also recommend *The Feeling Good Handbook* by David Burns. (See Recommended Reading at the end of this chapter.)

1. *Exaggerating or Overestimating Risk*
   Overestimating means to greatly exaggerate the odds of a dangerous or bad event happening, even if it has never occurred before. The italicized words below are events that could happen because there is no absolute certainty in life except death (see Chapter 4); however, they are highly unlikely to happen. Some examples:

   - Next time I panic, I could *faint*.

   - The pains in my chest (during a panic) must mean I'm having a *heart attack*.

   - If these panics continue and get worse, I will have a *nervous breakdown*.

   - If I drive on the freeway, I may get so anxious that I will *crash the car* into a wall or *drive off* an overpass.

   - I need to escape. I may *pass out*. I need to get fresh air, or I'll *suffocate*.

   - I'll *make a fool* of myself if I have to speak up in a group.

2. *Catastrophizing*

   Catastrophizing is closely related to Overestimating. Not only could the bad event take place, but extreme and *horrible consequences* are bound to follow. It involves imagining the worst-case scenario, often stated in "What if. . .?" terms. The person also *underestimates his or her ability to cope with the event*. Therefore, an emotion becomes deeply embedded into the scenario of the feared event. Some examples:

   - What if I go crazy in a panic and will not be able to take care of my son?

   - If I panic, I won't be able to function at work and I will surely lose my job. I won't be able to get another job.

   - What if others see me shaking so terribly and they think I'm crazy? I couldn't ever face those people again.

   - What can I do in a panic? I'm losing control. I don't want to scare anyone else. I'll feel so embarrassed.

   - What if I jumped out of the car and abandoned the children? Or what if I lose control and hit them? What if I hurt them so badly they'll need medical care? What if the child I'm holding falls and gets hurt?

   - I hope I won't have an attack. If I lose control, something awful will happen and I won't be able to cope.

   - What if I can't get rid of my panics? I'll get stuck at home forever and won't ever be able to leave.

   - If I faint in the store, I could fall and crack my head open and then I'll need surgery.

   - I think I'm going mad. I'm closed in. I can't do anything about it. I can't stand this. I'm going to lose control. I hope no one notices this. Somebody help me!

3. *Control at All Cost*

   People with panics become obsessed with two kinds of control: Wanting *control over outside events*, and wanting *full control over their emotions* at all times. Some examples:

   - I'll know that I'm in control if I never have another panic again.

   - I can't stand situations where I am not in control: Stuck in traffic, waiting in a waiting room, flying, being a passenger in a car, sitting in the middle of the row in a movie theater or auditorium, sitting in a group meeting, being at the dentist.

   - I must always appear strong and in control. If people notice my anxiety, they'll think I'm weak.

4. *Perfectionism or All-or-Nothing Thinking*

   Perfectionism goes hand-in-hand with "either-or" thinking. Either I'm a success or I'm a failure. If it's not 100 percent, it's no good. Everything is seen in black and white. An example:

   - This is so horrible. I don't want to lose my mind. I just don't want to live this way. Having panics makes me a defective person. But I must be perfect. (This example includes both catastrophic and perfectionistic elements.)

5. *Emotions as Evidence*

   Using emotions as evidence occurs when we consider our feelings to be all of reality, i.e., if something is felt, then it must be true. This involves the notion that the stronger something is felt, the more it is a sign of truth. Some examples:

- But when I feel so much fear, I know that something awful will happen.

- The pain in my left arm means I'm having a heart attack.

- If panics weren't dangerous, why would I have so much fear? One fears what is dangerous!

Unhelpful or Maladaptive Thoughts

Whereas Cognitive Distortions reflect exaggerated thinking and drawing illogical conclusions from the evidence, Maladaptive Thoughts may seem logical and reality-based. Yet these thoughts do not promote well-being and therefore are called "maladaptive" or "dysfunctional." For instance, a person feels unable to cope well with job stress and thinks, "When I see others handle a lot of stress on the job well, and I feel I can't handle it, I feel different. I feel bad and guilty because I can't handle it."

Being self-critical, worrying about something incessantly, or berating oneself over and over for past mistakes, is very unhelpful and ultimately unhealthy. You can determine if a thought is maladaptive by asking yourself:

- Is this thought helpful?

- Do I feel good about myself when I think this way?

- Does this way of thinking help me solve the problem?

- Are these thoughts productive?

1. *Disaster Expectation*

   Disaster expectation is a prime example of a common Maladaptive Thought in chronic worriers (which includes many panickers who become chronic worriers). Many people think that expecting the worst is a good approach to life. Now, I don't suppose that they started life thinking this way, but based on past hardships and difficulty coping, they adopt this mode of thought. The thinking goes, "I'll expect the worst. Then, if the worst does not happen, I'll be grateful. If something good comes out of it, I'll be really happy." There are two beliefs underlying this way of thinking.

   The first is that they could not possibly cope if bad things happened unexpectedly. The second is magical thinking. (Magical thinking is actually an Irrational Thought.) Few people will openly admit to thinking this way, but it is very common. It is the belief that worrying about a danger somehow insures that it will not happen. Let's assume that you worry intensely about going crazy during a panic. But several panics have passed and you did not go crazy. In the background may be the barely conscious thought, "I worried a lot and nothing terrible happened. Somehow, worrying saved me." In other words, when you worry intensely and nothing bad happens, this may reinforce the need to continue worrying, and worrying might easily become a habit.

   Another common example of magical thinking is seen in the person who holds tightly onto the airplane seat armrests for fear that the plane will crash. Intellectually, that person knows that holding onto the armrests doesn't keep the plane aloft, yet he or she repeats this behavior over and over when flying. Some people justify their thought patterns by thinking, "God will spare me. I paid my dues worrying. He would not have let me worry for nothing. But if I don't worry, I'll fall short and that's when the axe will fall."

2. *Giving Up*

   Giving up is the behavioral approach when someone's thinking is totally dominated by the expectation of a negative outcome. Some examples:

- Why even apply for that job? I won't get it anyway.

- I never get what I want, so why even try?

- I won't ever be able to drive on the freeway without anxiety, so why try? It is always going to be a struggle.

- I'll never be able to take a plane and fly; it's too scary. I can live without it.

3. *The Unanswerable Question*

Why? Why? Why? To always question why is an excellent way to plague oneself with questions that cannot be answered. The mind is so complex that even the best therapists seldom know *for sure* the why's. Sometimes asking why is not really a search for an answer but an instrument for self-torture or condemnation (think of a parent saying to the child—*Why* in hell did you spill the milk?). Asking why can distract you from working on solutions. Some examples:

- Why do I have this problem?

- Why am I anxious?

- Why did this panic come out of the blue?

- Why am I such a worrier?

Ask yourself instead "How" or "What" questions. They help to increase your awareness and promote finding solutions.

- How am I making myself anxious?

- What was I thinking that may have contributed to my panic?

- How can I learn to worry less?

One "how" question is tricky though, that's "How did this happen to me?" (What is really meant here is—"Why did this happen to me?")

Underlying or Core Beliefs

We saw in Chapter 3 that psychological vulnerabilities contribute to the development of panic disorder. These vulnerabilities can consist of underlying, deeply rooted, so-called "core" beliefs. Frequently, but not always, they are formed when we are children. They usually reflect our families', especially parents', world views and become our own. Most of the time this happens unconsciously, i.e., we do not realize that we are absorbing these beliefs.

At other times, because of difficult childhood experiences, people learn that they have little control over their lives, or that what happens to them in life is unpredictable. Underlying, or Core Beliefs, have a powerful impact on many of our attitudes, moods, and behaviors. They can set the stage for later development of problems, such as panic disorder. If many Underlying Beliefs operate on an unconscious level, how can you detect them to aid in your recovery from panic disorder? It is a challenge, but it is not an impossible task. The Automatic Thoughts that were described earlier can lead you to the discovery of your Core or Underlying Beliefs.

By now, you should have written down some of your thoughts, both on Worksheet 4. "Specific Thoughts I Have During a Panic Attack" and other thoughts that you may have jotted down as you were reading the subsequent text. Read through your list of thoughts and ask yourself, "Is there a pattern here?" Look at some of your behaviors associated with anxiety, e.g., avoidances. If someone behaves or talks in a certain way, what is the Underlying Belief that their behavior or speech conveys?

Let me make this more concrete and understandable. People who let others walk all over them may have the Underlying Belief that they are worthless or undeserving. People who complain that they have low self-esteem, fear rejection, and fear failure may have an Underlying Belief such as, "I don't measure up to others," "I'm not all right unless I'm liked by everyone," "I'm so hurt inside that I cannot deal with rejection," "Unless I'm perfect, I'm no good."

Here are some more beliefs. See if any ring a bell and apply to you. They may also help you recognize some other beliefs you hold.

- I'm sensitive and fragile.

- I'm very vulnerable and cannot deal with too much stress.

- I don't count.

- I shouldn't get upset over small things.

- One should worry a lot about things that *could* be dangerous.

- If I'm going to be seen as a competent adult, I must be perfect.

- It is terrible when people don't act as they should.

- I have to be loved and approved by all.

- I must be perfect to be worthwhile.

- I'm not lovable.

- No one cares about me.

- My opinions don't matter.

- If I have another panic (after a panic-free period), that proves there is no hope for me.

- Feelings don't lie. If I feel something, then it must be true.

- If something bad unexpectedly happens, then I won't be able to cope.

- I am vulnerable to anxiety and cannot cope with it. Therefore, I won't be able to overcome my anxiety.

- If I'm too happy, then a disaster will strike. It always does.

- The world is too dangerous for me. (This one could easily reinforce avoidance behavior.)

- Unusual physical symptoms always mean that something is wrong with the body.

As you can see from the examples above, Underlying Beliefs can be expressed in *blanket statements* (I'm not lovable), and in *"If . . . then" statements*. They are often judgmental, harsh, and unforgiving statements. They set you up for failure and make you feel hopeless (no one cares about me; I must be perfect to be worthwhile).

Can I change my Core Beliefs, you may now ask. That depends, in part, on how fixed or malleable your beliefs are. If changing a belief would severely threaten your self-image or world view, it is not likely to be changed. For example, there are people who were incest victims as children. Many deal with it in therapy and move beyond it. Others, no matter how much help they get, continue to feel that the abuse was so horrible that they continue to feel victimized forever.

Other people may have several relationships go sour. Maybe it is because they are self-centered and selfish, but they keep blaming their partners. You can see from these examples, that changing your Core Beliefs may be too threatening. But the more you can open your mind to looking at alter-

Worksheet 5: Core Beliefs That May Be Behind My Automatic Thoughts

1. _____

2. _____

3. _____

4. _____

5. _____

6. _____

7. _____

8. _____

9. _____

10. _____

11. _____

12. _____

natives, no matter how hard or unnatural it feels, the more likely it will be that you can alter your beliefs.

As you start to work on challenging your Automatic Thoughts, whenever you get stuck, pay attention to any Underlying or Core Beliefs and jot them down on Worksheet 5. You will be using this in Section 3 of this chapter.

The Belief in One's Ability to Cope with Fear or Self-Efficacy

Self-efficacy, a psychological term, means the belief in one's ability to cope with fear. Whenever a person is confronted with stress or danger, he or she assesses the degree of danger as well as the capacity for handling it. If you think that you cannot cope with the situation, you are much more easily overwhelmed, and you may resort to escape or avoidance behavior. At the moment, avoidance may feel good. Because anxiety is reduced by the avoidance, and the decreased anxiety is a positive feeling, you are inadvertently reinforcing avoidance, i.e., teaching yourself to further avoid fear-provoking situations. This only leads to further lowering of your self-confidence. You wind up feeling more vulnerable than ever and less able to cope.

Look at Figure 9.1, Perceived Danger, One's Ability to Cope, and Resulting Behavior. It is complex, but if you spend some time with it, you will find that it is another way of seeing how thoughts, avoidance, and self-efficacy interrelate.

The use of coping skills has been stressed in this book, but these skills can be short-lived. I would like you to achieve changes at a deeper level, by changing your unhelpful beliefs, so that you can cope better with anxiety and panic in the future. Your sense of self-efficacy would be greatly enhanced. You would not only cope better, but you would know that you can cope better. This is not to say that you will be perfect. No one is. But if you can change your thoughts and challenge your fears, you will be better prepared to deal with adversity, including panics, in the future.

Change Your Thoughts About
Danger and Challenge Your Fears:
You Will Become Less Vulnerable.

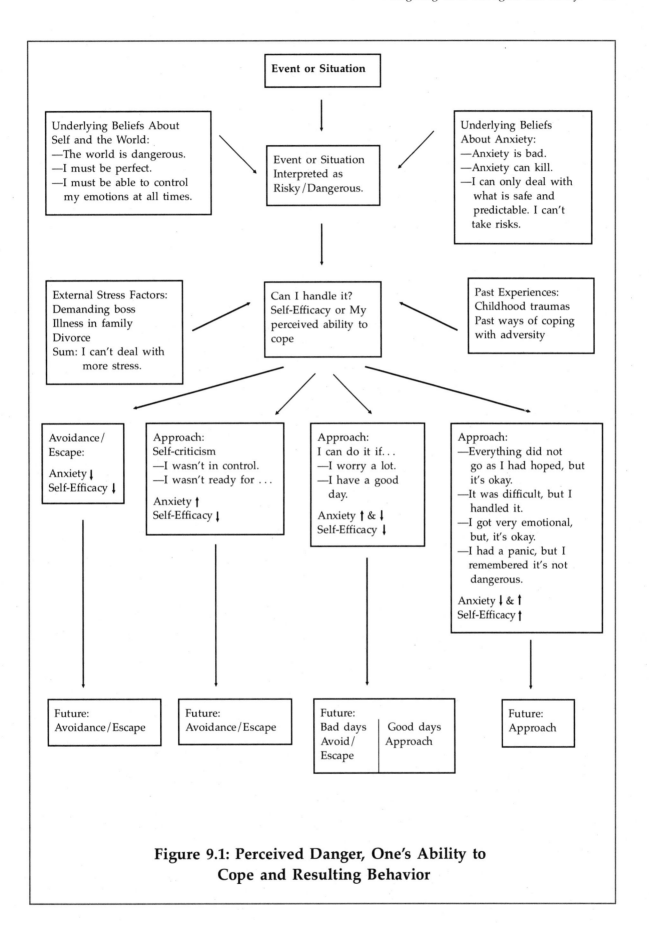

Figure 9.1: Perceived Danger, One's Ability to Cope and Resulting Behavior

Section 2: Changing Automatic Thoughts

Thoughts have power. Research has shown that the stronger a person's belief that a harmful event will happen, the more often the dreadful thoughts will occur and the more uncomfortable they will seem. If you have a strong belief that a bad panic will result in your having a stroke, it will nag you, consciously or unconsciously. Your anxiety about a stroke will keep you looking for any signs of danger, again, consciously or unconsciously. Since the danger is panic (panic = stroke), you will be looking anxiously for any signs of panic. You can become so sensitized that the mere thought, "What if I panic?" can bring on a panic. Thus, the more you think *fearfully* about not wanting to panic, the greater the likelihood that panics will return.

Targeting Your Thoughts to Decrease Fear

The aim of the preceding Section 1, "Identifying the Cognitive Component of Panic" was to help you recognize your fearful thought patterns. You are not the only one who has these. They are so common, in fact, that categories are used to classify them. Yet knowing which Cognitive Distortion or Maladaptive Thought your thoughts reflect is not enough. Procedures have been developed to help alter them. Now, you must challenge *your* Automatic Thoughts and change them to help your panic disorder.

I have included the following short section on strategies for coping with your fears while you work on achieving more profound changes.

Strategies for Coping While You Learn to Master Your Fears

Of course, it will take you some time before you learn how to overcome panic disorder. You are still faced with frightening attacks. While you learn the methods to overcome your fears, be sure to use one of the following three tools (Remember to add useful items to Worksheet 1: "My Personal Coping Affirmations."):

1. *Focus on your breathing* instead of catastrophizing about other physical events. Remember that breathing is the one autonomic (involuntary) function that you *can* bring under voluntary control, and it will eventually help to slow other physical symptoms of panic. (See Chapter 8). "Riding the wave" of panic while focusing on diaphragmatic breathing slows down the experience, instead of making you feel like running for your life.

2. *Talk to yourself.* Remind yourself of all the information you learned about the physiology of panics in Chapter 7. All of your physical reactions are *survival mechanisms*, preparing you for the fight/flight response. The body has built-in controls to protect itself from a reaction becoming too extreme. Panic attacks are in themselves normal fear reactions; the only aberration

is that they are triggered in the absence of a life-threatening situation. Describe to yourself the physical events as they take place: "My heart beats fast because . . . , I have discomfort and pains in my chest because . . . , I'm sweating because . . . , I'm lightheaded because. . . ." See Chapter 7 if you need to refresh your memory.

3. *Don't ignore the early stages of anxiety.* Proceed as soon as possible to the slow diaphragmatic breathing. It is always easier to deal with low levels of anxiety than with intense symptoms. Many panickers are so afraid of experiencing anxiety that they often ignore the early signs, hoping that they will go away. You are the best judge of whether this helps or hurts you most of the time. Whatever you do, don't fight or run from your anxiety and panic. It does not help. Face it squarely. You will learn to apply these strategies and thereby discover that you can cope with anxiety.

Stage 1: Moving from General to Specific Thoughts

At the beginning of this chapter, you were told to fill out Worksheet 4 with *specific* thoughts you have during a panic. If you did this, you are ahead. If you wrote down more thoughts as you went along, that's even better. Now, do the following exercise, "Questions to Help Make Your Thoughts Specific." Take a pen and pad and rewrite the general statements below, making them as specific as possible.

General Statements:

- I may stop breathing.
- I could make a fool of myself.
- I'll lose control.
- I'll be embarrassed.
- I'll die.
- I'll come unglued.
- I may go crazy.
- I can't stand this.
- I may have a nervous breakdown.
- I want the heat to stop. I can't stand it.
- I won't be able to handle a panic now. Something awful will happen.

Questions to Help Make Your Thoughts Specific

1. What exactly do you mean by _____? (Making a fool of yourself, losing control, being embarrassed, coming unglued, going crazy, not being able to stand it, having a nervous breakdown, feeling hot, something awful happening, not being able to handle a panic.)

2. How would _____ happen? (Dying, stopping breathing, etc.)

3. What is the worst that could happen if _____ took place? (E.g., a panic.)

You can use any approach discussed earlier, to help you state your thoughts in specific, rather than general, terms. PLEASE WORK ON THIS TASK NOW, before proceeding any further.

Worksheet 6: Challenging Automatic Thoughts

1	2	3	4	5	6
Date	Specific Trigger	Automatic Thought	My Evidence	Alternative Hypotheses	Face Up to Automatic Thought (Column 3)
	Physical sensation or situation	*Stated as a theory, identify which Cognitive Distortion or Maladaptive Thought it reflects. Probability of X happening 0–100%*	*for this Theory is: Then Refute!*	*Probability 0–100% of each being true*	*Just because X occurs, does not mean Y will, too. So what if . . .! Probability of 3 happening NOW 0–100%*

The space below is for you to practice with your thoughts.

Stage 2: Challenging Automatic Thoughts (Worksheet 6)

Worksheet 6 looks complex, and it is, but, if you stay with it, you can learn to do this piece of work and you will benefit greatly from doing it.

How to Use Worksheet 6 for Challenging Your Automatic Thoughts:

1. *Date.* Always write down the date. You will be repeating the challenge over and over, and later you will be able to compare your thoughts and challenges with earlier ones and evaluate your progress.

2. *Specific Trigger.* State what triggered the thought, either a physical sensation (feeling dizzy, feeling as if your heart had skipped a beat, feeling chest pain), or a situation (going to the mall, driving on the freeway).

3. *Automatic Thought.* Change your questions into *theories/predictions.* For example, "What if I can't breathe next time I panic?" becomes "Next time I panic I may not be able to breathe." State your thought in *specific* terms.

Questions to guide you:

- What exactly do I mean by _____? (losing my mind, losing control, the beginning of the end)

- What exactly am I afraid will happen if _____? (I become dizzy, my heart pumps a mile a minute)

- What would happen if I couldn't stop the feelings? (during a panic) _____

- What do I think could happen if I felt _____? (unreal, numb, tunnel vision, totally out of control)

- What is the worst that could happen if _____?

Identify your thought as representing which Cognitive Distortion or Maladaptive Thought. (See Section 1 in this chapter, especially "Automatic Thoughts and Perceived Danger," if you need to refresh your memory.) State the probability of the worst happening, using the 0–100% scale:

   0% = I do not believe my theory at all.

  50% = There is half a chance that my theory will become reality, half that it will not.

100% = I'm totally convinced that my theory will take place.

Use any number on the scale. For example, ask yourself, "Right now, how much do I believe that I will actually pass out in a panic?"

4. *My Evidence.* The evidence I am using for my theory is:_____. What exactly led me to conclude that my theory is valid? Why I believe it: _____.

   Then Refute! Does it hold up to objective scrutiny?

Questions/statements to guide you in refuting the evidence:

- Is my theory an absolute objective fact or is it just a hypothesis?

- What is the objective evidence?

- Has _____ ever happened before?

- Are thoughts necessarily accurate.

- I must remember that my feelings are not good evidence.

- Am I looking at all the evidence or am I exaggerating the negative possibilities?
- Because it happened once, does that mean it will always happen?

5. *Alternative Hypotheses*. State two to three alternative hypotheses for the symptoms/fears, with the probability of each being true, from 0–100%.

Questions to guide you:

- What are alternative hypotheses/explanations for my sensations?
- Could other people explain the same sensations differently?
- At other times, when I had similar sensations but was not scared, how did I explain them then?

6. *Face Up to Automatic Thought (listed in Column 3)*. Use the "Just because X, does not mean Y" and the "So what if . . . !" techniques.

Questions to guide you:

- Can I live with it?
- How bad/serious is it?
- Is it the end of the world?

State the probability of 3 (*Automatic Thought*) happening, as you see it NOW. What are the real odds, 0–100%?

Before I ask you to start work on changing your thoughts, let me give two examples.

Example 1

1. *Date.* 1-3-96.

2. *Specific Trigger.* I'm feeling this sudden heat wave going up my spine and into my head.

3. *Automatic Thought.* Oh, no! I'll have a panic. What if it's a bad one and this sensation gets much worse?

   Restate (specifically and as theory): The sudden heat wave means my blood pressure is shooting up, and I'll have a stroke. Example of Overestimation (a Cognitive Distortion). 20% probability of happening.

4. *My Evidence.* Feeling this sensation is not normal. At times I have had high blood pressure. Strokes do come on suddenly!

   Refute! Maybe I'm using the discomfort I feel about the physical sensations as evidence. I have had these sensations before, and they have led to panic but never to a stroke.

5. *Alternative Hypotheses*

   - The sensations could be due to anxiety, which can lead to a panic. 50% probability of this being true.
   - I'm just very tense lately because of these other problems I have. It could just be tension, similar to a tension headache. 60% probability of this being true.

6. *Face Up to Automatic Thought (Column 3)*. Just because I feel a heat wave in a panic, doesn't mean I'll have a stroke. What's so horrible about heat waves or even a panic, anyway? It's not the end of the world. 5% probability of my Automatic Thought happening.

Example 2

1. *Date.* 3-9-96.

2. *Specific Trigger.* Driving on the freeway and becoming very tense.

3. *Automatic Thought.* What if I become so dizzy that I'll lose control?

   Restate (specifically and as theory): The dizziness will get so bad that I'll lose control of the wheel and I'll crash the car. Then I'll be killed and my children will be miserable forever. Example of Catastrophizing (a Cognitive Distortion). 10% probability of this happening.

4. *My Evidence.* I have always pulled off the freeway when dizzy. But it might suddenly get so bad that I couldn't get off and the above disaster would happen.

   Refute! Does dizziness really lead people to let go of the wheel? If I feel dizzy, I always pay closer attention and try to be extra cautious. Maybe I tense up, but I don't go limp. I have felt dizzy many times before and have never gone limp or gotten myself in danger.

5. *Alternative Hypotheses*

   - Dizziness can come from hyperventilation. I could have been hyperventilating! 80% probability of this being true.

   - Because I'm apprehensive and fearful, I may be looking for sensations of dizziness and exaggerate any sensation with my fear. 90% probability of this being true.

6. *Face Up to Automatic Thought (Column 3).* Just because I feel dizzy does not mean I'll let go of the wheel of the car. So what if I feel dizzy? It's not the end of the world! 4% probability of my Automatic Thought happening.

Stage 3: Challenging *Your* Automatic Thoughts

Now that you have read the examples, it is time for you to do the work. Take two 8.5" x 11" pieces of paper and tape them together on the short side (horizontally), so that you wind up with an 8.5" x 22" chart-size paper that can fold like a brochure. That will give you enough space to write. Copy the names of the columns, draw a line underneath them, and use the space below. It will be much easier for you to work with the chart horizontally rather than vertically. Also, the chart format allows you a better overview. (You can write in a briefer fashion. The examples here were expanded to clarify the task.)

Now go back to Worksheet 4: "Specific Thoughts I Have During a Panic Attack" earlier in this chapter, and to any other thoughts on this subject that you may have jotted down. Start working on one thought at a time. Do *not* work with the most frightening thought and theory first (heart attack, stroke, suffocation); *start with something easier.* I suggest this so you can become used to doing challenging work before arriving at the "Focal Fears." (Focal Fears are the one or two worst fears that you have in a panic, the absolutely scariest ones.)

Take three days or more to work on this before you proceed further with the book.

PLEASE PRACTICE NOW.

I have worked on the chart copied from Worksheet 6.

I still don't know quite how to do it. I need more guidance. Turn to the next page.

I have done the work, but I don't think it will help my fears. Turn to page 94.

Yes, I am challenging my thoughts as you suggested. What next? Turn to Stage 4: "Working on Focal Fears" on page 94.

§ You still don't know quite how to do it. You need more guidance.

Let me give you two more examples to see if they help. When you look at these new examples, you will notice that, like the previous examples, they follow the format of the exercise "How to Use Worksheet 6 for Challenging Your Automatic Thoughts," on pages 89–90. Refer to those pages to get more practice in how you can best work on changing your Automatic Thoughts.

Example 3

1. *Date.* 8-8-96.

2. *Specific Trigger.* Feelings of unreality while shopping in the mall.

3. *Automatic Thought.* This is not normal. Am I abnormal?

   Restate: These feelings of unreality mean that I'm defective. I cannot accept that. Example of Perfectionism (a Cognitive Distortion). 30% probability of this being true.

4. *My Evidence.* Everyone else is okay compared to me. I have asked others if they have these sensations, and they say no. I'm abnormal!

   Refute! Unreal feelings are some of the symptoms of a panic attack. Many people must experience this, since so many people have panic disorder. Maybe I'm not helping myself by labeling myself as defective. Everyone is different.

5. *Alternative Hypotheses*

   • Overbreathing produces feelings of unreality. Maybe I'm doing it now. 60% probability of this being true.

   • Being a perfectionist doesn't help. No one is perfect. 95% probability of this being true.

6. *Face Up to Automatic Thought (Column 3).* Just because these sensations feel so strange, does not mean that I am defective. Also, so what if I'm not perfect? No one is! 0% probability of my Automatic Thought happening.

Example 4

1. *Date.* 9-14-96.

2. *Specific Trigger.* Feeling a little shaky from being in the mall.

3. *Automatic Thought.* What if the shaking gets worse and worse and I panic and embarrass myself?

   Restate: I may shake worse and then I'll panic. Everyone will notice, and I'll be embarrassed, and they'll think there is something really wrong with me. They will laugh at me and treat me without respect. Example of Catastrophizing (a Cognitive Distortion). 60% probability of this happening.

4. *My Evidence.* If I shake, people will treat me without respect. It has happened to me before. They may laugh at me.

   Refute! At times, people have treated me without respect, but not because I was shaking. Most of the time people don't even know when I'm having a panic attack.

5. *Alternative Hypotheses*

- When I get anxious, sometimes I shake. It is not that unusual for people to shake. I don't judge people harshly when I see them shake. I feel bad for them. 80% probability of this being true.

- I can't read people's minds, so I really don't know what they are thinking. 95% probability of this being true.

6. *Face Up to Automatic Thought (Column 3).* Just because I shake, does not mean others will act disrespectfully toward me. If some people do think there is something wrong with me, so what!! I'll be okay. 5% probability of my Automatic Thought happening.

Did these examples help? I hope so. Now return to page 91. Using your *specific* thoughts from Worksheet 4, do the exercise following the larger "Challenging *Your* Automatic Thoughts" chart that was described on page 91. When you have done the work, continue on to Stage 4: "Working on Focal Fears" on page 94.

§   **You have done the work, but you don't think that it will help your fears.**

You might be saying something like this to yourself: "I can do all this intellectually, but I know that it won't affect my fears." Initially, this may be true. You may find the exercises artificial and not believable. Nevertheless, I strongly recommend that you keep doing the challenges. You will have to do them *many times* before you start believing the new thoughts; eventually you will think a new thought instead of an old thought and your emotions will be affected as well.

It is a good idea to repeat the work, even using the same exact Automatic Thought. Take as many opportunities as you can to do the challenging work when you are aware of negative Automatic Thoughts. Do not copy the challenges from earlier dates. Rather, try not to look back at the beginning. At a later time, when you have done quite a bit more work, go back and compare the new challenge work to that of earlier dates. Then examine the progress you have made. For instance, you may notice that the percentages, which reflect how strongly you hold on to certain thoughts, have slowly changed.

This is very hard work. It is just like confronting phobias; it may take you quite a few trials. Your patience will be sorely tried, but the reward is it works! One day you will realize that your thoughts have changed. Your Automatic Thoughts will convey positive messages not negative ones. This can change your life profoundly.

If you need to, return to the instructions in "How to Use Worksheet 6 for Challenging Your Automatic Thoughts," on pages 89–90. Refer to those pages to get more practice in how to best work on changing your Automatic Thoughts. If you already did a number of practices, try just a few more. Then continue to "Stage 4: Working on Focal Fears" on this page.

Stage 4: Working on Focal Fears

Fear is the major element in Panic Disorder. That is why we are spending so much time on these exercises. By challenging your Automatic Thoughts you began to challenge your fears. The next step is to challenge your Focal Fears. By Focal Fear I mean the real, underlying fear—the fear that terrifies you most during panic attacks. Most people have one Focal Fear, some have two or even three. Focal Fears usually center on disaster in one of the following four areas:

- Physical (dying of a heart attack, stroke, or suffocation; fainting while driving)

- Mental (going crazy)

- Social (being criticized, scrutinized, judged, or humiliated)

- Behavioral (losing self-control)

You may have been aware of your worst fear when you started this book, or the challenging exercises may have helped you to become aware of it. If you still haven't identified it, turn to page 110. If you need to work on more than one of the fears that are listed below, you can choose the order that feels best to you.

If your Focal Fear is:

§   Dying from a heart attack. Turn to page 96.

§   Dying of suffocation. Turn to page 98.

§   Having a stroke. Turn to page 100.

§   Fainting. Turn to page 102.

Going crazy or having a nervous breakdown. Turn to page 104.

Losing control. Turn to page 106.

Being embarrassed or humiliated. Turn to page 108.

Feeling so weak that you cannot move or you might fall down. Turn to page 109.

You cannot identify your Focal Fear. Turn to page 110.

§   **Your Focal Fear is dying from a heart attack.**

Medical Fact: Panic attacks do not lead to heart attacks. On an electrocardiogram test (EKG), a panic attack shows up as just a slightly increased heart rate. If you have had a medical exam and your physician says that your heart is fine, trust your doctor! Furthermore, people who have had heart attacks report sensations that are very different from those felt during panic attacks.

Use the "Challenging *Your* Automatic Thoughts" chart (described on page 91) as a guide and write down your answers *as I ask the questions*. (Do not just read through the material.)

1. *Date*. Fill out.

2. *Specific Trigger*. What are the exact sensations that make you think that you might end up with a heart attack? Write them down in Column 2. Please do so NOW.

   I have a hunch they are one or several of the following: Your heart pounds or races, it can flutter so fast that you hardly feel it, it seemingly skips beats; you feel chest pain and tension; your pulse races (if you have gotten into the habit of checking your pulse).

3. *Automatic Thought*. State yours in a specific theory. Determine which Cognitive Distortion or Maladaptive Thought it is. State the probability of your specific theory happening, using the 0–100% scale. Please do so NOW.

   A client said: "When my heart flutters so quickly, I believe it will be damaged, and I will end up having a heart attack." This is an example of Overestimation (a Cognitive Distortion). His guess at the probability of this happening was 30%.

4. *My Evidence*. State your evidence and refute it. Please do so NOW.

   Client's example: "I just don't feel my heart. It goes so fast. That speed must be damaging to my heart."

   He *refuted*: "Let me look at this differently. My probability is 30%. I have had roughly 100 panics. If the probability of having a heart attack was 30%, I would already have had 30 heart attacks. But I have had none! So what does that tell me? My probability is off! My assumption may not be accurate at all!"

5. *Alternative Hypotheses*. Find other possible explanations. If you get totally stuck, ask other people. Rate the probability of each. Please do so NOW.

   Client's example:

   • "If my heart flutters when I get scared, it is part of the fight/flight response, and it won't kill me. The fight/flight response is there to protect me. 50% probability of this being true."

   • "I have been checked out and been told that my heart is okay. I should trust my doctor. 70% probability of this being true."

6. *Face Up to Automatic Thought (Column 3)*. How would you face up to your fear? Write in Column 6. Restate the probability of your original Automatic Thought as you see it now. Please do so NOW.

Client's example: "Just because my heart flutters, does not mean that it is dangerous, or that I will have a heart attack and die. I have to trust the medical findings. 4% probability of my Automatic Thought happening."

If you need to work on more Focal Fears, return to pages 94–95. Otherwise, proceed to "Changing One's Thoughts Is Difficult but Fundamental" on page 112.

§   **Your Focal Fear is dying of suffocation.**

Medical Fact: No one has ever died of suffocation during a panic attack. Many people *feel* as if they cannot breathe in a panic, but they are actually breathing all along, and probably are over-breathing! (See Chapter 8.) This is a *paradoxical* perception (a perception that is contrary to the truth).

Please use the "Challenging *Your* Automatic Thoughts" chart (described on page 91) as a guide and write down your answers *as I ask the questions*. (Do not just read through the material.)

1. *Date.* Fill out.

2. *Specific Trigger.* What are the exact sensations that make you think that you might end up dying of suffocation? Write them down in Column 2. Please do so NOW.

    Clients have told me: "When I'm closed in, I just can't breathe. If I try really hard, I start to choke."

3. *Automatic Thought.* State yours in a specific theory. Determine which Cognitive Distortion or Maladaptive Thought it is. State the probability of your specific theory happening, using the 0–100% scale. Please do so NOW.

    A client said: "When I'm in a panic, when I think about my breathing, it really slows down. I'm afraid that when I breathe too slowly, I won't get enough air. Then, I will suffocate to death." This is an example of Overestimation (a Cognitive Distortion). Her guess at the probability of this happening was 5%.

4. *My Evidence.* State your evidence and refute it. Please do so NOW.

    Client's example: "I find myself hardly breathing when I am really anxious and in a panic. It gets harder and harder to breathe. One of these days my throat could close up and I could die."

    She *refuted*: "I am making a very specific prediction. First, breathing is not a voluntary function. I'll breathe whether or not I think about it. Second, however much I have had the feeling, I've never stopped breathing. That should tell me something!"

5. *Alternative Hypotheses.* Find other possible explanations. If you get totally stuck, ask other people. Rate the probability of each. Please do so NOW.

    Client's example:

    • "I have always been afraid of suffocation. Maybe I'm obsessed with my throat. 30% probability of this being true."

    • "I don't hear of other people dying from lack of air just because they are anxious, unless they may have severe asthma or emphysema. I don't have those conditions. 45% probability of this being true."

    • "If there's enough air for everyone else around me, there is enough for me, no matter what I feel. The air does not just get sucked from my nose! 60% probability of this being true."

6. *Face Up to Automatic Thought (Column 3).* How would you face up to your fear? Write in Column 6. Restate the probability of your original Automatic Thought as you see it now. Please do so NOW.

Client's example: "Just because I feel like I'm not breathing, does not mean that I literally did stop breathing. I would have been dead long ago! 3% probability of my Automatic Thought happening."

If you need to work on more Focal Fears, return to pages 94–95. Otherwise, proceed to "Changing One's Thoughts Is Difficult but Fundamental" on page 112.

§   **Your Focal Fear is having a stroke.**

Medical Fact: Panic attacks do not lead to strokes. During a panic the blood pressure may rise, but it does not do so to levels sufficient to trigger a stroke. (Remember, the fight/flight response is activated to save the organism from danger, not to harm it.)

Please use the "Challenging *Your* Automatic Thoughts" chart (described on page 91) as a guide and write down your answers *as I ask the questions.* (Do not just read through the material.)

1. *Date.* Fill out.

2. *Specific Trigger.* What are the exact sensations that lead you to believe that you might have a stroke? Write them down in Column 2. Please do so NOW.

   A very common sensation leading to that fear is feeling a heat wave moving up from the spine and into the head.

3. *Automatic Thought.* State yours in a specific theory. Determine which Cognitive Distortion or Maladaptive Thought it is. State the probability of your specific theory happening, using the 0–100% scale. Please do so NOW.

   A client in my New Panickers Group feared a stroke. Several of his relatives, including his father and grandfather, had suffered from high blood pressure and strokes when they were about his age. He constantly checked his pulse. His Automatic Thought was: "When I feel my pulse going a mile a minute, tightness in my head, and I have a spacy feeling, I believe that I will have a stroke." This is an example of Overestimation (a Cognitive Distortion). His guess at the probability of this happening was 40%.

4. *My Evidence.* State your evidence and refute it. Please do so NOW.

   Client's example: "I'm just a prime candidate for strokes, and I know that, in a panic, the blood pressure tends to go up a bit. Maybe that's all I need to end up with a stroke. Or the blood pressure could shoot way up."

   He *refuted*: "Am I such a prime candidate, really? My life style is very different from that of the others in my family who had strokes. I eat healthy foods, exercise, keep a low weight, and don't smoke. I can only take care of myself the best I can. The rest is up to God or fate. Also, do I really believe I can stop a stroke by checking my pulse?"

5. *Alternative Hypotheses.* Find other possible explanations. If you get totally stuck, ask other people. Rate the probability of each. Please do so NOW.

   Client's example:

   • "Panics don't lead to strokes, unless maybe the person was going to have a stroke imminently anyway. 90% probability of this being true."

   • "Using anxiety emotions as evidence does not make good sense. Emotions are not evidence. I am sometimes suggestible, and now I am doing it to myself. 80% probability of this being true."

6. *Face Up to Automatic Thought (Column 3).* How would you face up to your fear? Write in Column 6. Restate the probability of your original Automatic Thought as you see it now. Please do so NOW.

Client's example: "Does it really help to do what I'm doing? Maybe while I'm worrying about a stroke, I will end up being killed in a car accident. Does it really help? 0.25% probability of my Automatic Thought happening."

If you need to work on more Focal Fears, return to pages 94–95. Otherwise, proceed to "Changing One's Thoughts Is Difficult but Fundamental" on page 112.

Your Focal Fear is fainting.

Medical Fact: People seldom faint from panics because the blood pressure goes up slightly during a panic. For fainting to occur, usually blood pressure goes down drastically. Theoretically, the person would faint before something damaging happened. In fact, clients have rarely reported fainting during a panic. When the setting involves potential danger, as in driving, the survival instinct takes over. If you ask people how often they have felt like they were fainting while in panic states, most report having felt it many times. This is a *paradoxical* perception (a perception that is contrary to the truth). Some people even say that they fainted when in fact they did not. *Feeling like fainting* is not the same as lying on the floor unconscious for a few seconds.

Please use the "Challenging *Your* Automatic Thoughts" chart (described on page 91) as a guide and write down your answers *as I ask the questions*. (Do not just read through the material.)

1. *Date.* Fill out.

2. *Specific Trigger.* What are the exact sensations that lead you to believe that you will faint in a panic? Write them down in Column 2. Please do so NOW.

   Clients have described feeling the following: Hot, unreal, confused, unable to concentrate, needing fresh air, unable to breathe at all, lightheaded, dizzy.

3. *Automatic Thought.* State yours in a specific theory. Determine which Cognitive Distortion or Maladaptive Thought it is. State the probability of your specific theory happening, using the 0–100% scale. Please do so NOW.

   A client said: "The symptoms of dizziness, lightheadedness, difficulty breathing, and tunnel vision mean that I'm going to faint. It would be a disaster if I fainted! I could cause so much damage!" This is an example of Catastrophizing (a Cognitive Distortion). Her guess at the probability of this happening was 35%.

4. *My Evidence.* State your evidence and refute it. Please do so NOW.

   Client's example: "I can barely function when I feel those symptoms. I am pretty sure that I'll collapse and faint if they get worse."

   She *refuted*: "I have never fainted as an adult. Do these symptoms really lead to fainting? If I believe the probability of fainting is really 35%, that would mean that I already must have fainted in over a third of my panics. But I never have."

5. *Alternative Hypotheses.* Find other possible explanations. If you get totally stuck, ask other people. Rate the probability of each. Please do so NOW.

   Client's example:

   • "I have talked to several people who panic. No one has fainted. It must be rare. 90% probability of this being true."

   • "In panic, one's blood pressure goes up slightly; for one to faint the blood pressure must go *down*. I'm even less likely to faint in a panic than normally. 90% probability of this being true."

6. *Face Up to Automatic Thought (Column 3).* How would you face up to your fear? Write in Column 6. Restate the probability of your original Automatic Thought as you see it now. Please do so NOW.

Client's example: "Just because I have those sensations, does not mean I'll faint. Even if I fainted, it would not be in a life-threatening situation. And anywhere else, so what? If people were around, they'd try to help me, not to punish me. 5% probability of my Automatic Thought happening."

If you need to work on more Focal Fears, return to pages 94–95. Otherwise, proceed to "Changing One's Thoughts Is Difficult but Fundamental" on page 112.

∮   Your Focal Fear is going crazy or having a nervous breakdown.

Medical Fact: Panic attacks never lead to insanity. They do not lead to nervous breakdowns. Someone might have panics in the context of a nervous breakdown, but then there are many other psychological and physiological processes going on than in panic attacks. Having strange sensations and feeling as if one were losing one's mind happens to most "normal" people. It is very different from the long-term loss of contact with reality that people with schizophrenic or manic-depressive psychoses experience.

Please use the "Challenging *Your* Automatic Thoughts" chart (described on page 91) as a guide and write down your answers *as I ask the questions*. (Do not just read through the material.)

1. *Date*. Fill out.

2. *Specific Trigger*. What are the exact sensations that lead you to believe that you might go crazy or have a nervous breakdown? Write them down in Column 2. Please do so NOW.

   Clients have described these sensations: Feelings of unreality and depersonalization, losing focus and concentration, feeling dominated and trapped by fear, thoughts scattering from one to another a mile-a-minute, and being unable to focus on any one thing.

3. *Automatic Thought*. State yours in a specific theory. Determine which Cognitive Distortion or Maladaptive Thought it is. State the probability of your specific theory happening, using the 0–100% scale. Please do so NOW.

   A client said: "I'll go crazy and never return to reality. I'll end up in a mental institution for the rest of my life, and I'll be forsaken. It would be unbearable!" This is an example of Catastrophizing (a Cognitive Distortion). Her guess at the probability of this happening was 2%.

4. *My Evidence*. State your evidence and refute it. Please do so NOW.

   Client's example: "I don't feel myself in such a bad panic, but they say schizophrenics are not in touch with reality. They do and say strange things. Maybe this is how it begins."

   She *refuted*: "Anxiety attacks do not lead to schizophrenia. If it were so easy to become psychotic, many panickers would be like that. And they are not. Furthermore, I have felt this way before and I did not become psychotic when the panic passed."

5. *Alternative Hypotheses*. Find other possible explanations. If you get totally stuck, ask other people. Rate the probability of each. Please do so NOW.

   • "My symptoms are some of the more common symptoms of hyperventilation. Maybe I was overbreathing. 50% probability of this being true."

   • "Even if I have strange feelings in a panic, going crazy is at the other end of the scale! 30% probability of this being true."

6. *Face Up to Automatic Thought (Column 3)*. How would you face up to your fear? Write in Column 6. Restate the probability of your original Automatic Thought as you see it now. Please do so NOW.

Client's example: "Just because I feel strange, does not mean I'm becoming insane. So what if I think these thoughts! I need to find better ways of dealing with anxiety. 0.5% probability of my Automatic Thought happening."

If you need to work on more Focal Fears, return to pages 94–95. Otherwise, proceed to "Changing One's Thoughts Is Difficult but Fundamental" on page 112.

§ **Your Focal Fear is losing control.**

Fact: *Losing control* is an extremely vague and "loaded" statement. Many people label crying as losing control. Sometimes people *do* cry in a panic. Yet, would you label a *normal* emotional response like crying when upset as "losing control"? Often, people fear that they will yell and run around uncontrollably and frighten others or hurt themselves or others. There are occasions when someone will bolt out of a room in a panic. But this behavior is hardly serious enough to "brand you" forever as a "crazy" person.

Please use the "Challenging *Your* Automatic Thoughts" chart (described on page 91) as a guide and write down your answers *as I ask the questions*. (Do not just read through the material.)

1. *Date.* Fill out.

2. *Specific Trigger.* What are the exact sensations that lead you to think that you will lose control? Write them down in Column 2. Please do so NOW.

    Clients have described the following: "I can't concentrate, I can't function"; "I want to run, I just feel like running"; "I'm not at all myself"; "I feel like I'm crawling out of my skin."

3. *Automatic Thought.* State yours in a specific theory. Determine which Cognitive Distortion or Maladaptive Thought it is. State the probability of your specific theory happening, using the 0–100% scale. Please do so NOW.

    A client thought: "If I were on a job and panicked, I would become totally disorganized by my feelings and could not sit still or concentrate. I wouldn't have control over anything. The work would not get done, and I'd lose my job." This is an example of Catastrophizing, Control at All Costs, and to some extent Emotional Reasoning (all Cognitive Distortions). Her guess at the probability of this happening was 10%.

4. *My Evidence.* State your evidence and refute it. Please do so NOW.

    Client's example: "I just can't function in a panic and will lose control at any time. I have lost control in the past."

    She *refuted*: "Well, I haven't really *totally* lost control. I have shed a few tears of fear and frustration at times. That's not so bad."

5. *Alternative Hypotheses.* Find other possible explanations. If you get totally stuck, ask other people. Rate the probability of each. Please do so NOW.

    Client's example:

    - "Someone could feel out of control and still keep acting normally. 70% probability of this being true."

    - "Crying is not necessarily a sign of losing control. 50% probability of this being true."

6. *Face Up to Automatic Thought (Column 3).* How would you face up to your fear? Write in Column 6. Restate the probability of your original Automatic Thought as you see it now. Please do so NOW.

Client's example: "Just because I feel out of control, doesn't mean I have no control over my actions. So what if I cry or am upset? It's not the end of the world. 2% probability of my Automatic Thought happening."

If you need to work on more Focal Fears, return to pages 94–95. Otherwise, proceed to "Changing One's Thoughts Is Difficult but Fundamental" on page 112.

⸸   Your Focal Fear is being embarrassed or humiliated.

Fact: It is impossible for anyone to go through life without sometimes saying or doing things that feel embarrassing or humiliating! Ask yourself: Is it something that I can survive? Can I let go of it and move on?

Please use the "Challenging *Your* Automatic Thoughts" chart (described on page 91) as a guide and write down your answers *as I ask the questions*. (Do not just read through the material.)

1. *Date.* Fill out.

2. *Specific Trigger.* What are the exact sensations/situations that lead you to think that you will be embarrassed and humiliated? Write them down in Column 2. Please do so NOW.

   Clients have described the following: Shaking, trembling, crying, blushing, unsteady voice, and feeling as if people are looking at them.

3. *Automatic Thought.* State yours in a specific theory. Determine which Cognitive Distortion or Maladaptive Thought it is. State the probability of your specific theory happening, using the 0–100% scale. Please do so NOW.

   A client said: "I may panic, start shaking and crying, and then I will be terribly embarrassed. People will know how insecure I am. I've got to be in control!" This is an example of Catastrophizing and Control at All Cost (both Cognitive Distortions). Her guess at the probability of this happening was 40%.

4. *My Evidence.* State your evidence and refute it. Please do so NOW.

   Client's example: "I can't stand my emotions going wild in public. Other people stay in control of themselves."

   She *refuted*: "Being a human being means that one's emotions go up and down. I have seen plenty of people throughout my life become emotional and cry at times."

5. *Alternative Hypotheses.* Find other possible explanations. If you get totally stuck, ask other people. Rate the probability of each. Please do so NOW.

   Client's example:

   - "I own my embarrassment. It's up to me how I judge myself, and whether I wind up feeling embarrassed. 70% probability of this being true."

   - "The more a person obsesses about being in control, the more anxiety she creates. 90% probability of this being true."

6. *Face Up to Automatic Thought (Column 3).* How would you face up to your fear? Write in Column 6. Restate the probability of your original Automatic Thought as you see it now. Please do so NOW.

   Client's example: "Just because I shake doesn't mean others are judging me badly. So what if I'm embarrassed! It won't kill me! So what if people think I'm insecure? I can live with that! 20% probability of my Automatic Thought happening, and I can let go of it!"

If you need to work on more Focal Fears, return to pages 94–95. Otherwise, proceed to "Changing One's Thoughts Is Difficult but Fundamental" on page 112.

Your Focal Fear is feeling so weak that you cannot move or you might fall down.

Medical Fact: People can feel extremely weak, numb, and stiff and still move voluntarily. Whenever someone describes feeling this way in my office, I ask the client to walk up to the door with me, and, of course, he or she is always able to do so! The perception of weakness feels much worse when you *assume* that you cannot move.

Please use the "Challenging *Your* Automatic Thoughts" chart (described on page 91) and write down your answers *as I ask the questions*. (Do not just read through the material.)

1. *Date.* Fill out.

2. *Specific Trigger.* What are the exact sensations that lead you to think that you cannot move? Write them down in Column 2. Please do so NOW.

   Clients have described typical sensations as numbness, tingling, extreme weakness, and feeling "wobbly."

3. *Automatic Thought.* State yours in a specific theory. Determine which Cognitive Distortion or Maladaptive Thought it is. State the probability of your specific theory happening, using the 0–100% scale. Please do so NOW.

   A client said: "I'm so weak that I can't walk and my arms and legs don't function" (demonstrating a body totally slumped over), "and I collapse. But foremost I can't risk it while driving, so I've given up on driving." This is an example of Overestimating (a Cognitive Distortion) and Giving Up (a Maladaptive Thought). His guess at the probability of this happening was 70%.

4. *My Evidence.* State your evidence and refute it. Please do so NOW.

   Client's example: "I feel so weak. I don't stand or move like this when things are normal. I can't even feel my legs."

   He *refuted*: "Well, I haven't really collapsed. So far I have not actually fainted or fallen down. Maybe I can drive after all."

5. *Alternative Hypotheses.* Find other possible explanations. If you get totally stuck, ask other people. Rate the probability of each. Please do so NOW.

   In client's example:

   - "The feeling of numbness or weakness may not mean that I really do not have command over my muscles. 50% probability of this being true."

   - "If I test out whether I can move one part of my body, and then another, and another, I bet I can move as I want. 80% probability of this being true."

6. *Face Up to Automatic Thought (Column 3).* How would you face up to your fear? Write in Column 6. Restate the probability of your original Automatic Thought as you see it now. Please do so NOW.

   Client's example: "I bet I can learn to stand up straight during a panic if I work on it! Just because I feel that way, doesn't mean I have no control over my body. 10% probability of my Automatic Thought happening."

If you need to work on more Focal Fears, return to pages 94–95. Otherwise, proceed to "Changing One's Thoughts Is Difficult but Fundamental" on page 112.

℘ **You cannot identify your Focal Fear.**

Please use the "Challenging *Your* Automatic Thoughts" chart (described on page 91) and write down your answers *step by step* as I lead you through them. (Do not just read through the material.)

1. *Date.* Fill out.

2. *Specific Trigger.* What are the exact sensations/situations that lead you to feel frightened about the panic attack? Write them down in Column 2. Please do so NOW.

   Examples could be: Panics are dreadful, I don't know why, other than being unbearable and feeling like impending doom.

3. *Automatic Thought.*

   Client's example: "Anything could happen and that's very scary. I don't know what will happen, but I know it is something bad!"

   Do you, my reader, identify with this? Stay with your feelings. Feel the nameless anxiety fully. Now, ask yourself, what is the absolute worst that can happen? State your ideas in a specific theory or as an image. Determine which Cognitive Distortion or Maladaptive Thought it is. Rate the probability of your theory or image happening, using the 0–100% scale. Please do so NOW.

   In the example above, the client was able to come up with the following: "I can see disaster coming, it's like total chaos. If I worry, it seems to get better; then the worst doesn't happen." This is an example of Catastrophizing (a Cognitive Distortion) and Disaster Expectation (a Maladaptive Thought). His guess at the probability of this happening was 25%.

4. *My Evidence.* State your evidence and refute it. Please do so NOW.

   Client's example: "I have always been able to prevent the disaster from happening. But I have to worry to do this."

   He *refuted*: "What evidence is there that worrying prevents disasters from happening? I'd love to believe it because then I could have more control, but objective evidence? No, there isn't any."

5. *Alternative Hypotheses.* Find other possible explanations. If you get totally stuck, ask other people. Rate the probability of each. Please do so NOW.

   Client's example:

   • "Maybe no disaster would have happened, even if I didn't worry. 40% probability of this being true."

   • "Other people have told me that they have occasionally felt chaos impending, because they were too overwhelmed with everything. They suggested that I might just be feeling overwhelmed with everything too. 20% probability of this being true."

   • "Maybe what I'm feeling is part of the fight/flight response. 30% probability of this being true."

6. *Face Up to Automatic Thought (Column 3).* How would you face up to your fear? Write in Column 6. Restate the probability of your original Automatic Thought as you see it now. Please do so NOW.

Client's example: "Just because it feels terrible, does not mean all is lost. I'll survive as I always have. 10% probability of my Automatic Thought happening."

If you need to work on more Focal Fears, return to pages 94–95. Otherwise, proceed to "Changing One's Thoughts Is Difficult but Fundamental" on page 112.

Changing One's Thoughts Is Difficult but Fundamental

Your old thought patterns chronically fed your anxiety; they needed to be restructured. Changing your thoughts is fundamental but not easy. However, you are now developing tools that will help you to change your thought processes. The more you succeed in altering the negative cognitions (thoughts and images), the greater the likelihood that your improvements will be long-lasting.

Sometimes there is a *sudden elimination of fear*. As your mind processes the new information via the challenging of Focal Fears, there can be a sudden significant shift in your Automatic Thoughts. More often, though, the cognitive changes take at least several weeks. As you know by now, the more diligently you practice, the greater the results you will see. Get into the habit of carrying a small notepad with you at all times and jot down the Automatic Thoughts that come up during panic and anxiety-provoking situations. Whenever you have a few spare minutes, try to do some challenging work. Remember, it does not matter how often you work on the exact same Automatic Thought; although, in fact, the more often you work on it the better. Over time watch how you change. Monitor how your estimates of the probability of fearful events changes. Do not let the lack of belief in the Alternative Hypotheses stop you. Initially, the new thoughts are awkward; they are not deep-rooted like the old, Automatic Thoughts. New thoughts may seem clumsy, or false. They are certainly not "automatic." It takes time and practice to get used to new thoughts, and, hopefully, to turn them into more adaptive and realistic Automatic Thoughts.

Imagine you are walking on a path of well-packed snow. Walking is easy, isn't it? Your old Automatic Thoughts are like that path. Your brain has the paths and the associations for them so well-established and rehearsed that it takes hardly any effort to think them. Now imagine walking on fresh snow. What happens? You sink in and it takes a lot of effort. That is how it is with new thoughts. It takes a lot of effort to think them, and you may be tempted to give up trying. The good news is that as you keep walking on new snow, eventually, it will become well-packed and you will be able to walk down that path easily. It's the same with your thoughts. As you practice, your new thoughts will become well-established and therefore more familiar and believable.

Coaching

You may still be experiencing significant difficulty in doing the challenges. If such is the case, consider using a coach. You would need a person who is willing to take the time and effort to read through this chapter and to work closely with you. It is not enough—as you know by now—for someone to say, "Just don't worry about this." If you can find a coach to work diligently with you, it can help tremendously. Frequently, people suffering from anxiety disorders do not share their *exact* thoughts with others—often because of feelings of shame—and those thoughts therefore remain unchallenged. In my practice, I have often been impressed by the way that hearing *someone else's* Alternative Hypotheses can cause clients to question the truth of their Automatic Thoughts.

Repetition

My motto for changing Automatic Thoughts is: Repeat, repeat, and repeat the work! What is the reward? As you puncture holes in your Focal Fears, many of your more superficial fears will quickly vanish. This is because the Focal Fears perpetuate the fear in panic. In turn, the Focal Fears are fed by deeper Core Beliefs. At times, when you work on the Automatic Thoughts associated with your overt symptoms of fear and anxiety, your Underlying, Core Beliefs are changed as well. This does not always occur, however, and you may therefore wish to do additional work on your Core Beliefs. If this is the case, continue working with Section 3: "Changing Underlying or Core Beliefs" in this chapter.

nging Underlying or Core Beliefs

ights can be phenomenal. This persistence does not mean that
ject these thoughts. What it does mean, as many researchers have
underlie Automatic Thoughts. Naturally, these Core Beliefs have
(as reflected in certain Automatic Thoughts), and thus on your

sk. Let's say that you tried to challenge your thoughts, using the
ghts" chart (described on page 91), but because of the effort in-
much trouble. Was it just that? Is it possible that you were ready
ay hold some Core Beliefs that interfere with your progress. Such
ways be a prisoner of my anxieties," "I won't succeed in life," "I
can t cope with life anyway, so now could anything help?" (See page 82 for a more complete list of
such beliefs.) Let us look at "I can't cope with life anyway." Automatic Thoughts related to panic that
emanate from this belief could be: "I'm losing control and won't be able to function." (Overestimating
& Catastrophizing) "I'm going to die. This will never go away, so why try?" (Overestimating and
Giving Up) "I need to escape, I may pass out." (Overestimating) "It's too hard, and I can't do it."
(Giving Up) "Oh, my God, I can't breathe. I want to run out of the room so no one can see me. It's
too much. I don't want to die here. I may go crazy." (Catastrophizing) "Why did this happen to me?"
(The Unanswerable Question) These kinds of thoughts only increase your anxiety level and decrease
your ability to cope.

Stage 1: Unfolding the Belief (Using the "Top Down" Technique)

How can you become aware of your Core Beliefs? You go from the top down, questioning every
step along the way, as suggested by David Burns in his book, *The Feeling Good Handbook*. He labels
this top down technique the "Vertical Arrow" technique. I call this work "Unfolding the Belief." See
Example 1 for an example of how this is done. Then, you will use Worksheet 7: "Unfolding the Belief"
to discover your Core Beliefs.

Questions and Statements Used to Unfold Your Beliefs

1. State the belief as a *theory*.

2. Be as *specific* as possible.

3. If _____ happened, *why* would it be *so upsetting* to me?

4. And *then what*?

5. *Why* would that be *upsetting*?

6. And what would that *mean* to me?

7. What's *the worst* that could happen?

Automatic Thought	Unfolding the Belief (top down)
What if I lose control in a panic?	Please state it as a theory.
I may lose control in a panic.	Please be more specific.
I may lose control over my behavior and act fearfully and irrationally.	If that happened, why would it be so upsetting to me?
People will think I'm crazy.	If people thought so, why would that be so upsetting to me?
If people see me as crazy, maybe they are right.	And what would that mean to me?
Maybe I will go crazy.	What would it mean to me to go crazy?
I'll wind up in a mental hospital.	And then what?
I'll be there forever like my grandmother was.	So because my grandmother was confined in a mental hospital, I think I'll end up there. How long have I held this belief?
Ever since I was about 15 and the family said I looked a lot like my grandmother. But I never told anyone of my fear that I would inherit her mental illness.	

Example 1: Unfolding the Belief

Worksheet 7: Unfolding the Belief

Automatic Thought	Unfolding the Belief (top down)

At the very end of the unfolding process, you should be able to remark regarding your Core Belief:

8. So *because* _____ , I *believe* _____.

9. And follow that up with: *How long* have I held that belief?

Stage 2: Worksheet to Challenge Core Beliefs

Now that you have uncovered your Core Beliefs, it will become possible to challenge them. In Example 2, I will unfold one client's Core Belief and then I will analyze and challenge it.

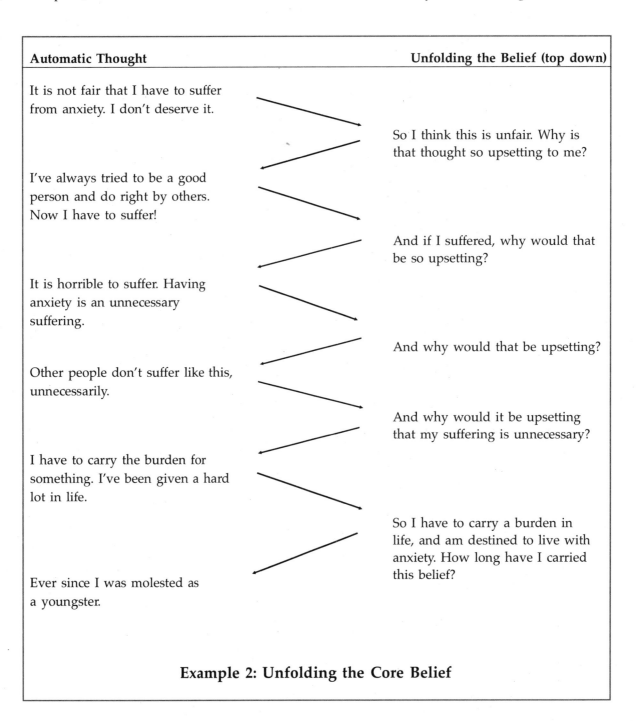

Automatic Thought	Unfolding the Belief (top down)
It is not fair that I have to suffer from anxiety. I don't deserve it.	
	So I think this is unfair. Why is that thought so upsetting to me?
I've always tried to be a good person and do right by others. Now I have to suffer!	
	And if I suffered, why would that be so upsetting?
It is horrible to suffer. Having anxiety is an unnecessary suffering.	
	And why would that be upsetting?
Other people don't suffer like this, unnecessarily.	
	And why would it be upsetting that my suffering is unnecessary?
I have to carry the burden for something. I've been given a hard lot in life.	
	So I have to carry a burden in life, and am destined to live with anxiety. How long have I carried this belief?
Ever since I was molested as a youngster.	

Example 2: Unfolding the Core Belief

How to Use Worksheet for Challenging Core Beliefs

1. Is there an *objective basis for my belief*?

2. Does it *add to my life or take away*?

3. Can I *bring in a modifier*? (Instead of "always," "never," and similar absolute terms insert "sometimes.")

4. *Can I question* my need to hold on to the belief?

5. What statements will make the *belief more user-friendly* (to me) or help me to *change the belief*?

Now, let's analyze Example 2. This woman's Core Belief, based on her childhood molestation, was that she had to carry a burden in life, and, consequently, she had to live with constant anxiety. Let's see how she can challenge that belief.

1. *Objective Basis for Belief?* "I was molested as a youngster. I have suffered from hardships all my life."

2. *Adds to My Life or Takes Away?* "It takes away. I always feel like a victim and that bad things will keep happening."

3. *Can I Bring in a Modifier?* "Well, I can't really say all my life was filled with hardships. I have had some good moments. I have had many really big hardships, though, that I wouldn't wish on anyone."

4. *Can My Need for the Belief Be Questioned?* "I guess, though it's extremely hard to trust when you have been molested.

5. *Make Belief More User-Friendly or Change Belief.* "My life has been tough, but it has had some rewards. Who said life is fair? I don't want to let those early bad experiences ruin the rest of my life. Anxiety is not the end of the world. It does not kill me. Maybe I can learn to cope with anxiety.

Now let's return to you. Look for the Core beliefs you wrote down on Worksheet 5 in Section 1 of this chapter. It is now time for you to work on your own Core Befiefs, challenging them using the format given in Worksheet 8. This may be very hard work to do on your own. If it is too difficult, enlist the aid of someone you trust.

Stage 3: Old and New Beliefs—Their Relationship with Behaviors

If your old Core Belief is that you have been given a difficult burden to bear in life and, therefore, you *must* suffer from anxiety, a possible related thought is that you do not really believe anything major can change and, consequently, this will affect you behaviorally. You will give up easily when working on your panic attacks and phobias, and you will probably find one way or another to defeat yourself.

If your New or Modified Belief is that you do *not* have to carry an old burden and be branded forever, that you can learn to cope with anxiety, some possible related behaviors are as follows: You *will* stick with a program, even when it's hard; you *will* be willing to challenge yourself more in your work with thoughts and behavioral practices; and you *will* be more willing to seek professional help if your own efforts fail. As J.B. Persons (1989) states, you can ask yourself whether a particular behavior supports your old or new Core Belief. You even might be willing to engage in behaviors that will directly challenge your old belief. What does your behavior tell you?

Let's explore one more example using the format of Worksheet 9. On page 82 in Section 1 of this chapter I gave the following example as a Core Belief, "I must be perfect to be worthwhile." You would list it under the Old Belief column. The equivalent "New Belief" would be something like, "I am worthwhile even if I am not perfect." The behavioral change of not having to push yourself beyond work hours to finish a project would be compatible with the New, not the Old Belief. Allowing your house to stay messy when you are really tired would be compatible with the New, not the Old Belief. Trying again after failing to do an exposure practice would be compatible with the New, not the Old Belief. But, helping your friends out at all costs to retain their approval at all times would be compatible with an Old rather than a New Belief.

Use Worksheet 9 to help you look at what your behaviors say about you. Since no one can be totally objective about himself or herself, ask family members and friends you trust to give you some input in this exercise in addition to the work that you do.

To end this chapter, remember that Core Beliefs are learned, they are not absolute truths.

Did you find any particulary useful thoughts, ideas, or actions to take in this chapter to add to Worksheet 1: "My Personal Coping Affirmations"?

What is your Fear Barometer doing now? If you had a bad panic right now, how much fear would it evoke in you? What is the number, using the 0–100% scale? Determine what the number is NOW. Write it in: _____.

Did your fear decrease while you were working on this chapter? Did you follow *all* of the instructions in this chapter? What is still keeping your fear alive? Perhaps Chapter 10 will help you to answer that question.

Recommended Reading

Barlow, D.H., and Craske, M.G. 1994. *Mastery of Your Anxiety and Panic II.* Albany, N.Y.: Graywind Publications, Inc.

Burns, D.D. 1989. *The Feeling Good Handbook.* New York: William Morrow & Co.

McKay, M., Davis, M., and Fanning, P. 1981. *Thoughts and Feelings: The Art of Cognitive Stress Intervention.* Oakland, CA: New Harbinger Publications.

Worksheet 8: Challenging Core Beliefs

1	2	3	4	5
Objective Basis for Belief?	Adds to My Life or Takes Away?	Can I Bring in a Modifier?	Can My Need for the Belief be Questioned?	Make Belief More User-Friendly or Change Belief.

Worksheet 9: Relationship Between Behaviors and Beliefs

List Behaviors Below	Old Belief (State *yours* here) _____ Behavior compatible with this belief?	New Belief (State *yours* here) _____ Behavior compatible with this belief?
1. _____	Yes ____ No ____	Yes ____ No ____
2. _____	Yes ____ No ____	Yes ____ No ____
3. _____	Yes ____ No ____	Yes ____ No ____
4. _____	Yes ____ No ____	Yes ____ No ____
5. _____	Yes ____ No ____	Yes ____ No ____
6. _____	Yes ____ No ____	Yes ____ No ____
7. _____	Yes ____ No ____	Yes ____ No ____
8. _____	Yes ____ No ____	Yes ____ No ____
9. _____	Yes ____ No ____	Yes ____ No ____
10. _____	Yes ____ No ____	Yes ____ No ____

10

Overcoming the Fear of
Physical Symptoms in Panic

The work in this chapter is based on ideas and research developed by two psychologists, Drs. David Barlow and Michelle Craske, and their colleagues at the Center for Stress and Anxiety Disorders, at the State University of New York at Albany. I first heard about the concept of "interoceptive exposure" in 1987 at a workshop given by the two doctors in San Francisco. Although other researchers also have developed behavioral interventions, the particular interventions that I teach must be credited to this very creative team. I owe special thanks to Dr. Craske, under whose guidance I have perfected the techniques.

In Chapter 7, I described and elaborated on the three components of anxiety and panic: Physiological, cognitive, and behavioral. If you are like most panickers, your initial and, possibly, current fear of panics is fear of the physiological sensations. In Chapter 9, you did a great deal of cognitive work. Now, let me check in with you on your Fear Barometer.

How fearful would you be if you had a "bad" panic right now? If you truly have *no* fear, I would suggest that you should still go through this chapter to be absolutely certain that your fear is vanquished and to strengthen and reinforce your gains. Most likely, though, you are still experiencing some fear.

Now, think of a high-anxiety situation that you experienced some time before you had your first panic attack. I'm talking about situations such as your first job interview or a final exam in school. What happened when you got anxious? Do you recall your heart beating faster or starting to sweat more than usual? Were you afraid of those sensations back then? Most likely not. Yet they revealed your anxiety, and you may then have tried to calm yourself down. But now it's different, isn't it? Not only do you suffer from anxiety, but from *fear* of the anxiety, and as mentioned frequently in this book, fear intensifies your physical sensations.

The more you fear the physical sensations of panic, the more you develop hypervigilance, even to *normal* bodily sensations. In other words, you start to monitor normal changes in your body. Even "harmless" (i.e., nonpanic) sensations can then elicit panic, because *to you* the sensations signal danger.

Viewing panics as dangerous has become a part of your experiential mind, which is that part of your mind rooted in emotionally important experiences. (See Chapter 2.) The best way to change this view of panics is to have "corrective" experiences, which is what interoceptive work provides.

In sum, panic disorder is like being phobic about your own internal sensations, except that, unlike other phobic fears, you cannot run away from your body or the symptoms it produces. It is a learned fear of your own physical sensations. You need to relearn that they are not dangerous. In the past you used distraction and other means to minimize or avoid the sensations. In this chapter you will do the opposite; you will learn through direct experience that they are harmless. If you then *respond differently to the sensations*, the sensations will no longer produce anxiety.

The type of practice you will learn from is called *interoceptive exposure*, which means *to expose oneself directly to one's internal sensations*. The conditioned (learned) fear of panics will diminish, becoming weaker and weaker. As you keep practicing, you will slowly *decondition* yourself. This is a proven, highly effective method for overcoming fear in panic disorder (see Barlow, 1990, 1992; Craske and Rodriguez, 1994; Margraf et al., 1993).

The cognitive work of Chapter 9 was crucial, and it still is, but now, you need to deal with the sensations themselves. You must confront rather than avoid them. As you can see, this work is equivalent to deliberately exposing yourself to fearful situations and places in agoraphobia. You need to desensitize yourself through *interoceptive deconditioning* to achieve your prepanic level. That is, to return to the state where your internal bodily sensations do not frighten you.

Interoceptive Deconditioning: Eliminate Fear of Panic Sensations

Desensitization to the physical sensations of panic is achieved by eliciting sensations similar to those in panic. If this sounds scary to you, that demonstrates how limited the cognitive work is in addressing the behavioral aspect of panic disorder. In addition to the extensive work that you did with your thoughts (making them manifest and visible with paper and pen), you now have the opportunity for more concrete and tangible work. This work will allow you to *test your thoughts* about the *uncontrollability and catastrophic nature of panic*. We'll complete a full circle. The behavioral tests, in turn, will strengthen your new set of thoughts and beliefs.

Integrating the Behavioral and Cognitive Work

When you do the exercises and feel uncomfortable sensations without the feared catastrophic consequences taking place, your old Automatic Thoughts are put to the test (for example, the Automatic Thought "I will faint when I feel dizzy and unreal."). Thus the behavioral tests are not done in a vacuum. You need to apply the cognitive strategies you learned in Chapter 9 and thereby work with your experiential *and* rational minds. Your aim is to achieve the *new experience* of feeling panic-like sensations without fearing them. Eventually, these new experiences will lead you to the understanding and belief that panics are harmless. The *integration* of behavioral and cognitive learning

---

Learning Must Be So Convincingly
Profound That It Can
Counteract Catastrophic Thoughts
During *Peak* Anxiety.

---

solidifies through repeated practice: A cognitive shift takes place in your mind, and the fear of panics will no longer control your life.

Interoceptive Work and Medications

If you have been taking medications for panic disorder, and plan to stop taking them while working through this program, this is the best time to taper off. The interoceptive work is most fruitful if you can fully experience the sensations produced. Otherwise, when you later discontinue medications and you have a "bad" panic, you might not be sufficiently prepared for it. You might remain too vulnerable. It is best to taper off slowly, collaborating with your physician, and continue working on the exercises as you cut back on the medications.

The tapering off from medication will become, in fact, another form of interoception, with you learning to tolerate higher levels of anxiety that were formerly masked by the medication. First with reduced and later no medication, your challenge grows. Naturally, you will experience higher levels of anxiety for a while, but, remember, this heightened anxiety is temporary. The harder you work on these cognitive-behavioral methods, the faster you will override this anxiety.

Exclusions

You are **cautioned not to do these exercises** if you have epilepsy or a history of seizures, serious asthma, chronic arrythmia, heart or lung problems, a history of fainting and/or *very low* blood pressure, or if you are pregnant. If you have any doubts, consult your physician. Describe the specific exercises to your physician, who will easily tell whether any of the exercises are contraindicated for you.

There are some other conditions that may limit you. For instance, there is one exercise where you are asked to sit in a chair with your head bent down between your legs. The ideal is to have your head below the heart level. If you have a stiff back, however, it is likely that you will not be able to do the exercise as instructed. Some clients in my groups either pass up this exercise or do the best they can, depending on their condition. Additionally, the person with a bad back is not advised to spin around standing up, but *may* be able to do the spinning exercise while sitting in an office-type chair. So, my advice is to use your common sense, and do the best you can without hurting yourself.

If your physical condition limits you from doing most or all of the physical exercises, you may still be able to do some of those that primarily involve your mind rather than your body, such as those where you stare at a spot, relax and daydream, and so forth.

Preparing for Interoceptive Work

The sensations that we want to bring on include: Rapid heart beat, dizziness, lightheadedness, tingling, heat, stomach discomfort, suffocation, shortness of breath, chest tension, choking sensations, throat tightness, imagining fearful symptoms, and feelings of unreality. These are among the primary panic sensations. To keep things in perspective, let me remind you that these symptoms are not scary for everyone. Some people seek them out: Children like to spin like tops to make themselves dizzy, people of all ages go on amusement park rides, watch horror movies and sports events, and sometimes even engage in such potentially destructive ways as taking illegal drugs to feel some of those sensations! The personal interpretations of these symptoms can be either excitement or fear and can be viewed as either comfortable or uncomfortable. As you learn that the symptoms are *not dangerous,* your anxiety sensitivity (i.e., fear of the symptoms) should decrease and your view of "comfortable" and "uncomfortable" should expand.

Some exercises almost always bring on certain kinds of symptoms, with, of course, individual variations. Other exercises may not bring on any sensations at all. By now you have developed some skills to help you: Diaphragmatic breathing, and cognitive methods to modify your thinking so your thoughts will lower rather than raise your anxiety.

Many of the exercises can be incorporated into your daily life. Their effect is usually less predictable and controllable than previous work you have done. In other words, you will be "graduating" from exercises where the effect is usually immediate to others that are not, and which are more a part of daily life.

Actually, you have already done one of the interoceptive exercises. That was the overbreathing test in Chapter 8. Here I will use the term "Hyperventilation" to refer to the same test.

What You Need to Know Before Doing the Exercises

1. Some exercises produce the sensations *while* you are doing them, some *right after*. Therefore, right after you finish the exercises, sit (or stand) still and pay attention to the feelings and thoughts you are having.

2. You can do the exercises *in any order*. It is recommended that you start with the ones that seem easiest for you.

3. You can modify the times, especially when starting. If you cannot tolerate the sensations, stop earlier. However, keep in mind that eventually you want to *feel* the sensations to their fullest. If the time given is unrealistic for you, wait till you feel the sensations, and then continue for 20 to 30 seconds longer (except for the holding breath exercise).

4. If you are too fearful to do the exercises alone, use a coach. Do not ask an anxious person to be your coach. You want someone calm. Ask your coach to be a cheerleader for you. If you wish, you can follow this plan: (a) Have the coach do the exercise first. (b) Do it with the coach. (c) Do it while your coach watches you. (d) Do it alone. All exercises eventually should be done alone (to develop your coping skills and to achieve self-efficacy).

5. Use SUDS = Subjective Units of Distress Scale. 0 = Totally calm, no anxiety or fear. 50 = Moderate level of anxiety/fear. 100 = Intolerable level of anxiety/fear. Use the number from 0 to 100 that best describes your anxiety/fear level.

6. Follow the first time limit given for each exercise in version (a), and keep repeating it, till your SUDS is 20 or less. Then follow with version (b), and keep repeating the exercise, till your SUDS is 20 or less.

7. It is extremely important that you distinguish between *sensation intensity* and *anxiety/fear*. You can feel very strong sensations and they may be very uncomfortable, but do they produce *fear*? For instance, one of my clients always got extremely strong sensations while hyperventilating, but his SUDS level decreased from a 75 to a 10.

8. The intensity of the sensations themselves (aside from anxiety/fear) *may* decline in strength as they lose their novelty or they may remain high. It is perfectly normal to continue to experience strong sensations, as long as your anxiety (SUDS) diminishes to 20 or less.

9. You may ask, "What if I panic while doing the exercises?" It can happen, but it has not happened often. If it were to happen, take it as a challenge. Use your skills, diaphragmatic breathing and cognitive work. Later, repeat the exercise again as soon as possible.

10. If some exercises produce strong anxiety, this is actually very good, since you then have something concrete to work with to help reduce your fear. If the anxiety level is high when you start with an exercise, and you keep working on it, the effect of watching the anxiety decrease is very powerful.

11. If the sensations produced are very *similar to those in panic*, this is excellent. But even if the sensations are different, it is good practice for decreasing your general vulnerability. As I mentioned before, beyond diminishing fear of panics, the goal is also to lower your general anxiety sensitivity. Also, some day you may have a panic with different sensations than you have experienced, this could help you in such an event.

12. If an exercise produces a SUDS below 20 the first time, try version (b). If it remains 20 or less, go to another exercise.

13. MAKE A SCHEDULE FOR PRACTICE. Plan on doing these exercises five days a week. Do the exposures several times in a row, either the same or different exercises. Remember, the more diligently you work, the faster your progress. If you find yourself avoiding doing them or doing them less well, get support from your coach.

14. Plan rewards that you really look forward to, especially if you find yourself putting off doing the exercises.

NOTE: The exercises work if you try to do them as instructed; otherwise, you defeat their purpose. A client who was terrified of suffocation (he was a chronic overbreather) told me several times that the straw breathing did nothing for him. I was skeptical and asked him to show me how he did it. I watched him closely. As I had guessed, he was letting air out through his mouth whenever the breathing became difficult, rather than letting it out through the straw. Yet this was a crucial exercise for him to master if he were to ever get beyond his "obsession" with suffocation.

Items You Will Need

1. A timer. (Do not just use a watch or clock because you would have to stop to look at it, which would be too distracting in most exercises.) You want a timer that sounds an alarm when the time is up.

2. Pad and pen.

3. Coffee stirrers or cocktail straws. These are the *thin* straws, usually red and white, with a tiny hole. (A regular straw would defeat the purpose of the test. I have found that the small straws differ greatly in diameter. Some straws have a division in the middle, rendering two very tiny holes, which may be too small. Some of the small straws have holes that are a bit large, so the test does not feel very challenging. You may have to look around for straws and try out a few.)

(A paper bag will not be used this time around. By now, you can use diaphragmatic breathing, which is a much better way to slow down the sensations after doing the exercises. It is better not to depend on an *object*.)

Each exercise is listed in Table 10.1 with detailed instructions on how to do it. When I work with clients in my office, I always demonstrate and do the exercises with them the first time around (i.e., the ones that I *can* do in the office, including drinking coffee, eating chocolate, and turning up the heat). As with my clients, I will provide you with a worksheet to work with, and describe how to proceed.

TABLE: 10.1 Interoceptive Exercises

Exercise	Length of Time*	Instructions
1. Shake head side to side	(a) 30 sec. (b) 40 sec.	Lower your head *a bit* and shake it loosely from side to side with your eyes open. When the timer goes off, *suddenly* lift your head and stare straight ahead for a little while.
2. Head between legs	(a) 1½ min. (b) 2 min.	Sit in a straight chair. Bend your head down between your legs, trying to keep it lower than your heart level. When the timer goes off, *suddenly* lift your head and stare straight ahead for a little while.
3. Run in place	(a) 1 min. (b) 2 min.	Jog in place. Jog vigorously. (Or run upstairs.)
4. Complete body tension	(a) 1 min. (b) 1½ min.	Make fists with your hands, tense your feet, bring your shoulders forward and tense your chest and entire body. Breathe deeply throughout.
5. Hold breath	(a) 30 sec. (b) 35 sec.	Just as you begin timing, take a deep breath and try to hold it for 30 sec. (later 35). *If you cannot hold for that length of time, you should stop before the 30 secs. are up.*
6. Spin	(a) 1 min. (b) 1 min. and walk immediately thereafter	Spin around yourself at a *good* pace. Give yourself room and have a wall nearby to put your hand on if you lose your balance. Or use an office chair that spins and push against the floor as you spin.
7. Straw breathing	(a) 2 min. (b) 2 min. (pinching nose)	Place the thin straw in your mouth and breathe in and out through the straw. Do (b) while also *slightly* pinching your nose with your other hand.
8. Hyperventilate	(a) 1¼ min. (b) 1½ min.	While *standing*, breathe deeply in and out through your *mouth* (like panting, but slower, and breathing *out* more than breathing *in*). Make it audible, i.e., make a sound that can be heard across the room.

* Do (a) first and keep repeating it until your SUDS is 20 or less. Then do (b), and keep repeating until your SUDS is 20 or less.

TABLE: 10.1 Interoceptive Exercises (Cont.)

Exercise	Length of Time	Instructions
9. External pressure on throat	(a) 1 min. (b) 1½ min.	Using either your thumb or two fingers, apply pressure to the middle of your throat. Apply pressure until it feels uncomfortable, but not extremely so.
10. Stare at a spot	(a) 2 min. (b) 3 min.	Pick a spot on an empty wall and stare at it *without deviating your gaze* at all.
11. Lump in throat		Swallow as quickly as you can 4 times in a row.
12. Focus on your worst sensation in imagery	(a) 2 min. (b) 3 min.	Remember your worst panic sensation. Now close your eyes, imagine a very bad panic, and totally focus on that feared symptom. Or think of a feared thought or image, such as your "losing control" or "going insane," (imagining yourself in an insane asylum), etc. Do not allow yourself to be distracted.
13. Ingest caffeine[**]	(a) Coffee (b) Coffee and chocolate	Drink a cup of caffeinated coffee or tea (not too weak). For part (b) either drink 2 cups or combine 1 cup with a piece of chocolate. Here you want to work on sensations brought on by caffeine. One advantage is that the maximum effect of the caffeine is not immediate, allowing you to practice with greater unpredictability.
14. Relax and daydream	(a) 5 min. (b) 10 min.	Sit and try to relax. Allow yourself to just daydream without focusing on anything planned or anything that needs your attention.
15. Create heat	(a) 15 min. (b) 30 min.	Turn up the heat (in house or car) and sit with very hot clothing on.
16. Stare at your mirror image	(a) 1½ min. (b) 3 min.	Stare at one spot on yourself *without deviating your gaze* at all.
17. Tight clothing around neck	(a) 15 min. (b) 30 min.	Wear something tight around your neck, i.e., a scarf or collar.
18. Vertigo	(a) 30 sec. (b) 1 min.	Stand by a *tall* building and look up its exterior wall.

[**] Many panickers have stopped drinking coffee or tea for fear of the sensations produced. Although the idea here is not to get you back to ingesting caffeine on a regular basis, it is better that you learn not to be so *afraid* of its stimulant effects.

More Interoceptive Exercises

- Hold your breath briefly and immediately do the hyperventilation exercise for 1 minute. (Item No. 8 in Table 10.1)

- Stand up suddenly from a lying down position.

- Run up a few flights of stairs.

- Do aerobics or other vigorous exercise, for about 15 to 30 minutes, depending on your stamina. (If you exercise regularly already, Great! But then this is not an interoceptive challenge for you. Please do another.)

- Sit in a sauna; from 5 to 15 minutes.

- Watch something suspenseful (mystery movie, sports event); 1 to 2 hours.

- Go on an amusement park ride.

- Drive in a car with the heat turned to the maximum, windows closed, and wearing a sweater; up to 30 minutes.

- Place the palm of your hand 6 to 8 inches from your face. Stare at one spot without deviating your gaze for 3 to 5 minutes.

- (a) Raise up one hand. With your other hand apply pressure to your upper arm, so the circulation is restricted. (b) With one arm hanging loosely at your side, grasp your upper arm with the opposite hand. Grip the upper arm tightly and press and turn it firmly against your torso. Do both from 30 seconds to 1 minute. (These two exercises were demonstrated by Dr. Alec Pollard in a workshop at the 1995 conference of the Anxiety Disorders Association of America.)

How to Use Worksheet 10 to Record Your Interoceptive Exercises

1. *Date.* Always date. It will help you keep track of your progress.

2. *List Exercise.* List the exercise you are going to do.

3. *Alone or with Coach.* List whether you did it alone or with a coach.

Instructions on How to Do the Exercises

- Allow yourself to fully feel the sensations. Pay attention to them. Do not distract yourself!

- Determine your SUDS level.

- Take one to two minutes afterwards to stay with the experience. Pay attention to any thoughts and/or feelings.

You can now apply the cognitive strategies you have learned!

If anxious, challenge yourself mentally (or have your coach help you):

- What *exactly* am I *afraid of right now*? What is the worst that can happen right now?

- Which Cognitive Distortion or Maladaptive Thought does *my* thought reflect?

- What is my evidence? Refute!

- Are there alternative hypotheses?

Worksheet 10: Practicing Interoceptive Exercises

Fill Out Before Practice			Fill Out After Practice		
1	**2**	**3**	**4**	**5**	**6**
Date	List Exercise	Alone or with Coach	Length of Time	Describe Sensations	SUDS: Anxiety/ Fear

- So what if . . . ! Just because *X* happens, does not mean that *Y* must happen. You can use Worksheet 6: "Challenging Automatic Thoughts" from Chapter 9 to help with this part of the work. It is better, however, to start doing the cognitive challenging more and more in your mind. You will not always have paper, pen, or the opportunity to write down the challenging work at the moment you need it. You want your new thought patterns to come quickly to really confront your old Automatic Thoughts.

If less anxious than last time you did the same exercise:

- What is different now?

- What am I learning?

Do diaphragmatic breathing

- See how quickly you can now restore your body to a low-arousal state.

Fill in Columns 4 through 6 NOW. Writing immediately after the exercises may distract you from the mental work you need to do first.

4. *Length of Time.* State the length of time you did the exercise. It will help you keep track of your progress.

5. *Describe Sensations.* Describe the sensations you became aware of.

6. *SUDS: Anxiety/Fear.* List your SUDS level.

Reward yourself just for having done the exercise. You should be very pleased with yourself and give yourself a lot of credit. You may also want to reward yourself with something tangible.

If doing any of the exercises produces nausea feelings in you, just take it easy with that exercise, perhaps not doing it more than once at any given time. This happens on occasion to some of my clients. No one has thrown up, and the nausea feelings usually go away quickly.

To Achieve Mastery

1. Remember to keep repeating each exercise (unless limited by health) until your SUDS measurement drops to 20 or less. *As long as you fear the symptoms, practice on the interoceptive exercises.*

2. Since each single trial can present different challenges to you, *do the cognitive work again each time.*

3. Practice at least five times every week. On any given day you can practice on the same exercise several times in a row or on different exercises. For example, you can do hyperventilation three times in one day; or hyperventilation once, straw breathing once, and aerobics once in a single day. The more work you do, the faster you will progress. It is possible to finish the entire interoceptive deconditioning phase in two to four weeks.

4. This work is worthwhile only if it *applies* to different situations.

   - After doing exercises with a coach, you need to do them alone.

   - Do them when you are alone at home (no one else around).

   - Do some of them outside, e.g., in a *parked* (not moving) car. For instance, in a parked car you could do hyperventilation, holding your breath, and straw breathing. You could do some of them while at a relative's or friend's home. Another challenge would be to hold your breath for 15 to 20 seconds while standing in line (no one would know, since you can do it subtly).

In Worksheet 10 in the column *List Exercise* specify where you did your practice, e.g., "Hyperventilation in car," and "Holding breath while standing in line," and so forth.

5. There is no limit to one's creativity in expanding the practices. You can also get ideas from people close to you, who know what you are working on.

One client had a lifelong obsession with panic sensations and the fear of suffocation. The group came up with the idea of her practicing at home by placing a pillow over her face—at first for a minute and later for a longer time. The task was *totally predictable and under her control.* Although, initially, the thought of it was frightening, she did try it. It worked very well. She was able to desensitize herself. She was no longer obsessed with that fear! Note that often there are specific traumas behind such fears; in her case she even remembered some childhood situations when she was scared that way. Nonetheless, it was very liberating for her to overcome that fear.

6. If you do the exercises less than well, you may be practicing a subtle form of avoidance. The ideal is to feel the sensations strongly, especially if they produce a great deal of fear during your panics, and to learn to no longer fear them.

7. *You are finished when all the exercises have a SUDS level of 20 or less!*

PLEASE DO THE EXERCISES OVER THE NEXT TWO TO FOUR WEEKS. Check out this page for possible stumbling blocks. If there are no stumbling blocks and you have done the work well, you'll be ready for the next task on page 135.

Question
How did it go?

Answer

- You may ask, Is this really necessary? Turn to the next page.

- You were progressing very well with the exercises, and then had a bad panic. Now you are having a setback. Turn to page 133.

- Most of the exercises don't seem to apply to you. They don't produce symptoms like the ones in your panics. Turn to page 134.

- You feel that you have learned a lot from doing these exercises, and you are ready to continue with the next task. Turn to page 135.

§ You may ask, "Is this really necessary?"

Your apprehension is very understandable. In the past, the emphasis was on slowing down the physical reactions with relaxation. However, research has shown increasingly that one has to confront fears, face them, and deal with them. This is partly because *fear grows in the absence of the fearful sensation or situation.* By now, you have acquired a lot of knowledge about panics, and appreciate how important it is to overcome the *fear* of the symptoms of panics. There is no way around this.

Of course, some people cannot do the exercises for health reasons, and they have a tougher time ahead, because they cannot put their beliefs to the test the same way you can. Keep in mind that the behavioral and cognitive changes will produce biochemical changes in your brain.

If this task seems too difficult for you, take two approaches, already mentioned. The first is: Do the exercises with a coach. Ask your coach to do them while you watch before you try them yourself. This is not a sign of weakness. Most of my clients would not do them either, if they did not do them first with me and/or the group. The other is to start with *whichever exercise* seems easiest to you. It can be either from Table 10.1: "Interoceptive Exercises" or from the list "More Interoceptive Exercises" on page 128. Proceed in whichever order you wish.

Keep up the work! Return to page 126.

You were progressing very well with the exercises and then had a bad panic. Now you are having a setback.

What do you consider a setback? Maybe it is not as bad as you first thought. In reality, occasional setbacks are quite common. Let us say that you have progressed with all the working chapters so far, Chapters 7 through 10. Then you had a "bad" panic attack and everything you learned seems to have flown out the window. You are afraid, you are catastrophizing, and so on. I would bet that your tendency is to criticize yourself. Instead, try to think of it this way: If you succeeded once, *you can succeed again*, and the next time will be less costly, both in time and energy. Just because you are now familiar with this book, does not mean that going through it again will not be helpful. In fact, when I give my clients handouts with even a small portion of material to digest, they often say that they benefit more each time they reuse the materials. Learning takes time, especially correcting old thought patterns. It does not happen overnight.

Or suppose that you had good intentions to get off medications but were unable to do so. Work hard on the interoceptive exercises while you are on medications. Challenge your limits. If your physician agrees, you can try to taper off medications at a later time. Do cognitive and interoceptive work again at that time. In order to succeed, however, you must be willing eventually to take a small amount of calculated risk and accept the discomfort of higher anxiety.

Occasional Setbacks Can Make You Appreciate Your Progress Fully.

I suggest you revisit the work in this chapter. Return to page 126.

Most of the exercises don't seem to apply to you. They don't produce symptoms like the ones in your panics.

There is no way of knowing in advance which exercise will produce precisely which symptoms in you. There is a general idea of what one can expect, but there is enough individual variation to warrant testing them out. That is why it is better to do all of them at first. You really don't need *many* exercises to be relevant to your panics. But it is crucial to find some that will produce the sensations that relate to *your* fears. Then you have something concrete to work with.

The exercises that do not seem to relate to your panics but still evoke some anxiety are very worthwhile for you to work with. They may relate to the fear of bodily symptoms in a more subtle way. Look beyond the panic attacks themselves. Try to overcome fear of uncomfortable but harmless physical sensations. It is an investment in your future.

PLEASE DO THE EXERCISES UNTIL YOU NO LONGER FEAR THEM. Return to page 126.

§   **You feel that you have learned a lot from doing these exercises and you are ready to continue with the next task. CONGRATULATIONS! Continue reading on this page.**

Achieving Mastery in Phobic Situations

The more the mastery over your fears generalizes (spreads) to different places, situations, and activities, the better prepared you are. You were already instructed to do some interoceptives outside the home. Next, when you work on overcoming fear in different situations (see Chapters 11 and 12), repeat the interoceptive exercises. Practice them in places where you especially fear the occurrence of panics, work, restaurants, buses, or the place where you had your first panic. You can practice hyperventilation, holding your breath, and straw breathing in a parked car. Either do it so no one else can see what you are doing, of if you don't care whether you are seen, even better!

When you are out and about, you may have to modify the interoceptives slightly, but the most important thing is not to avoid the sensations. Again be the participant-observer: Be aware of your sensations, describe them in detail to yourself. Without making situations dangerous, you can find ways to manipulate your sensations. For instance, you can deliberately tense up your body while driving, then relax, then tense up again, and thus achieve a sense of control. If you are in a phobic place like a mall, and you have a fearful sensation, can you make it stronger? Learn to manipulate it. Make it stronger, weaker, stronger, weaker, to produce control.

Work also with feared symptoms in situations where you have felt embarrassed. For instance, if you fear turning red, use blush deliberately (making it look like you *are* blushing); if sweat on your face embarrasses you, place water drops on your forehead to look sweaty.

Most likely, you will not want to do interoceptives right at the beginning of your exposure to fearful situations. However, as you master the different steps, do some of the interoceptives in those places, as appropriate. If you can produce the sensations in those situations, then you will truly experience again what "control" is: *You* will be the master in the situation, not fear.

Mastery Over the Fear of Sensations
Raises Self-Efficacy.

Recording Your Progress

Self-reward is so important that I have prepared Worksheet 11: "Interoceptive Achievement Record" for you to record your progress. Get in the habit of patting yourself on the back, and giving yourself a tangible reward. Working through these chapters on your own is a tremendous feat. Become your own best cheerleader!

Moving On

If you have been experiencing fewer panics, or none at all, you may feel confident and be thinking more positively. However, you will know the true degree of your progress if you still have occasional panics and no negative cognitions. The interoceptive and the cognitive work go hand-in-hand. Each reinforces the other in a positive or a negative cycle. Your intervention for a healthy cycle at any point is invaluable, because you can turn the entire experience around.

Did you find any particularly useful thoughts, ideas, or actions to take in this chapter to add to Worksheet 1: "My Personal Coping Affirmations"?

Now, what is your Fear Barometer doing? If you had a "bad" panic right now, how much fear would it evoke in you? What is the number, using the 0–100% scale? Determine what the number is NOW. Write it in: _____.

If there is still fear (aside from phobic situations, which you will work on in Chapters 11 and 12); can you determine where it is coming from? Do you need to review the physiology of fear and panic in Chapter 7? Do you need to rework Chapters 9 and 10? It may be wise to do so. Look at it this way: The more you learn and relearn, the more the material will sink in and the less you will be plagued by negative Automatic Thoughts about panic.

Recommended Reading

Barlow, D.H., and Craske, M.G. 1994. *Mastery of Your Anxiety and Panic II*. Albany, NY: Graywind Publications Inc.

Worksheet 11: Interoceptive Achievement Record

List	*Alone at home*				*Alone outside*			
Exercise	Date Achieved	# Trials	Final SUDS	Self-Reward	Date Achieved	# Trials	Final SUDS	Self-Reward

PART III

CHALLENGING AND MASTERING
PHOBIC SITUATIONS

11

Assessing the Extent of Your
Panic Disorder and Setting the Stage
for Your Phobia Work

How Agoraphobia Develops

Agoraphobia is defined in Chapter 3 as "the fear of places or situations where in case of a panic: (a) help is not immediately available and/or (b) escape is difficult because of physical or social constraints." This translates in practical terms to the fear of leaving a "safe" place, like home, venturing into crowded areas, or doing things without a "safe" person. If you go to many places and do many things, but *only* with a companion, you also have agoraphobia. Agoraphobia includes the fear of staying home alone.

Avoidance behavior often occurs as a consequence of the fear of panics. It becomes the "solution" to fear. Unfortunately, this is a false illusion of safety and actually causes the fear to grow. Many people avoid the place of their first panic. In these cases, fear of the place/activity occurs partly through "conditioning" (where a fearful experience, such as panic, is associated with a "neutral" event, like driving and later the driving itself provokes fear). Then generalization occurs: The phobias

If You Have Not Begun to Avoid,
Don't Start!
If You Are Just Starting to Avoid, Try to
Confront the Situations as Soon as Possible.

spread to similar (sometimes symbolically "similar") situations. Some people become housebound after their very first panic. Others begin to avoid as their panics progress. In some instances, no agoraphobia develops. Note that people who do not avoid typical situations may, nevertheless, still have some subtle avoidance patterns.

Fear Feeds Upon Itself

The more you surrender to fear, the more the fear grows. Left alone, fear spreads like a weed. The more places you avoid, the narrower your life becomes. Agoraphobia is the worst part of panic disorder. Furthermore, as the person becomes increasingly used to avoidance, it becomes harder and harder to treat.

The generalization of fear to places other than the place where the first panic occurred is not simply a mechanical event. It involves other psychological processes. Having felt extremely fearful and vulnerable, the person with panic disorder may want absolute certainty in any potentially fearful situation. Yet as we know, there is no absolute certainty or safety anywhere in life. The more you *try* to control risk and uncertainty in one area, the more you will find other areas you want to control.

When you fear panics, you start to scan your body and the area around you for cues that represent "danger." One common concern is whether you can escape easily in case of a panic attack. You don't want to feel trapped, and thus you focus on all possible ways that you *might* be trapped. Furthermore, you label entrapment as not being in control. In reality, there is always a way out of most situations. Think about it. Two of my favorite examples are: (1) "If you became violently ill and had to throw up, would you leave whatever situation you were in?" and (2) "If there were a sudden, serious earthquake, would you try to get out of a confining or dangerous situation, no matter what?" In the first example, if you would allow yourself to leave a movie theater because you were going to throw up but not because of feeling anxious, you would be entrapping yourself. Keep in mind that other people would not necessarily know why you suddenly left. I am not advising you to escape from fearful situations. But *if you don't allow* yourself even the *idea of an "out"* and thus feel trapped, you are actually *entrapping yourself*.

Further, as you overpredict danger (either due to panic or to an external situation that is really frightening), you feel increasingly vulnerable and unable to deal with the event. You believe that you don't have the inner resources needed to cope. As a result, instead of creating more control in your life, fear controls you. Also the more you *expect* to experience fear in various situations, the more you start to anticipate anxiety before you even get there. This is called *anticipatory anxiety*. Frequently, anticipatory anxiety is worse than the fear in the *actual* situation and it is often harder to eliminate.

Avoidance Becomes a Pattern

Why is avoidance often so pervasive and persistent? Avoidances can become very "comfortable" and therefore difficult to change. Not only do people get used to avoiding uncomfortable sensations, but avoidance feeds the illusion that somehow they can control the terrifying uncertainties in life. Sometimes the pattern of avoidance goes on for so long that the person does not recognize it as a problem related to fear. It is much easier to say, "I don't really like to go to parties anymore" rather than "I'm afraid of going to parties." In other words, the activities that people *say* they don't want to do can be activities they are *afraid* of doing.

Phobic situations, like panics, often elicit a number of Automatic Thoughts, which are related to the person's Core Beliefs (see Chapter 9). The Automatic Thoughts of a person with agoraphobia might be:

• This anxiety and panic might last forever. What if they get worse and worse? I may never get rid of them!

- If I'm not in control, I can't cope with the situation.

The Core Beliefs of the person could be:

- I'm weak and vulnerable and cannot deal with too much stress and anxiety.

- I'm very sensitive and can't cope with life as well as others can.

As J.B. Persons explains in her very useful 1989 book, *Cognitive Therapy in Practice*, these types of Core Beliefs have a powerful effect on how people view themselves and therefore affect their behavior enormously. Core Beliefs can thus support avoidance behavior. They can interfere with your recovery by influencing you to give up too easily or to think that there is no hope for you.

Earlier in this book I discussed the example of my client Jennifer who, after having been house-bound for a long time, finally made the decision to go out, even if she were to die! To her, dying of a panic seemed very probable. After all, her friend had died of a heart attack while a passenger in her car. Jennifer had stayed home for a number of months, thinking that only by remaining house-bound could she prevent herself from dying of the same fate. One day she realized that her life was literally "hell," and she decided to put her fear of dying to the test. As she experienced being alive and out in the world—not dying in spite of her fear—she slowly gained confidence. What you can learn from her example is that you too must be willing to put your ideas to a *behavioral* test. Your actions must prove to you that your fearful thought is irrational, that is, disaster does not follow activity. When you see that you survive, your sense of self-confidence will grow.

In the panic work, you put your assumptions to behavioral tests. When working with phobias, you need to do the same, in order to realize that there is no danger. According to Craske and Rodriguez (1994) arriving at *that* realization is highly predictive of the ability to overcome phobias.

If I No Longer Fear Panics, How Come My Agoraphobia Persists?

If agoraphobia were related only to the fear of internal sensations, then it should follow that if you no longer fear panics, your phobias will dissipate. Unfortunately, this is not the case. The psychological structure that maintains agoraphobic avoidance is much more complex than simply the fear of internal sensations. More danger is attributed than previously to the *situation itself*. Let me give an example to illustrate what I mean. Initially, you might be afraid of panicking and losing control of your car on the freeway. With agoraphobia you might now also think that freeways are terrible places where most people drive carelessly, and someone is sure to injure you. You exaggerate your perceptions to make these into imminent life-and-death situations. Many panickers develop new sets of worries. A number of clients have told me that after their first panic they began to worry about many things that had not worried them previously. Most of these worries have to do with issues of uncertainty and lack of safety.

Phobias Take on a Life of Their Own.

I hope that working through Part II has helped prepare you for your agoraphobia work. We will be using some of the same principles and exercises in the work that follows.

Agoraphobia Treatment: Research Findings

In Vivo Exposure

For years *in vivo exposure* has been the treatment of choice to overcome fear of places and situations. In vivo exposure means to repeatedly confront fearful situations. There is a great deal of research and clinical experience showing that it is effective. It is believed that exposure works through habituation. *Habituation* is a term that means by repeating the exposure to a fearful situation, your psychic distress and bodily reactions gradually diminish in intensity. For instance, heart rate decreases quickly with repeated exposure, even in situations that arouse strong fear.

Distraction

In the long run, habituation is greater when you *focus on the feared situation* rather than distracting your mind away from it. Many people with phobias and many therapists use distraction as a coping mechanism and find it very helpful. As comfortable as it may feel, most prominent researchers and clinicians ask people *not to distract* themselves. It is generally better not to do so for two reasons: (1) Distraction prevents you from testing out and disputing your Automatic Thoughts (see Chapter 9). (2) It becomes another form of avoidance. (Although most researchers do not use distraction, we do not have the final answer on it yet, according to Rodriguez and Craske, 1993.)

Frequency and Length of Practice

The more often you practice, the more rapidly you will achieve results. For example, if you went to a mall and stayed for a while on a "good day" but did not repeat the exposure for two to three weeks, you might not see an improvement the next time you went. This is because the fear grew again during the "long" break. It is best to practice at least three to five times a week on the same situation. *The ideal is to practice daily.* It has also been shown that the *longer* you stay in a fearful situation, the better. Ideally you would experience the highest point of anxiety and watch it subside, before you left the situation. For that to happen, you would need to stay in the situation for one and one-half to two hours. (If the event itself is of short duration, such as riding in elevators, you would want to repeat it many times in a row in order to get a more lengthy exposure.)

In the Absence of the Feared Situation, Fear Grows.

Mastery Exposure

In vivo exposure, as I said, requires that the person face the fearful situation and pay attention to the sensations and thoughts evoked. The more exposures and the longer they are, the better. The guided mastery approach (therapist as a guide) is a modified version of in vivo exposure (Williams, 1990; Williams and Zane, 1989). The theory behind guided mastery exposure suggests that people *avoid mainly because they feel that they lack coping ability.* By preparing yourself in the exposure practices to feel a little more confident, you obtain evidence that *you do have the coping skills needed.* This strengthens your sense of mastery.

The emphasis is on gaining mastery rather than on tolerating high levels of anxiety. In other words, if you can face the situation with only a small degree of fear, that's fine. It is believed that this approach helps generalize (spread) the gains made more than traditional in vivo exposure: The more confident you are in dealing with the expected adversity in one situation, the more easily you will master other situations.

Usually, this type of mastery work is done first with a therapist, who soon may enlist the aid of the client's spouse or friend. If you have extensive avoidance, ultimately you may need to work with a therapist. If you do have strong and extensive avoidance but want to try it on your own, be prepared for agonizingly slow progress at times. I will try to give you as many guidelines and therapeutic principles as possible for you to succeed. It is very exciting that some people have turned their fears around on their own. Even 15 years ago, when the field was in its infancy, some people used the self-help manuals available at the time and did well.

I will be using the term Mastery Exposure, which means exposure with emphasis on mastery techniques designed to promote self-efficacy. Mastery Exposure often uses a guide who can provide assistance via modeling and encouragement. It also utilizes aids (including safety signals and safety behaviors) when working on the tasks step-by-step, and extensive strengthening of the gains made. *The aim is for you to have a greater sense of control and coping ability*, although as you recall, *total* control is an illusion.

Ultimately, and as soon as possible, you are to do the practices alone and without the use of aids. This is extremely important. The reason is that if you see your success as related to a "person," "thing," or "behavior," it will not help increase your own self-confidence. Your improvements will not be entirely "yours." In such a case, your fears about danger will be kept alive, you will not improve very much, and you are likely to relapse.

What Is Avoided in Agoraphobia

1. **Places/Situations Commonly Avoided**

    Driving and/or being a passenger

    Walking outside

    Supermarkets

    Shopping malls

    Crowds

    Public transportation

    Being far from home

    Being home alone

    Movies/Theaters

    Bridges/Tunnels

    Waiting in line

    Meetings

    Elevators/Escalators

    New places

    Walking across open spaces

2. **Other Feared Experiences/Activities**

   Exercise

   Excitement brought on by movies, news on TV, ball games

   Relaxation and inactivity

   Optional social events

   Situations that can lead to disagreement or arguments, i.e., create intense emotions, such as anger and excitement

   Setting limits with others, when their wishes conflict with yours

   Changing jobs

   Taking college classes

   Caffeinated drinks

   Eating in front of others

3. **Safety Signals/Safety Behaviors**

   These are seen as preventing bad things from happening (Craske and Barlow, 1994).

   "Safe" person

   Medications, or empty pill bottles

   Small brown paper bag

   Water/Sodas

   Telephone numbers of nearby hospitals

   Lucky charms (supposed to prevent panics)

   Focusing on escape plans

   Holding one's breath

   Grasping the steering wheel with "white knuckles"

   Always driving in the slow lane

   Driving with radio on

   Leaning on shopping cart

   Sitting near exits

   Knowing where bathrooms are

   Tensing up

   Distractions

   Doing things on sunny vs. cloudy days

   Doing things on "good" vs. "bad" days (on "bad" days you expect panic or disaster and thus let your physical state dictate your day)

   Having a "safe zone" beyond which you feel you can't cope

   Any object or behavior that supposedly can save you from panics or other phobic fears

Typical Fears Behind Agoraphobic Situations

- Having a panic attack with its feared consequences

- Loss of urinary or bowel control

- Feeling hot/unable to breathe

- Losing control, making "a fool" out of oneself, standing out too much

- Showing signs of anxiety

- Collapsing of weakness

Assessing Where You Stand

When you look over the preceding lists, do you relate to any of those situations/experiences? Do you have any outright phobias? If not, are there any other activities you avoid? Do you have to do things in just a particular way to avoid panics? In sum, has your life changed as a result of panics, and if so, how?

The reason I encourage you to grapple with these questions is twofold: As long as something is supposed to "save" you from panics, you remain vulnerable. Without your "safety signal" you would be lost and unwittingly invite a panic to come. You would anticipate a panic and probably make it happen. The other reason has to do with the quality of your life. Let's assume, for example, that you no longer can exercise because of fear. You know how important physical exercise is for your health. You are jeopardizing your health *more* by not exercising than by having some panics! Are you allowing the panic disorder to dictate the conditions of your life?

In my New Panickers Group the members have all had a recent onset of panics and do not have phobias. Quite a few of them are initially apprehensive about some situations, e.g., exercising. At this point, their avoidance tendency is flexible enough so that corrective information quickly gets them to stop avoiding. If you are a new panicker, it is very helpful to return to the place of your first (or worst) panic as soon as you have the coping skills you need. This may neutralize the situation for you, so you will be able to feel as you did before the panics.

I cannot emphasize enough the value in ridding yourself of any limitations (avoidances of any kind), no matter how subtle. If it proves difficult, follow the guidelines in Chapter 12. One of my clients had a relapse recently. She had worse panics than ever before. Although she did not avoid anxiety-provoking situations, she was on the brink of doing so. I told her that she was placing the panics on a very prominent pedestal, because all of her thinking revolved entirely around her panics. We started to work on removing her safety signals and safety behaviors (like carrying Ativan with her at all times and taking it whenever she felt uncomfortable). Although she thereby risked being totally at the "mercy" of panics, she took charge of her life again; and she improved soon thereafter. Her recovery was quicker than the first time around. (Keep that in mind. Once you have overcome fear of panics and phobias, if they return, you are likely to master them again, and much faster the second time around, so long as you *work with the fear*.)

Whatever you do, do not give in to the temptation of seeking safety by avoiding. You won't rid yourself of fear. Anxiety and panic will follow you that way.

Making a Commitment to Change

You don't *feel* like addressing your fears, because it is such an unpleasant task. Who wants to do something they dread? Yet behavioral methods like the ones I'm proposing require you to do precisely that. It would be nice if there were indirect ways, such as just talking about fears; but as we have seen, talking does not allow you to test out—with your body and your mind—the idea that a situation is not unduly dangerous or embarrassing. You cannot learn to cope with adversities and difficulties in your mind only, just as you cannot raise your self-esteem by merely thinking about it. You need to engage in an activity that will prove to you that there is no danger and that you can cope.

Summary of Parts I and II

1. Objective danger is the same for everyone. We all have to grapple with the uncertainty of life.

2. Taking risks leads to growth.

3. If you are willing to go through temporary discomfort, you are investing in greater self-confidence.

4. Anxiety is uncomfortable but it does not kill.

5. Anxiety and panic will dissipate.

6. You must accept that you will feel anxiety and fear.

7. Panic attacks won't hurt you, physically, mentally, or socially.

8. You *can* cope with panic. You won't go crazy, have a heart attack, faint, have a stroke, or act hysterically (screaming and running around uncontrollably).

9. You *can* learn to interpret symptoms as reactions, not as signs of catastrophe.

10. You *can* look at panics as inconvenient and uncomfortable annoyances, not as catastrophies.

11. Avoiding panics at all costs is *not the goal*. If the only way to avoid panic attacks is by avoiding, *the cost is too high*.

12. Avoidance *feeds* fear.

13. The more you avoid a fearful situation, the more the fear grows.

14. Fear entraps you.

15. You can look at situations with fresh eyes: *You can see how you are not trapped.* You can exercise the *control you do* have.

16. You are not the center of the universe. People are not watching every move you make. They have their own lives to live and think about!

17. You *can* free yourself from worrying about what strangers might think of you.

18. Even if some of your anxiety symptoms do become visible, don't exaggerate the probability of being laughed at, thought of as weird, or of embarrassing yourself. And if it happens, so what! Remember that *we all* act at times in embarrassing ways and survive. Only death is the point of no return.

19. Just because you are anxious does not mean that you lose your integrity or personal worth.

20. We cannot grow in life without experiencing uncertainty and anxiety.

Recommended Reading

Craske, M.G., and Barlow, D.H. 1994. *Agoraphobia Supplement to the Mastery of Your Anxiety and Panic II*. Albany, NY: Graywind Publications Inc.

12

Mastery Over Fearful Situations

Section 1: Doing Mastery Exposure—Step-By-Step

Setting Goals

Right from the start, I want you to *list your goals,* not your fears. It is often recommended that goals be listed in sequence from the easiest to the hardest, and to start working on the easiest one. I prefer a more practical approach. You can start with the easiest one, the one you most want to achieve first, the one you *can* work on most often, or the one with which you think you will succeed best. In other words, start anywhere, except with very difficult goals or goals that cannot easily be broken into small segments (notably, flying or having surgery). It is *preferable* to first choose goals that you can work on *at least three times a week*. You can work on more than one goal at a time, but don't get sidetracked in the process.

Examples of Goals

1. Shop for three hours in a very crowded mall.

2. Drive on freeway for a distance of 100 miles from home.

3. Go to movies and theaters, sitting anywhere.

4. Walk alone outside, anywhere.

5. Socialize: Go to lunch with coworkers, attend parties/weddings, have small dinner parties at home.

List your goals on Worksheet 12. PLEASE DO SO NOW (before proceeding further).

Worksheet 12: List of Goals

1. _____

2. _____

3. _____

4. _____

5. _____

6. _____

7. _____

8. _____

9. _____

10. _____

11. _____

12. _____

Using the Mastery Exposure Chart

General Guidelines

When working on your phobias, you want to feel that you can cope with the situation. Feeling that you perform a task well gives you a sense of mastery. To help you gain that, you need to ask yourself, "What do I need in order to feel that I can master *this particular practice*?" I want you to go out equipped with tools. These tools can help you cope better, whether or not you become highly anxious. Mastery can be achieved using physiological change (breathing), cognitive challenging, or behavioral means. Examples of behavioral means are using a coach as a model, using safety signals and safety behaviors, taking one step at a time, and working on subtasks before you move on. A subtask is a single aspect of an activity that may pose a stumbling block and impede your progress.

NOTE: It is very important to wean yourself from the coach or safety signals and safety behaviors *as soon as possible.*

Examine Worksheet 13. Fill out items A to D *before* the exposure, items E to H *after* the exposure. It is extremely important to do items C and D *before* the exposure, or you will defeat much of the goal of your mastery exposure. Although items E and F are part of the planning in D, state afterwards what actually took place. Try to follow your plan (do not change it depending on whether you have a "good" or a "bad" day). The same instruction goes with G, *Diaphagmatic Breathing.* State afterwards whether you actually did it. This chart, like previous worksheets, helps you assess your progress. Record keeping has been shown again and again to profoundly affect behavior, because you can actually measure your progress in black and white. Worksheets 12 and 13 will guide you in this phobia work.

How to Use Worksheet 13 to Record Your Mastery Exposures

As with previous worksheets, record your work on paper. Notice that Column C is the work you did with Worksheet 6: "Challenging Automatic Thoughts." Here, you will challenge your thoughts in preparation for your exposure to fearful situations. I hope that you are now familiar enough with Worksheet 6 so that it flows more easily for you. Although I'm asking you to write it all down for the present, I hope that eventually you will be able to challenge your thoughts in mind without needing to write them down. The long-term goal is for you to quickly work with your mind when encountering potentially fearful situations. Some of my clients have been able to apply these strategies successfully even in real life-threatening situations. But for now, please bear with me, and to the task!

Working on Goal. State your long-term goal. See your List of Goals in the beginning of the chapter, on Worksheet 12.

Frequency of Mastery Exposures

Set a general time frame to accomplish subtasks, but use it only as a guide. It will help you keep track of your general progress and whether you are moving at the speed you want. On the average, how often will you work on it? The ideal is for you to work on the steps three to five days a week (if less than three days, your fear may increase in between). If you choose to work on them seven days a week, you'll progress that much faster.

Time of Mastery Exposures—Plan Ahead

On the day before you do the mastery exposure, plan exactly what time you will do it. If you leave it up to doing it when you feel like it, or you "want to see how my day goes," you'll never feel like it. By following a schedule, you won't build up too much *anticipatory anxiety.* Decide on the exact step you will work on the next day and plan the specifics ahead of time (see B in Worksheet 13). This will also allow you to make plans with your coach if you will

Worksheet 13: Mastery Exposure Chart

Working on Goal: _____

	Fill out Before Practice			Fill out After Practice			
A	B	C	D	E	F	G	H
Date	Specific Task (small step)	Challenging Automatic Thoughts	Raised CAPS to: 0–100	Alone or with Coach	No S/S or with S/S	Diaphragmatic Breathing	Self-Reward

Legend:

CAPS = Coping Ability in Phobic Situation, stated in 0 to 100.

How confident you are that you can manage the upcoming task.

0 = No confidence at all.

50 = Moderate confidence in my ability to handle the upcoming task.

100 = Fully confident in my ability to handle it.

S/S = Safety Signal/Safety Behavior

be using his or her assistance. (Note that the coach may need more advance notice.) *Follow your plan as closely as possible.* Do the cognitive work (C in Worksheet 13) before your exposure.

A. *Date.* Always enter the date. This will provide you with the best measure of your progress over time. How long did it really take to reach your final goal? Once you have had some successes, you may want to move faster with another goal.

B. *Specific Task.* Work on one step at a time. Work in small, manageable steps. The harder the task, the smaller the steps. Ultimately, each step will take you to your long-term goal. Start where you are *now*.

   Once you have mastered a task, do it without a coach and safety signals/safety behaviors. Introduce a number of variations. While removing the last self-restrictions, move on to the next step (while still perfecting your first step). Eventually, you want to *leave a task only when it is fully mastered.* You no longer will accept *anything* restricting you in the performance of that task.

C. *Challenging Automatic Thoughts.* Do the cognitive work, using Worksheet 6: "Challenging Automatic Thoughts" from Chapter 9. Note whether that work helped to lower your anxiety level. Did the probability of the event occurring change as a result of your work, i.e., how did the percentage number (from Columns 3 to 6) change? Given any apprehensions you may still have, after working on this, you can plan your next step, D, in Worksheet 13: "Mastery Exposure Chart."

D. *Raised Coping Ability in Phobic Situation (CAPS).* You want to raise your CAPS as much as possible before encountering the fearful situation.

   Ask yourself, "How can I best prepare myself for this exposure so that I will maximize my sense of mastery?" Ask yourself further, "What do I need in this upcoming task?" (Do not project onto later tasks.) Ask, "What is fearful to me about this step only?" Keep in mind that by exposing yourself to your fears you'll put them to the test. Rehearse the difficulties you expect, and plan on how to best handle them. "What can I do to help myself cope?"

   In addition to the cognitive work that you have already done, you can do diaphragmatic breathing, make the steps so small that they are manageable, use a coach, use safety signals/safety behaviors, or any other approaches. Look at Examples 1 through 4 below.

Perceived Control

"How can I face the anxiety?" Because control is usually such a big issue, try to change it around. Instead of trying to fight anxiety or avoid it, *give up attempting to "control" it.* Instead, look at other means of exerting control. And apply them!

Stay in the Here and Now

No matter how well you prepare yourself for the task, *you will feel discomfort and anxiety.* Be prepared for it. *When you feel it, that does not mean you've failed.* At some times you will feel more anxiety than at others. In the long run just repeating reassuring phrases to yourself is not helpful. Do not run ahead with your thoughts. Forget projecting into the future! Stay in the here-and-now, with this task only! *Think in the present moment.* Pay attention to your sensations and thoughts. Keep the "participant-observer" stance toward yourself. When your anxiety level is high, this stance is a very powerful tool for challenging your catastrophic thoughts.

Planning "Exits" at the Beginning of Your Mastery Exposure

I make a distinction between "exit" (an idea I first heard of from Dr. Alec Pollard) and "escape." When you "escape" you leave prematurely, because you got too uncomfortable; when you "exit" you leave according to your prepared plan. Because the fear of entrapment is so dominant in agoraphobia, begin working on each of your goals with plans to exit the situation. Find out how often you can leave a situation, and try it out, maybe even several times: Leave from a line, the middle of a row in a movie or theater, a mall, or a store. As a passenger in a car, as a passenger in a bus or tram, get off at the next stop. On the freeway take the next exit. Leave meetings and classrooms (unless you might jeopardize a job or a test), parties, and restaurants.

Plan on leaving these situations—for good—5, 15, or 30 minutes after your arrival. Make note of what happens with your feelings of entrapment. *Do not allow imaginary social constraints to stop you.* If these constraints do stop you, it is *your* doing. In that case, you need to repeat exiting those situations over and over until *you no longer care!* The reason most people do not feel easily entrapped (and probably you felt this way too, before your panic disorder) is that they know that they can leave most situations when and if they want to.

You need to use good judgment, of course, when planning exits so as not to create costly or dangerous situations for yourself. To give a few examples, it would be unwise to try to persuade a flight crew to land a plane prematurely unless you really were having a heart attack, to stop a surgical or dental procedure, or to stop a car on the shoulder of a freeway or on a bridge.

How to Cope with the Urge to Leave or "Escape"

First, accept that some days will be more difficult than others. The measure of success is how much you are able to do *in spite of anxiety*, whether your anxiety level is low or high. You will raise your self-confidence faster if you do the work when you are *not feeling your best.* Be the "participant-observer" that I asked you to be earlier: Observe how you handle the situation. You want to observe yourself function even when things are not ideal.

If you find yourself too uncomfortable to carry out the task as planned, or feel that you cannot cope, plan to leave. But whenever you plan to leave, ask yourself: "Even though I feel very anxious right now, can I handle staying here for a few more minutes?" It is best if you leave when the anxiety has lessened a bit. If you do leave, can you recoup and go right back? When you escape, try to return *as soon as possible.*

E. *Alone or with Coach.*

Guidelines for a Coach:

The coach is someone who gives support in guiding, assisting, and giving feedback. The help can be provided in the form of modeling, or helping with coping strategies for behaviors and responses, e.g., standing on a high balcony and looking down while keeping the body relaxed. Also the coach can explain verbally how to try out something. This person is not supposed to take over the practice but to help you achieve a sense of personal accomplishment. Ideally, he or she would help initially, then you would do the work relying on yourself. As an intermediary step between these two stages, the coach could be available over the telephone.

The coach should reassure you that assistance is there in case of your feeling overwhelmed (helpless and disintegrated behavior). However, in many cases, you may worry more about more subtle forms of behavior. One of the more useful ways a coach can assist, is in giving you corrective feedback about possible awkwardness in your behavior. *This should always be followed with specific suggestions on how you can do better*. It is important in mastery exposure that you feel really sure about how you are being perceived. Feeling better *inside* follows later. Finally, the coach should give ample praise.

> ## If You Use a Coach,
> ## Do the Same Task Alone
> ## as Soon as Possible.

F. *No Safety Signal/Safety Behavior or with S/S.* You need to identify all your safety signals and safety behaviors. You can first do the task with an S/S, then do it without, or you can eliminate it from the start, if you wish. If you use an S/S, however, eliminate it *as soon as possible.* Once you are rid of the S/S, vary the task, do it differently, do it relaxed, faster, and so forth.

The reason the S/S must be removed is that with it you will expose yourself only partially. Partial exposure does not work: You do not accomplish full mastery of the situation, and relapse is much more likely. An S/S keeps the danger alive. It reinforces the notion that you are vulnerable. Ultimately, you need to test your erroneous beliefs. Only when you experience that disaster does not follow the test, can you gather evidence that you can cope in anxious situations.

> ## If You Use Safety Signals/Safety
> ## Behaviors, Abandon Them
> ## as Soon as Possible.

G. *Diaphragmatic Breathing.* State Yes or No (as a reminder). Breathing helps manage the physical aspects of anxiety. Many clients find it extremely helpful. Do it *immediately before* you enter a situation and *during the situation,* as well, if at all possible.

H. *Self-Reward*: Incorporate self-rewards into your plan. Reward each small step you take. The most effective reward is one that immediately follows your exposure. Although some rewards may include other people, you do not want the reward to depend on other people, the weather, or any other circumstances outside of your control.

Planning for your next exposure

Plan your next task, partly depending on how you fared on the previous task. It may be another small or a bigger step.

Here are four detailed examples, all from the "Examples of Goals" list on page 149.

Example 1

Working on Goal. Socialize: Go to lunch with coworkers.

A. *Date.* 4-14-96.

B. *Specific Task.* Lunch at work cafeteria with one coworker.

C. *Challenging Automatic Thoughts*

　　1. *Date.* 4-14-96.

2. *Specific Trigger.* Going out to lunch with coworker.

3. *Automatic Thought.* What if I start to shake?

   Restate (specifically and as theory): I may shake and Mary will think that I don't have my act together. Example of Overestimation. 70% probability of happening.

4. *My Evidence.* I often do shake when I'm very anxious.

   Then Refute! I cannot read Mary's mind and know whether she thinks that I don't have my act together.

5. *Alternative Hypotheses.*

   - Maybe I won't shake. 30% probability of happening.

   - She may think I'm a little nervous. 50% probability of happening.

   - Mary may think I'm a total loser for shaking. 30% probability of happening.

6. *Face Up to Automatic Thought.* So what if I shake! Is it the end of the world? What's the worst that could happen if Mary thinks that I don't have my act together, or that I'm a total loser, for that matter? Just because someone may think I'm a loser (for shaking, mind you!), that does not mean I am one. Wouldn't that thought say more about Mary than about me? 10% probability of my Automatic Thought happening.

D. *Raising My Coping Ability in Phobic Situation (CAPS).*

   - I can have Mary meet me in the cafeteria. I will try to get there earlier, sit down with at least a soda to drink, and settle down before she joins me.

   - I'll do diaphragmatic breathing while I wait for Mary.

   - I'll tell Mary soon after we both sit down with food that my hands are shaking, and I feel jittery. (It will take some of the pressure off if I just put it out there.)

   - I'll try to pay attention to what Mary says, so I'm not overly absorbed with my own symptoms and thoughts.

Raised CAPS to 40.

E. *Alone or with Coach.* Alone.

F. *No Safety Signal/Safety Behavior or with S/S.* With S/S. (Went into cafeteria earlier.) That's okay. It is one step. Another time I'll do it without an S/S.

G. *Diaphragmatic Breathing.* Did diaphragmatic breathing.

H. *Self-Reward.* Right after lunch with Mary I called my husband at work and told him how it went. (He had already agreed to take this call.) His supportive attitude is great.

Planning for your next exposure

My next task will be as above with Mary again (or Liz, if Mary is unavailable), but without an S/S.

Example 2

Working on Goal. Drive on freeway for a distance of 100 miles from home.

A. *Date.* 5-21-96.

B. *Specific Task*. Drive from A to B (about 6 miles) on freeway, near home.

C. *Challenging Automatic Thoughts*

1. *Date*. 5-21-96.

2. *Specific Trigger*. Driving on the freeway from A to B.

3. *Automatic Thought*. My legs may feel so rubbery that I won't feel the accelerator or the brake; I'll lose control of the car and crash. Example of Overestimation. 10% probability of happening.

4. *My Evidence*. I have felt my legs become really rubbery. So far nothing has happened because I have gotten off the freeway fast.

    Then Refute! If I can move my left leg, it'll be evidence of control in spite of the rubbery/numb sensations. Then I have control of my right leg as well. I have never jeopardized my own or my family's safety.

5. *Alternative Hypotheses*.

    • I could have been hyperventilating. It brings on weird sensations of numbness at times. 10% probability of happening.

    • Numbness and weakness are common panic and phobia symptoms. It can be a horrible sensation, but does not have to lead to loss of control over my body. 40% probability of happening.

6. *Face Up to Automatic Thought*. Just because it feels awful, does not mean I'm actually losing control of physical functioning, especially not in a life-threatening situation. My sense of survival is stronger! 5% probability of my Automatic Thought happening.

D. *Raising My Coping Ability in Phobic Situation (CAPS)*.

    • Since I still fear not being able to control my legs in a panic by a 5% margin of probability, I will have my friend Jane follow me in her car. She can drive two to three cars behind me. That way, in the worst case scenario, I can get off the freeway at the next exit, and she'll follow me there.

    • If I get off the freeway before I reach point B, it will be okay. In that case, I'll try to continue after a brief break. If the trip is interrupted, I'll make sure to do diaphragmatic breathing to help me calm down. I'll try to go from A to B nonstop tomorrow, in that case. I have the time set aside for another practice.

    Raised CAPS to 30.

E. *Alone or with Coach*. With coach.

F. *No Safety Signal/Safety Behavior or with S/S*. With S/S. I planned a way out for myself and used it. But I did ask myself first, "Can I manage going a little farther before I get off?" and I did go a little farther than my first impulse to exit would have taken me.

G. *Diaphragmatic Breathing*. Did diaphragmatic breathing.

H. *Self-Reward*. Jane agreed to take me to a discount store that I wanted to find out about afterwards. That was fun! I like her company.

Planning for your next exposure

I wanted to get off after the second exit, but I felt I could manage a bit longer, so I got off at the third exit. Jane and I stopped only for about two minutes before I felt ready to continue my trip! Tomorrow I'll try to drive straight through, this time still with Jane following me.

Example 3

Working on Goal. Shop for three hours in very crowded mall.

A. *Date.* 4-5-96.

B. *Specific Task.* Go to mall, pick one small item and stand in a long line. (Waiting in long lines is a particularly difficult part of being in the mall for me).

C. *Challenging Automatic Thoughts*

   1. *Date.* 4-5-96.

   2. *Specific Trigger.* Standing in long line in the mall. If I panic, I may have to leave.

   3. *Automatic Thought.* People may think I'm crazy. I can't stand it when someone thinks there's something wrong with me! Example of Catastrophizing and Perfectionism. 60% probability of happening.

   4. *My Evidence.* I sometimes judge others when they suddenly leave a line. I wonder if they are anxious.

      Then Refute! I really cannot read other people's minds, so I don't know what their reasons are.

   5. *Alternative Hypotheses.*

      - People might think that I forgot an item. 40% probability of happening.

      - The people behind me may feel relieved because their wait was just shortened! 70% probability of happening.

      - Most likely people have other things on their minds than whether or not I'm standing in line. 55% probability of happening.

   6. *Face Up to Automatic Thought.* Just because I leave a line, doesn't mean I'm crazy. And if somehow I found out that someone thought I was crazy, so what! It reflects more on them than on me. Many people who are not crazy leave lines. 8% probability of my Automatic Thought happening.

D. *Raising My Coping Ability in Phobic Situation (CAPS).*

   - I'm ready to take the challenge alone this time! If I panic, I'll ride the wave. I'll keep doing my breathing. I'll stay in the here-and-now, and I'll challenge my thoughts, again!

   Raised CAPS to 50.

E. *Alone or with Coach.* Alone.

F. *No Safety Signal/Safety Behavior or with S/S.* No S/S.

G. *Diaphragmatic Breathing.* Did diaphragmatic breathing.

H. *Self-Reward.* My reward to myself for this big test was to rent this movie I wanted to see and watch it at home. I finally took the time to see this movie!

Planning for your next exposure

My next task will be to spend half an hour in the mall, pick one small item and stand in a long line.

Example 4

Working on Goal. Walk alone outside, anywhere.

A. *Date.* 7-8-96.

B. *Specific Task.* Take a 15-minute walk during lunch time.

C. *Challenging Automatic Thoughts.* Did not have enough time to do it in written form. Did it mentally.

D. *Raising My Coping Ability in Phobic Situation (CAPS).*

- Lea Ann knows about my problem, and she likes to walk. I'll ask her to walk a distance behind me to judge how I seem; whether I look nervous or "lost" or "weird." I really want to know.

- I'll watch other people walking and observe how they seem.

Raised CAPS to 25.

E. *Alone or with Coach.* With coach.

F. *No Safety Signal/Safety Behavior or with S/S.* No S/S.

G. *Diaphragmatic Breathing.* I did the breathing just before but not during the walk. It's hard to do when walking.

H. *Self-Reward.* I rewarded myself by calling Sally when I got home from work.

Planning for your next exposure

My next task will be to do the same without a coach. (Lea Ann assured me that I looked perfectly normal.)

Now start doing exposure practices. You have had a great deal of information and practical guidance. It is a lot to digest. As relevant as the next section is, I recommend that you take a break from the book and begin to work on exposures. Then, at any time, proceed to Section 2: "Working on Specific Goals and Looking at Difficulties."

PLEASE PRACTICE NOW.

Section 2: Working on Specific Goals
and Looking at Difficulties

Give yourself a pat on the back. You did it! Every step counts.

What is the best way to work on specific goals?

The following pages will give you ideas on how to divide your long-term goals into manageable steps. If your goal is to be able to perform the following actions for prolonged periods, follow the instructions below. Remember to keep using Worksheet 13: "Mastery Exposure Chart."

    Staying in small, enclosed spaces, such as an elevator or a small room with the door closed; or riding in the back seat of a car with the windows closed. Turn to page 161.

    Driving. Turn to page 163.

    Going to stores and malls. Turn to page 164.

    Going to movies; using public transportation. Turn to page 165.

    If none of the above apply, turn to page 166: Other situations that provoke fear.

enclosed spaces, such as an elevator or a small room
g in the back seat of a car with the windows closed.

if you are not getting enough air, especially when it is hot
ng with the fear of suffocation, turn to Chapter 9, page 98
Work through the "Challenging Automatic Thoughts" chart
nd. Then, fill out Worksheet 13: "Mastery Exposure Chart"

rk alone as soon as you can.

tor. Enter and exit the elevator. Then stand there for 30 sec-
. Next, allow the doors to close and stand in the stationary

in elevator, with coach.

e floor that the elevator will stop.

away, out of your sight.

ne floor.

ator on different floors.

increasingly more floors.

solution to the problem in advance. First, there is plenty of
ou will probably not spend the rest of your life in it. What
ss the alarm button, or *any* button for that matter, if necessary.
n button or the electricity went out? What if nothing worked?
d as you can and yell for help. One of my clients once said,
"But I couldn't do that. That would be out of control behavior!" In such a situation, I think most of
us would not consider it out-of-control behavior but rather very *purposeful* behavior. I certainly would
do anything I could to draw attention to my plight and to get help as soon as possible.

To increase mastery:

- Do hyperventilation in the elevator, when you are inside with a coach. Ask your coach to
  do it with you.

- Do hyperventilation in the elevator, while alone.

- Similarly, you could hold your breath (not long enough to pass out) and do straw breathing
  while with a coach or alone.

Small room with door closed

- Work alone or with a coach.

- Sit (or stand) inside the room with the door closed for increasingly longer periods of time.
  You may start with five minutes, or less, if necessary.

To increase mastery:

- Do any of the interoceptives you worked on in Chapter 10.

Riding in back seat of a car with the windows closed

This task is particularly challenging if it is done in a two-door car.

- While the car is parked, preferably in a garage, sit in the back seat with the windows closed, starting with a 5-minute period and working up to 30 minutes. For the longer time periods you may want to bring along something to do. If this sounds a bit much, have a family member check on you every 5 minutes or at longer intervals. In this task you are in perfect control: You *can* leave at any time.

- Have your coach or someone else who is willing to take a break after 5 minutes drive you. You can open the window or step outside. Repeat the 5-minute trips several times.

- Increase the length of time without an "exit," depending on your "CAPS" score, for as long as 30 minutes, and later for 1 hour.

To increase mastery:

- Once comfortable in the parked car, do hyperventilation, holding your breath, and straw breathing.

- Do hyperventilation, holding your breath, and straw breathing while you are a passenger in the back of the moving car.

Return to page 160 for other specific goals, or proceed to page 166.

Your goal is driving.

Any driving

- If you don't drive at all because of fear, start with really small steps.

- Sit in the car, while the car is parked, at first for short intervals, and later for longer periods of time. Then, turn on the ignition. Next, move the car out from wherever it is parked.

- Once you have mastered the step above, just drive around the block.

- Gradually increase the distance you are driving.

- You should drive with a coach at first. As soon as possible, drive alone. Your coach may follow in a separate car (see below under Freeway driving).

- Use the same principle for major roads and highways.

Freeway driving

- Use a coach if necessary. Wean yourself as soon as possible.

- If getting on the freeway is difficult, drive on a major highway first, if there is one near you. The ideal simulation would be one where you can drive up to 45 or 50 miles an hour, and the highway is rather straight.

- Drive only the distance between the on ramp where you enter the freeway and the first off ramp or exit. In other words, get on the freeway and take the next exit. Ideally, choose a freeway entrance where you won't have to merge with the traffic; where the same lane that you used to enter the freeway will also allow you to exit.

- As you keep practicing, loosen your grip on the steering wheel, do diaphragmatic breathing, and try to relax your body.

- If you are using a coach, let the coach follow you in another car, with longer and longer stretches of roadway between the two of you.

- Change lanes, drive at different times of the day, with different amounts of traffic, in rain or shine, on good or bad days.

- Drive increasingly longer segments.

- Bridges cannot be broken up into small segments. Work on them later.

To increase mastery:

- *While the car is parked:* Do hyperventilation, straw breathing, and holding your breath. Do it in places where others won't see what you are doing (unless you don't care, which would be even better).

Return to page 160 for other specific goals, or proceed to page 166.

§

§ Your goal is going to stores and malls.

Here the frequent fears are feeling shaky, fainting, losing control, and otherwise making a spectacle of yourself. If you are still grappling with those fears, turn to Chapter 9, Example 4 on pages 92 and 93. Work through Worksheet 6: "Challenging Automatic Thoughts" with the specific situation you fear in mind. Also fill out Worksheet 13: "Mastery Exposure Chart" in this chapter.

Stores/Malls

- If you are using a coach, have your coach wait for you inside the store or mall. You enter, spend five minutes, and leave, without purchasing anything.

- The coach can be a few steps behind you, with longer and longer distances between you, while you purchase something.

- If you use a cart, loosen your grip on the handles. Make sure you can be in a store without a cart as well.

- The coach waits outside, you enter, and stand in a short line to purchase an item.

- You spend increasingly more time inside, select more items to purchase (e.g., groceries), stand in longer lines. In fact, at times look for the *longest* line you can find!

- Go inside the mall via different entrances and exits.

- Do it without a coach as soon as you can.

- Spend increasingly longer periods in store/mall, up to two hours or more, at one time.

To increase mastery:

- If you fear feeling dizzy, go up to the clerk in the mall store and say, "I'm feeling dizzy, can I sit down?" Don't make it look so serious that they call 911.

- Go to the bathroom or fitting room and spin around. Walk while dizzy out to the store floor. (*I tried this out.*)

Return to page 160 for other specific goals, or proceed to page 166.

Your goal is to go to movies and to use public transportation.

In theaters and on public transportation, some people tend to feel trapped, without an exit. Much of the sense of entrapment has to do with social apprehensions. If you fear being embarrassed, turn to Chapter 9 on page 108 "Your Focal Fear Is Being Embarrassed or Humiliated." Work through Worksheet 6: "Challenging Automatic Thoughts" with the specific situation you fear in mind. Fill out Worksheet 13: "Mastery Exposure Chart" in this chapter also.

Movies

- You should probably do this one with a coach, at least at the beginning.

- Go to a movie and choose a seat near the aisle.

- *Plan in advance how* long you think you can stay there. It may be 10, 15, or 30 minutes. Excuse yourself when your time limit is up and leave the theater. That is, *leave on purpose.* (In any situation where you feel trapped, whenever possible, see how often you can get out of the situation.)

- Go to the movie and sit *several seats from the aisle. Plan to take a break* at a certain time (e.g., 15 minutes after your arrival), go to the bathroom or out to the lobby and return 10 minutes later.

- Go to the movie and sit in the middle of the row.

- Try to look very "panicky" when you leave. (By doing this you create a "paradoxical" situation. If you are afraid of looking a certain way, do it on purpose to see that you can survive it.) Return later.

To increase mastery:

- Now, go to the movie *alone.* Make sure you leave, as planned, and return.

- Go alone and remain for the *entire* movie.

Public transportation

- For some people the fear here is to wait at the departing station, where the train or bus may sit for a while with the doors open. You may feel torn: "Do I leave, or do I not, do I leave, or do I not?"

- Go in, sit for a while and *leave* before the train leaves.

- With a coach, go to the next station when there are few passengers.

- With a coach, go farther by train or bus.

- Have the coach take an earlier train or bus and meet you at a specified station.

- Take the public transportation alone.

To increase mastery:

- Take public transportation during a busy time of the day.

- Go alone during rush hours as far as the last station and then return.

Return to page 160 for other specific goals, or proceed to page 166.

§ Other situations that provoke fear.

Walking across open spaces

Fact: This fear is at times called "space phobia." It is most often found in seniors. (I once had a client who needed to hold onto *something*, even a grass straw, to feel steady!) In reality, people with these fears do not usually fall down, even if they feel unsteady (unless they are very frail).

- Have a coach follow you, keeping increasingly longer distance between the two of you. Have your coach give you feedback on how you seem to be walking.

- If you "look drunk" because you are so wobbly from the fear, so what! You know you are not drunk.

Sitting at the dentist

Fact: Fear of dentists is *so common* that nearly all dentists are familiar with dental phobia.

- Work with an understanding dentist.

- Tell the dentist/hygienist that you are nervous.

- Plan to have a small job done first.

- Plan to ask for a few seconds' break when one is not offered (allowing you to feel in charge of the situation).

Heights

Fact: Fear of extreme heights is very common in humans, and may be partly genetic. It is not a "phobia" unless it interferes with your life. Here, I am assuming that it is a problem for you. Many people with this fear feel "drawn" to the precipice and think that they may jump. In fact, no matter how strong the urge and the fear, people do not actually jump for fear.

- This is a good task to start with a coach.

- Work up slowly, with an easy item first.

- Approach a balcony, railing, or window while staying close to the wall.

- Stand comfortably.

- As you increase your mastery, approach it differently, faster, slower, from the left, the right. Look far out, look straight down.

- Look straight down for five minutes nonstop.

Fear of being looked at

You may fear getting up during a meeting, from a dinner table (as in a restaurant), in a movie, theater, or other places, because you are afraid that people will look at you and judge you.

Fact: When everyone is sitting, it is natural for the eyes to move to the person standing up. The "stimulus configuration" (or the "picture," if you will) has changed. It is the same as if you looked into a can with all black marbles, except for one red marble. Your eyes would immediately and automatically be drawn to the one item that is different. It does not mean that people are then judging you negatively when you stand up. People *may* be momentarily annoyed if you block their view while getting up from the middle of the row in a movie, or similar situations. The annoyance or irritation is very short-lived. Have you not felt annoyed at a small inconvenience? How long did you dwell on it afterwards?

Other social apprehensions

These limitations can be extremely powerful and are a big part of agoraphobia. Work on overcoming them. Instead of hiding something, use a paradoxical approach: Do it on purpose. Test out if you can survive the feared symptom. The degree of freedom you can achieve is remarkable!

- If giving a speech, say you are nervous and predict that you will probably blow it.

- If you fear looking crazy, practice in front of a mirror for five minutes while looking as crazy as possible. Decide whether that's the way you look when you are outside.

- If you fear blushing, use blush or other means to make yourself look very flushed.

- If you fear sweating in front of others, apply drops of water onto your forehead to look as if you were sweating.

- If you are very fearful of showing imperfection because you may be judged adversely, make a mistake on purpose.

I'm Having Difficulties

The worst part for me is that . . .

    I've repeated the exposures many times, but I'm still very anxious. Turn to page 169.

    I can do practically everything. But I still have a *lot* of anticipatory anxiety. Turn to page 170.

§ You have repeated the exposures many times, but you still feel anxious.

1. First, check on your use of any possible safety signals/safety behaviors. Can you say to yourself, "As long as I do . . . I'm okay," "Phew, I made it!" or "I made it today." If these statements are true for you, you may not fully have tested out your fears. Are you carrying something with you, or behaving in a way that prevents you from fully achieving mastery? For instance, are you keeping yourself close to the exit, doing things only when it is uncrowded, and so forth? As long as you don't fully test out your fears behaviorally, they tend to return. This also happens if you believe that as long as your body "behaves," you'll be okay, but not otherwise. That is why partial exposure does not work.

2. Second, remember always try to push *beyond* the limits you want to achieve. If your goal is to spend three hours in the mall and to wait in line with five people in front of you, and those are the limits you work up to, you are still vulnerable and on the "edge." At times five people in front of you may be a problem. When you approach the three hours in the mall, you may get anxious. Push your limits! Only by doing so can you secure the comfort zone. As long as you avoid situations you are at risk for relapse. *Don't consider your work finished until you have mastered all avoidances!*

3. Third, try not to think in self-defeating ways. Remember all the useful cognitive techniques for influencing your thinking that you have learned. Apply them!

In sum, a complete attitudinal and perceptual shift must take place for you to fully overcome agoraphobia. With a great deal of mental and behavioral work this shift can be achieved.

If You Leave Yourself an Out— No Matter How Subtly—You Are Not Really Testing What You Fear.

If you need to, return to page 168. Otherwise proceed to page 171.

You can do practically everything. But you still have a lot of anticipatory anxiety.

Very often in agoraphobia, the anticipatory anxiety is much worse than the fear experienced in the actual situation. This again demonstrates how powerful the cognitive component of anxiety is. If you only felt fear in the actual situation, the argument could be made that it was pure conditioning. However, people play many "What if . . ." scenarios in their minds. This is the future-oriented state that was discussed earlier. It is not staying in the here-and-now. You must replace the "What ifs" with "This is how I'll cope with . . ." scenarios. Reprogram your mind to generate new coping thoughts rather than replaying and being overcome by old fear thoughts.

Overcoming anticipatory anxiety may be, if not the hardest, the most tenacious aspect of fear to conquer. It will stubbornly resist your attempts to rid yourself of it.

Anticipatory anxiety is the last step. It will *not* go away before you overcome your avoidances and the fear you feel in anxiety-provoking situations. It will not go away until you have rid yourself of the *social fears* that have entrapped you.

If you need to, return to page 168. Otherwise proceed to page 171.

Using Imagery to Combat Phobias

I believe that the body and the mind strive for health and that they are able to heal themselves. This healing is not always easy because we often have formidable forces to contend with that threaten our well-being. Using our minds to create healing images can influence the healing process.

You may recall from Chapter 2 that the experiential mind can be influenced by imagery. But just as with the previous practices set forth in this book, imagery must be learned and practiced to produce results. You can find very useful visualization and relaxation techniques in two books, *The Relaxation & Stress Reduction Workbook* by M. Davis, E. Robbins-Eshelman, and M. McKay (1988) and *The Anxiety and Phobia Workbook* by E.J. Bourne (1990).

All relaxation and meditation methods have one aspect in common: That is, an emphasis on diaphragmatic breathing as the natural relaxant to which we all have access, and which can be used as a conduit for mental peace. If you have learned and practiced diaphragmatic breathing, you can use it in your imagery work, although a more extensive relaxation method may be preferred. Here, I will present the brief version of an imagery method that I often use with my clients. You can do this in preparation for a specific task, or to deal with general anticipatory anxiety.

To do imagery rehearsal, it is important that you sit or lie in a quiet, comfortable place. (Do not lie down if that position leads you to fall asleep; you defeat the purpose then.) Loosen any tight or restrictive clothing. Assure yourself that you will not be interrupted by the phone or by other people. Visualize each step in *as minute detail* as possible. Custom-design it for *yourself*. Take *at least* 15 minutes to go through this sequence, and repeat it *at least* three times a week.

Step 1. Do diaphragmatic breathing. Move the diaphragm/stomach area *slowly* out and in, as you breathe in and out, respectively. (Try not to breathe faster than 8 to 10 breaths per minute.) Allow yourself to feel how the area expands and contracts, placing all your attention there. Allow yourself to enjoy the sensation and the calmness that is produced. Scan your body and your mind for any tension, tightness, anxiety, or bothersome thoughts, and if you detect any, let go of them, more and more with each exhalation. Visualize *life* coming into you when you breathe in, and exhale undesirable sensations and thoughts. Cleanse yourself in this way. Give yourself permission to do so, for just a little while. Offer this moment to yourself as a gift. Soon, if you wish to, you can return to tension, fears, and worries, but not now. Do it for yourself for this moment.

Step 2. Try to become "one with your breathing." That is, place your mind in your diaphragm/stomach area and fully sense the area expand out and in, slowly and comfortably. Let go of all your thoughts. Just feel the breathing *as if you were your breath.* You and your breathing are *one.* If your mind wanders at any time, gently and without judgment, bring it back to focus on your breath. This is your totally carefree moment. As you stay with yourself and your breathing, feel yourself become light and joyful in spirit and body.

Step 3. Think of a time before your phobias began and how you engaged in the activities that later produced fear in you. The activity might be driving, using elevators, standing in line, being in crowded stores, or in an enclosed space with door and windows closed, or any others. You were not only free from fear, but in some situations you may even have felt exhilarated. For instance, several of my clients have described how they once loved long-distance driving. You can recapture that sensation and your self-confidence. Remember that you are the same person, and what you could do then, you can do now. In fact, you have more experience now. For instance, now, you can appreciate better the importance of driving safely.

Step 4. Place yourself in the future, at a time when you have no phobia. See yourself as supremely skilled at doing the different activities. You are driving, flying, public transportation, going on jury duty, going to movies and theaters comfortably, all with confidence in yourself.

Envision social situations where you are yourself and engaged in animated conversations. Instead of being totally focused in worrying about what you can say or how you come across, you are showing interest in the other person, listening, sharing of yourself, all the while maintaining good eye contact.

Step 5. Imagine difficult situations that could arise. It could be heavy traffic, interpersonal tension, getting stuck in an elevator, etc., and then imagine being able to cope with the situation. What pride you would have in yourself! Visualize yourself moving through these situations with confidence. Feel a light emanate from your being.

Step 6. Thank yourself for the gift you just gave yourself. Decide if you want to take a piece of the experience with you as you leave this. Return to your breathing. Be aware of your surroundings. Open your eyes and stretch.

Did you find any particularly useful thoughts, ideas, or actions in this chapter to add to Worksheet 1: "My Personal Coping Affirmations"?

What is you Fear Barometer doing now? If you had a bad panic in one of your phobic (perhaps *previously* phobic) situations, how much fear would it evoke in you? What is the number, using the 0 to 100% scale? Determine what the number is NOW. Write in the number: _____.

Recommended Reading

Bourne, E.J. 1990. *The Anxiety and Phobia Workbook*. Oakland, CA: New Harbinger Publications.

Davis, M., Robbins-Eshelman, E., and McKay, M. 1988. *The Relaxation & Stress Reduction Workbook*. Oakland, CA: New Harbinger Publications.

PART IV

ADJUNCTS TO SUCCESS

13

Accepting Your Feelings and Standing Up for Yourself

Look at Your Issues: Learn to Take Control

A woman who had recovered from panic disorder gave a self-help workshop at a recent conference of the Anxiety Disorders Association of America. She told the audience that for years she had grappled with the question "Why me?" both on her own and in therapy. Never arriving at an answer she finally said to herself, "And why not me?" Once you ask the second question, you become more open to looking at all the factors in your life that may have contributed to the development of panic disorder. The goal of this chapter is to help you examine the relevant aspects of your life. Panic disorder is not eliminated in a vacuum. Examine the context in which it developed. Aside from panic disorder, are you truly at peace with yourself? If not, where are the problems? What can you do about them?

One major problem area for many panickers is the difficulty they have in standing up for themselves. If this applies to you, you may need to read books and practice asserting yourself, or take assertiveness-training workshops, or learn to be assertive with the help of a therapist. I will illustrate how this works with several examples, from my practice, of people who learned how to accept their feelings and to stand up for themselves.

Paul Changed His Attitude

Paul had a job he did not like. He found the work boring. On top of that, his boss yelled at the employees. He would stand over a sitting employee, point his finger at him or her, and yell at the person in public. Paul was totally intimidated, as were his fellow workers.

This issue came up in a group session soon after Paul had gained control over his panics and no longer feared them. But he felt powerless at work. The group spent a great deal of time on his situation and helped him plan how to achieve some power at work. After the group session, he went to work with the strength of the entire group behind him. Paul's attitude changed. While he still tried to do his best at work, he no longer stretched himself beyond reasonable limits as previously.

A day or two later, his boss had another angry outburst. Paul was prepared. With his boss practically leaning over him, he nonetheless wriggled himself out of his chair and stood up and faced the angry man. His boss no longer seemed so intimidating and he was shorter than Paul! The finger pointing stopped soon (it's harder to point upward than downward) and his boss calmed down. Paul was exhilarated. He shared this in the next group session. He had decided, on his own, that he would never again, in any job, remain sitting if he was being reprimanded by someone towering over him.

Chuck Began to Set Limits

When Chuck was leaving the New Panickers Group, he described his gains and explained what steps had helped him to overcome his panic. They were:

1. Having a physical exam, where he was reassured that he was in good health.

2. Learning about panic physiology.

3. Learning to recognize his negative thinking patterns and seeing how much he had been catastrophizing, and changing this.

4. Getting the group support and realizing that he was not alone.

5. Becoming more assertive.

Regarding assertiveness, he told the group that he had always agreed to work overtime whenever asked, even if the request came at the last minute. But Chuck had become aware of his need to be more assertive. Just prior to leaving the group, he began to put into practice all he had learned. For the first time he told his boss that he could not work overtime on the upcoming weekend because of prior plans.

Jose Got in Touch with His Feelings

Jose came to the New Panickers Group saying that he was unaware of any stressors that might have triggered his first panic, which had occurred about a month earlier. After about three sessions, he mentioned, in passing, that he had cosigned a loan for $6,000 for a good friend. His friend had defaulted, and Jose was stuck with most of the loan. He judged the likelihood of recovering the money as almost nil. He showed little feeling over this, even though he was struggling for his livelihood. Everyone else in the group was outraged! It was pointed out that he needed to get in touch with his feelings of intense anger and to reevaluate his friendship. (One great benefit from group therapy is that, although any member may be blinded to his or her own situation, the others can see it clearly and give useful feedback.)

Cindy Is No Longer Emotionally Abused

Cindy was in the Panic/Phobia Group, and although this is a more structured group than the New Panickers Group, we work on assertiveness issues in both groups. When working on these issues, she told the group how deeply hurt she was by her mother, who for most of Cindy's life had set her aside, put her down, and, after Cindy reached adulthood, continued to criticize her and her family. Cindy wanted very much to win the approval her siblings had; but to no avail. She worked through the loss of hope in the group. Finally, she decided that she did not want to allow herself to be emotionally abused, not even by her mother. She made several more overtures and then gave up. Thereafter, she chose to maintain only a minimal relationship with her mother.

Janet Learned to Fully Accept Herself

Janet was a woman in her mid-fifties who had known for a long time that she was homosexual. She had had a few lesbian relationships and had always hidden this truth from others, and half of the time from herself, because it was totally contrary to her upbringing and religious beliefs. She had gone out with men but only to keep up appearances. She never married. Slowly, she brought up bits and pieces of this history in the Panic/Phobia Group. In her last group session, Janet shared very movingly that she was making her first "public" announcement that she was lesbian. Although the other members were not homosexual, they were touched by her decades-long struggle for self-acceptance and gave her a great deal of warm support.

Gerald Made a Plan and Took Control

Gerald managed 12 employees, one of whom was always half an hour to one hour late. Gerald was a friend of this employee and did not have the heart to set clearly stated limits. Whenever he brought the subject up, the employee told him to just deduct the time from his legitimate compensatory time. Nonetheless, the situation remained troublesome for Gerald, because he could not plan the work that needed to get done, and it also disturbed the other employees. In the group, the following compromise was suggested: Gerald was to make an arrangement with the employee to arrive at work at 10 a.m. instead of 9 a.m., using compensatory time for the extra daily hour. If the employee came later than 10, he was to be dealt with as any other employee would be, with reprimands, and so forth. Understandably, in order for Gerald to follow through with the plan, his feelings had to be explored in depth and he was given a great deal of support. The plan allowed him to take control over the situation.

Esther Recognized Her Rights

Esther was the epitome of perfectionism. Her parents had raised her and her siblings to be "perfect." If the youngsters got a grade lower than an A, they were put on restrictions. If, while playing sports, they missed catching a few balls, they were lectured for an hour afterwards. It was this way with everything. Esther was a sharp young woman, a "go-getter." She did everything well. At her job, she was so good that her supervisor gave her many of her own managerial duties to perform (without extra pay, of course). Often, Esther worked through her lunch hours and breaks, while the supervisor took long lunches.

One day Esther had an out-of-the-blue "bad" panic attack and, not knowing what was wrong, ended up in the emergency room. Luckily, she came to my group soon thereafter. After some initial work on panics, which allowed her to understand them and to gain a sense of control, she began to examine her life. Although initially she was proud of her accomplishments, she soon realized how limited her life was and that her health was more important than her job.

She changed drastically over the next four weeks. Even though she continued to do a very good job, she no loner pushed herself to the utmost limit. She always took her breaks and lunches. Initially, she "blamed" her need for breaks and lunches on her panic disorder, but she soon got beyond that. She recognized her rights and saw how she had been ill-used—with her own consent. Soon, she decided that the job was too limiting for her future growth, and she quit. Then, she took a part-time job and went to college to pursue an interesting career. Although she dearly loved her parents, Esther recognized that the family "tradition" of perfectionism was grossly exaggerated and came with a big price. She learned that she could do her best without "killing" herself in the process and without having to suffer from panic disorder.

David Learned Not to Worry About What He Could Not Control

David's father was seriously ill in another state. David loved his father. Much of the time he felt guilty for having chosen to live in California, which kept him far from his parents. While David was in the New Panickers Group, his father took a turn for the worse. David immediately flew to see him for a short, four-day visit. Upon his return, we explored his guilt feelings. He felt guilty for not being there more often to give his father company and comfort. He waited, terrified, of news that his father might have died. Although two other grown children lived nearby and visited frequently, David was emotionally closer to his father. His father had told only David the details of his medical condition and his fears about further deterioration.

David had already formed the habit of calling his father daily and was ready to fly to see him again on a moment's notice. He learned, with the help of the group, to look at the positives: The time, concern, and money (for the calls and flights) that he contributed to staying as close to his father as distance would permit. He came to realize that this was all he could do and that he did not need to feel guilty. David also struggled with control issues. He learned that ultimately he could not control whether his father stayed alive or died. Instead of constantly dreading the inevitable, he started to more fully enjoy and savor every minute of phone contact and visits. He began to live the present and found new peace within himself.

Empower Yourself: Take Charge of Your Life

What are the common links in these examples? To summarize very briefly: Paul had been unable to stand up for himself (literally to stand up from a sitting position when he was being reprimanded) vis-à-vis his boss; Chuck had worked many overtime hours when he did not want to; Jose was in denial that he was furious with his "friend" for defaulting on a large loan; Cindy continued to seek approval from her mother when none was forthcoming; Janet had tried very hard to deny her homosexuality; Gerald could not set clear limits with his chronically tardy employee; Esther's need for perfection blinded her to the fact that she was being taken advantage of; and David felt guilty for not doing more for his ailing father because he did not live nearby.

These examples reflect one of the three following themes:

1. Not standing up to others;

2. Not accepting one's own feelings and ending up feeling guilty or in denial;

3. Being a perfectionist.

In all of these categories *control,* or rather, the lack of it, is at the heart. If I don't stand up to others, I certainly don't feel that I have control in interpersonal situations. If I deny my feelings and suppress them, I allow tremendous internal pressure to be created; these pressures exact their toll one way or another. Am I in control then? If I'm a perfectionist, I cannot judge what is *reasonable* to accomplish at any given time. I do not allow room for my human needs but rather allow the quest for perfection to control me.

As you know, control issues are at the core of panic and phobia problems. The relationship is not simple or sraightforward. Yet, from my clinical experience, these issues add significantly to the development of panic disorder. What strikes me is how unaware these clients had been, prior to treatment, of the influence of these scenarios on their lives. Perhaps they were too used to them. And yet they were so surprised when they began having debilitating panic attacks! Once they began to explore these life issues, they saw that they had to make significant life style changes before they could even hope to overcome their panic disorder. *You too* might not be aware of what a toxic environment you may have helped create for yourself.

As Dr. Manuel Smith says in his book, *When I Say No, I Feel Guilty*, these response styles are linked to the fight/flight response. We can try to solve the problems of living by fighting or fleeing, or we can try to communicate. Many people fight, if not physically, then verbally, e.g., by being verbally aggressive, hostile, and attacking. Fleeing is a very common response for which people are not "punished" (in contrast to aggressive behavior). We may withdraw from ourselves and our own feelings or from others for fear of conflict. Thus, we can passively escape from problems by pretending that they are not there or that they are unimportant.

The threat of failure and disapproval is a very common source of fear in society. Using fight/flight mechanisms to deal with our anxieties and insecurities, or to solve interpersonal problems, is not very productive and can lead to very serious problems such as anxiety disorders, depression, or both. Learning how to solve problems verbally is, therefore, a must if you want to deal better with anxiety. When you acknowledge and accept the "dark" and "light" sides of yourself, and when you embark on the arduous task of teaching others to treat you appropriately by asserting yourself, you gain mastery and self-confidence. And, as you know by now, empowering yourself and gaining mastery are precisely what you need to overcome panic disorder.

By Facing Issues, You Empower Yourself and Gain Mastery.

Here is a list of principles for achieving proper self-care and assertiveness. These are simply reminders. If you need to learn how to be more assertive, I suggest that you read Manuel Smith's *When I Say No, I Feel Guilty* or Pamela Butler's *Self-Assertion for Women*.

1. *Be kind to yourself.* This is an important point of departure. Sometimes people show more compassion to others than to themselves.

2. *Take care of yourself.* No one will watch out for your interests as you will. You can expect everyone to look out for himself or herself first.

3. *There is not just* one *reality.* Everyone experiences life differently. Our own values and preferences may not be those of the next person. This also means that just because others react differently, doesn't necessarily mean they are insensitive.

4. *Strive for excellence but do not attempt to be perfect.* Feeling angry, anxious, and "down in the dumps" is human. Telling yourself that you shouldn't feel a certain way reveals a perfectionistic and harsh attitude toward yourself. Taking every failure as a disaster is bad for your self-esteem.

5. *The main goal with assertiveness is to express yourself.* Naturally, you want to achieve something with an assertive statement. If you express your wants, you are much more likely to get them, but that is not guaranteed. You can hope to influence others but you are not likely to control them. Putting others down or attacking them does not work.

6. *Being assertive includes expressing uncomfortable feelings, setting limits, and taking positive risks in life.*

7. *Your feelings are your indisputable truths.* But, remember, the way to know whether you are expressing *feelings* is if you can say them in *one* word. If you use more words than one or

you have to preface your statement with "that," e.g., "I feel that . . . ," you are probably not describing a feeling and thus can be disputed and argued with.

8. *You don't have to be "sick" to say No.* Do not use physical illness, anxiety, or panic as an "excuse" to set limits. If you need to set limits, do it because you have the right to!

9. *Don't let your anger build.* When you are in a state of high frustration and anger you are less likely to express yourself constructively and to solve the problem at hand. Also, you may be labeled by others as "upset" or "hysterical"; and they may expect it to pass.

10. *Know what you want.* You are ineffective if you do not know what you want. If you are unsure, you can most often "buy time" by saying, "Let me think about it. I'll get back to you in an hour/tonight/tomorrow." Follow through by getting back to the person. Also, you have the right to change your mind.

11. *You don't have to justify your wants.* Ultimately, you are your own judge, not the other person.

12. *Stand face-to-face and maintain eye contact.* Diverting your gaze weakens your verbal message. (It works like avoidance.)

13. *Use "I" not "You" statements.* Stay close to yourself, using "I" statements, "I feel . . ." "I react this way when. . . ." Ultimately, we are responsible for ourselves and our feelings. When using "You," you are on more precarious grounds.

14. *Use the Broken Record technique.* This is very useful in business interactions. Persist in stating what it is you want. Keep your statements as brief as possible. The more words you use, the more likely it is that you will be distracted from the issue at hand. No matter how much the other person tries to push you off track, repeat your request (e.g., wanting a refund), if needed, over and over.

15. *When criticized, accept the criticism instead of becoming defensive.* Use statements like, "You are right, . . ." "That may be true, . . ." "I can see how you'd think that. . . ."

16. *Invite further and precise criticism.* Do so especially in interactions with people who are important to you. "Exactly what bothered you about what I said?" "Exactly how am I not paying attention to you?" "Exactly how is my performance not up to par?" "What precisely do I need to do differently to raise my evaluation score the next time around?"

17. *Setting limits with friends.* If saying "No" to being taken advantage of ends a friendship, perhaps the friendship was based more on what the other person got from you and less on friendship than you thought.

Recommended Reading

Butler, P.E. 1981. *Self-Assertion for Women.* San Francisco: Harper & Row Publishers.

Smith, M.J. 1975. *When I Say No, I Feel Guilty.* New York: Bantam Books.

14

Coping with Stress and General Anxiety

Although a number of panickers were worriers prior to their first panic, many become chronic worriers after developing panic disorder. Besides worrying about panic attacks and all that comes with them, they also worry excessively about their and their family members' health, finances, work, relationships, and so forth. How does this occur? In my clinical experience, this increase in worry seems to result from the increased sense of vulnerability that comes with panic disorder. Panickers feel less secure and not in control. Further, they expect that they will not be able to cope when bad things happen. Is this the case with you? Even if you have diligently worked through overcoming panic and phobias, you may still be left with considerable apprehension, anxiety, and worry in general. Unfortunately, remaining apprehensive increases the likelihood of relapse. So I will address four main areas here: limiting your stress level; examining what lies behind worry; the importance of relaxation; and biological toughening up.

Know Yourself and Limit Your Stress Levels Accordingly

People have different genetic predispositions and psychological profiles, including past and current life experiences. In order to grow, they seek out challenges. The problem arises if you put yourself into extremely stressful situations and ignore certain limitations of your emotional and physical strength, or time and resources. Too often people make major decisions based on fantasies. They ignore the realities at hand. Instead of asking themselves, "Given that this is what I have, what I have to work with and live with, what is my best course of action?" they make decisions based on how they think things *should* be. This can create tremendous discrepancies between what is desired and what is possible. I believe in holding an optimistic rather than a pessimistic outlook and, certainly, to achieve anything, you must stretch your mind and look beyond your immediate circumstances. Nonetheless, it is one thing to see a path ahead of you and another to totally ignore where you actually are, ending up stressed out and continuously disappointed.

Consider these examples: A new panicker in my group, while still working on overcoming her panic disorder, said that she now had to take on two jobs and attend college full time, just as she had done prior to her first panic. The other group members thought that this plan sounded unduly stressful. She said that she had to prove to herself that she was still able to do the same things she used to do. Another client had been at a job for four years. He was not promoted as he had expected to be and was often put down one way or another by his boss. A very dedicated worker, he believed that this might have been due to his minority status. Repeatedly, over a few sessions, he said that his boss *should* be different and *should* treat his employees respectfully. Filing a grievance did not improve his situation. He was distressed by panic attacks and sleepless nights.

Both of these examples illustrate nonadaptive responses. We know, as we learned earlier, that the first panic is often preceded by stressful events. Yet, too often, the person then becomes "obsessed" with the panic while ignoring his or her life situation. *Think of a panic as a "wake-up call."* Because the initial panic is elicited during a particularly stressful phase of life, it gives you a unique *opportunity to look at the panic as a signal that something in your life is not right and is negatively impacting your physical or mental well-being* (see Chapter 13).

In the first example, the client was intent on proving that things could and should be as they had been before the panics. Wanting to be so busy was partly her fear of free time. She was afraid that if not busy she would be confronted with her deeper thoughts and emotions. She needed to reassess her life and see what could be *changed* for the better. Although she made excellent progress otherwise, we were unable to convince her to modify this view.

The other client held onto a Cognitive Distortion that I did not list in Chapter 9, namely "Shoulds, Oughts, and Musts." Maybe in an ideal world everyone follows the "right rules"; however, we do not live in an ideal world. The man in the second example could have chosen to pursue his grievance with further legal steps or to cut his losses and look for another job. Being stuck on the "shoulds" was not helpful or adaptive. I myself often use the expression, "You gain some, you lose some." Not all battles are worth fighting. Sometimes I accept that the cost of fighting an issue is too high compared with the potential gain. At other times, I think that unfortunate events happen and are part of life.

We Don't Live in an Ideal World— Unfortunate Events Happen.

Looking Beyond Worry

A woman in my Senior Anxiety Group had suffered from claustrophobia for many years and had developed panic disorder in the past three years. During the initial interview, I asked her what her exact fear was while in a crowded elevator. She was unaware of any thoughts. I inquired what would be her worst fear in that situation. She said, "What if the elevator gets stuck?" I replied, "Yes, *what if* the elevator gets stuck?"

Then she told me that she had used the "What if . . . ?" question in many other situations and it had helped her to successfully curb her tendency to worry. She continued, "It never occurred to me to use this line of reasoning to my phobic situations." She learned to apply the "What if . . ." logic to her fears fairly effortlessly, because she was so familiar with the technique and had used it successfully for years!

Studies on worry have shown that it is sometimes used as a way to cope with the expectation of danger, where the person has no control over a situation; for instance, worrying that your young adult son or daughter has an auto accident while out at night. This is an example of a Maladaptive

Thought mentioned in Chapter 9 called Disaster Expectation. People find their worries are so intrusive they try to act in ways to neutralize them. This may include acting in a ritualistic way. In this example, the ritualistic act could be repeatedly phoning your child's friends or staying up at night until he or she arrives back home.

A different kind of worry arises, however, when people worry to prevent other, more threatening and unwanted *thoughts* from coming to the surface. Sometimes they will use negative self-labeling or self-punishing terms for "even having" these thoughts. They may use seemingly "harmless" statements such as "That was dumb/stupid of me." All of this can further lower self-esteem and lead to more complex emotional problems.

How can you overcome general worry? Facing and dealing with problems that you can resolve rather than trying to avoid them is one way. Another way is to learn to let go of things that you cannot control.

Let Go of Things That Are Beyond Your Control.

Thought Stopping

Many people find Thought Stopping a useful technique when dealing with recurring worry thoughts. Although facing and challenging worry thoughts (as you did with your worries about panic) is the ideal way to produce a "shift" in your thinking, you will find that worries can be exceptionally persistent. Sometimes, you may not have the energy, time, or opportunity to do the challenging work.

This is where Thought Stopping can prove helpful. As soon as you become aware of the undesired thought, say in your mind (or out loud if you like) "STOP!" Say it vigorously. You may want to imagine a Stop sign in front of you. Then think about something else. Think of something pleasant, something funny, or something requiring your concentration (such as remembering the words to a poem). You can use pleasant images and or fantasies (i.e., where you'd go on your dream vacation). Most people can think of something else *momentarily*. Yet, before you know it, the unwanted thought will be back. As many times as that happens, keep using the Thought Stopping technique. Say the word "Stop" and visualize the Stop sign as many times as you need. This is usually the hardest part: Staying committed to using Thought Stopping over, and over, and over. If you stay with it, it works!

Learning from Your Experiential Mind

I said earlier that learning to use your experiential and rational minds *together* can provide a good balance. When the two disagree, there is often tension. Your rational mind will tell you how you *should* respond, not how it *is*. You can access your experiential mind and learn about your moods and emotional frame of mind by allowing any positive or negative Automatic Thoughts to emerge. (Remember, many Automatic Thoughts are good and adaptive.) If you do not know what influences your moods, they will control you.

Dr. Seymour Epstein, in *You're Smarter Than You Think*, describes "focusing" as one way to open your mind. He recommends becoming a "passive observer" and letting your thoughts come up spontaneously. Then, when a thought comes up, you are to check it against different feelings till one "clicks." You do that by asking yourself, "Am I angry in this situation?" "Do I feel sad?" "Am I possibly feeling jealous?" This is one way to become aware of the connection between your general mood and your experiential thoughts.

Dr. Epstein's focusing technique reminds me of a somewhat different avenue to self-understanding that I learned how to use as a teenager when I would find myself feeling sad or worried for no apparent reason. One day I sat down and asked myself, "What changed?" I had been content or at least feeling neutral but then suddenly I found myself very "keyed up." I reviewed everything that had happened that day, including my thoughts. I said to myself, "Oh, yes, that happened; is that bothering me?" I answered, "No, not really." "I was thinking of such and such; is that bothering me?" "No, not really." Finally, I came up with something that "clicked." "Oh, yes, that is eating away at me under the surface!" However, to my amazement, when I revisited the issue, it seemed much less overwhelming than it had earlier. I insisted on finding a solution or making peace with it, since I didn't like that "keyed-up" feeling. After using this approach many times over, I realized that when I was feeling "down," there was *always* something *very specific* that brought me there. Often it was not even an important issue. But if I left it unresolved, it would continue to nag me.

So, ever since I was a teenager I haven't accepted the notion that feelings occur in a vacuum. Today, my approach is somewhat different. I have learned not to ignore issues as easily as I used to. If I find myself too anxious and ill at ease, I decide to apply diaphragmatic breathing as a calming, coping skill and to give myself a two-minute respite. Then, when I return to the issue, I seem to be able to look at it with a fresh mind. Then I try to find a solution or I make peace with it. ("I win some, I lose some, that's life.")

Pessimism is associated with negative expectations in life, and people who are pessimistic tend to act in less hopeful ways. If you are a pessimist, you probably think that you have little control over events and that, instead, events control you. Changing such a basic outlook can be very difficult but it is not impossible. I hope that this book is helping you to experience a more positive outlook, not just in dealing with panic and phobias but in other areas as well.

Renata was a dyed-in-the-wool pessimist. She went through my Panic/Phobia Group. When I first interviewed her, we established that in addition to panic and agoraphobia, she suffered from generalized anxiety disorder and some social phobia. She was in great distress. Her family of origin had been abusive to her. She recalled being very fearful since early childhood and she had become a worrier and a pessimist. Her self-confidence was minimal. In the group she made moderate progress and when she felt that she had her panics under control, she left the group. When she called me a few months later, she chose to attend my Anxiety Support Group. This group is a once-monthly drop-in, loosely structured group. It is open to past "graduates" from my other groups who at times need additional support.

At this time, Renata was more concerned about her chronic worry than her panic and phobias, which were largely in control. She was always tense and anxious. At various times, I strongly suggested a medication referral, but she always declined. Although I tend to be hopeful about the recovery of my clients, I must admit that I was less so about her. She did come to the monthly meetings, however. She said that she always felt good after leaving the group, though the good feelings did not last long. After attending about six sessions over a six-month period, one day she surprised me. She told the group several examples of how she was learning to control her worrying. From then on, over the next few months, she repeatedly and successfully curbed her habit of worrying.

She had achieved what I call a "shift" in her mind, and discovered that *worry was reversible*. She discovered that she had choices about the thoughts she thinks. She learned to speak up, to truly accept herself, to set limits on how much stress she would submit to, and to distinguish between what she can and cannot control (see Chapter 4). She became an avid walker and pursued her interest in reading. Her life was not easy, and I am certain that she will continue to struggle. Yet I felt profound joy when I heard every success story she shared. It was important to keep pointing out that her success was *her own doing*.

Renata had not set out to change her basic pessimistic outlook, and she did not become an optimist in any true sense of the word. Yet, as a result of her gains in assertiveness, diminished worry, and accepting what she cannot control, she developed a more open mind toward herself and the world. She found some long sought-after peace within herself.

No matter how much I help my clients, ultimately they are alone in fighting the demons of their fears. Somehow, they find the courage deep within themselves to face devastating problems. The success they achieve is due to their hard work. Likewise, if this book helps you, it is only a tool to guide you to do the hard work of empowering yourself.

Fight the Demons of Your Fears—
Find Courage Deep Within Yourself.

Relaxation and Fun

Sometimes stress and tension are inevitable. They cannot be eliminated from life. Stress can be brought on at work, at home, by illness, or other events. General anxiety is associated with a significant amount of physical tension. When stress and tension are chronic, emotional and physical problems can result. Therefore, it is imperative to balance the negatives with fun and relaxation. I am often amazed at how people think they *should* be able to live with stress without being affected by it. They do not create balance in their lives because they do not realize how much their stressors are affecting them.

I see many people in psychotherapy who have no interests, no hobbies, nothing that they really enjoy or strive for. They live for the day. It is not surprising then that they end up feeling empty and governed by anxiety and depression. If there is a void, being human we will fill it, somehow, with something—anything. If we do not have real, imminent concerns or goals, we will create an endless stream of imaginary worries.

I recommend that you make room and time in your life for fun and entertainment, which should include things you do outside as well as at home. Although watching television can often be an escape for many people and helps them to relax, I have never heard anyone describe having gained a sense of "fulfillment" or "challenge" from it.

If You Have No Dreams or Goals
to Strive for, You Will Fill the
Emptiness With Imaginary Worries.

Another useful way to handle stress is to learn some relaxation techniques. It is not within the scope of this book to teach you those. However, I would like to recommend an excellent book, *The Relaxation & Stress Reduction Workbook* by M. Davis, E. Robbins-Eshelman, and M. McKay. It teaches a number of relaxation techniques as well as some other coping skills, and you are bound to find one that fits you.

Biological Toughening Up

Although relaxation is very important to combat general stress and tension, it does not appear to help significantly with panic attacks themselves. Furthermore, however much you learn about leading a more relaxed life with new attitudes and new habits, sooner or later you will be confronted with stressful events.

As I mentioned in Chapter 7, it appears that stress can lead either to positive physical outcomes and emotions, or to negative ones, depending on how you interpret the event: Whether you perceive it as challenging or threatening. Challenges, even if they are very stressful, seem to lead to biological "toughening up," according to the very interesting studies done by Richard Dienstbier (1989; 1991). Why is it so important to toughen up? Because being tougher leads to better performance and learning, to greater emotional stability and resistance to depression, and to better physical health. Both positive and negative stress activate increased adrenaline and noradrenaline surges, but in a situation perceived as a threat, excess amounts of the hormone cortisol are also released, which is not desirable. In sum, which kind of hormonal arousal is generated depends on how the event is interpreted.

Toughness feeds upon itself, but weakness does the same. You know this in the context of panic and agoraphobia. If you practice avoidance, that is likely to lead to further avoidance. If you feel a sensation, e.g., dizziness, and you interpret it as a threat (terrible things may happen as result of dizziness), it will lead to more of those sensations, which in turn will increase your fear. The continued fear and perception of panic attacks as threatening is what leads to panic disorder.

There are two ways in which you can enhance your biological toughness, which in turn enables you to deal better with stress: They are doing regular physical exercise and developing coping skills. Coping skills are defined here as the ways you find to cope better with a stressful situation (see Parts II and III). If you feel that you have some degree of control and that you will cope relatively well, even if it is difficult, the harmful hormones are less likely to be activated and released into your bloodstream. If you feel that you can't cope, the pituitary-adrenal-cortical arousal increases the likelihood of you ending up feeling anxious and depressed.

Now, I know that my advice to exercise sounds like a cliché but consider it. It has been shown that aerobic exercise (essentially any exercise stimulating the cardiovascular system) produces sympathetic nervous system (SNS) arousal. With repeated activation, use, and depletion of adrenaline and noradrenaline, and recovery periods in between (as happens when you exercise regularly), the body is trained to deal better with increased stress.

If You Are Too Fearful to Carry Out Your Exposure Task, Exercise!

Conclusion

I have a suggestion for you regarding Mastery Exposure. Whenever you feel too frightened to expose yourself to a situation for fear of not being able to cope, do physical exercise instead! The problem here is, of course, motivation and self-discipline. But think about it. If the findings on toughening up are true, then exercising when you find exposure too difficult would greatly help you. Instead of feeling down for not accomplishing your planned task, the exercise would help you feel good about yourself and would actually prepare you for the rigors of confronting your upcoming exposure tasks.

Unfortunately, as paradoxical as it seems, many people, though extremely anxious, would rather worry than take action. But remember, *action absorbs anxiety.*

Recommended Reading

Davis, M., Robbins-Eshelman, E., and McKay, M. 1988. *The Relaxation & Stress Reduction Workbook.* Oakland, CA: New Harbinger Publications.

15

Setbacks: Making Sure
They Are Temporary

If you are feeling great and think that you don't need to read this chapter now, you are *wrong*. Please read this chapter very carefully and review it now and then.

When some of my clients experience setbacks, and I ask them how they became fearful of panics again, they say that on leaving the treatment program, they believed that they would never have another panic. I ask them if that idea was in any way conveyed by me. They reply, correctly, "No," but say, "I just thought it wouldn't happen again."

I tell my clients that they are finished with the treatment when they can say, "I haven't had a panic for a while and that's good. But if I have another one, so what!" This is quite a contrast to them saying, "I haven't had a panic for a while, and I expect I never will have one again!" Yet no matter how much I stress the first idea, some still leave with the expectation that they will never have to worry again. (Often these are the same people who stop practicing the skills they learned in treatment.)

The medical profession sometimes compares panic disorder with a disease like diabetes, implying that people will have it for the rest of their lives and need medication from that time on. It is true that some people, no matter what treatment they try, struggle with fears throughout their lifetime. Many, however, are more fortunate. I have seen lots of people overcome their panic disorder. This does not imply a guarantee of their never having another *panic attack*. In contrast, I firmly believe that once you have had a panic attack and developed fear of it, you will have another one sooner or later. Your mind and your body are "primed" for panics. Otherwise, what explains the fact that you can exist for years with intermittent high anxiety, but once you have a panic, you have another one and another one and another one in close proximity to each other? This is where the fear of panics comes in. Fear feeds the panic cycle. Even if you learn not to fear panics, the priming, or recognition if you will, remains imprinted in your psyche.

Tina, after having successfully "graduated" from the New Panickers Group, came back eight months later requesting a medication referral. She had been experiencing her worst panics ever, and they occurred mostly at night. She had never before experienced night panics, so she was terrified. She felt that her life was falling apart. When interviewed again, she admitted to having left the group with the belief that panics were gone from her life forever. She thought that she no longer needed to apply the learned coping skills. Because of her high distress, she was prescribed Ativan by a fellow psychiatrist with whom I work. The understanding was that she would get off the medication very soon. Reapplying the breathing and cognitive skills happened quickly, since she had already learned them well before. She had also learned to be more assertive. But now more material came up about her relationship with her in-laws. Tina had to learn to set limits with them as well. As she confronted deeper issues about herself and her relationship with others, she experienced more profound changes than she had the first time around. Unfortunately, she had to learn about the persistence of panics the hard way.

While seeming to progress, Tina was relying heavily on the medications to make her feel better. Though on a very small dose, she quickly became psychologically dependent on them. When the psychiatrist instructed her to taper off and to flush the remaining pills literally down the toilet, she reacted as if her life support system was being taken from her. But she saw our confidence in her and somehow she found the courage to follow the instructions. As scared as she was at first, she realized that now it was really up to her. No longer having the tranquilizer to rescue her, her improvement soared. After a few more sessions, she was confident and willing to take better care of herself.

Tina learned that she was more vulnerable than she had previously thought. She left the very brief second treatment with the understanding that the panics might return again. Yet she felt in control of her life. She would be better prepared the next time and would not hesitate to seek professional help again if needed.

Don't Be Caught by a Surprise Setback More Than Momentarily. Have Your Arsenal of Tools (Learned Skills) Ready.

While you cannot guarantee against a future panic attack, you can prepare yourself not to have panic disorder return. *If you have no fear of panics and have made some changes in your thought patterns and your life style, a panic is likely to remain an isolated event.*

On the other hand, you may be one of those rare people who *does* have a lifelong struggle with panic disorder. You may have had treatments and nothing seemed to work. You could need medications continuously. Every person is unique. If medications rather than cognitive-behavioral approaches work, that is perfectly acceptable. The important thing is to find what works for *you*.

It is possible that you have other emotional problems as well as panic disorder or certain personality characteristics that make it difficult to overcome the disorder. For instance, if you tend to be extremely dependent on others and have become used to having others solve your problems, you could be more prone to developing and maintaining agoraphobia. However, it has also been demonstrated that with proper treatment, some of the personality characteristics such as dependency, subside. If you have a marital partner, who wants you to remain dependent, this person may sabotage your progress. It is the experience of most clinicians, however, that if the panic disorder is treated and the person improves, his or her partner will support the changes.

How Fear Can Return with a New Panic

When some clients had a panic attack after experiencing a period of no panics, and their fear of panics returned, they provided the following "explanations":

1. *It came unexpectedly. I was not under any particular stress.*

   Even out-of-the-blue panics can occur again. Recall that at times the fight/flight response fires unexpectedly, or there is a dysfunction in another biological system. You are also "primed" by having had panic disorder previously. Although some panics do occur without any clue as to why, and *may* have a biological basis, I recommend that you take the occurrence of a new panic as a "wake-up call." Ask yourself, "Is there *something* I'm not accepting, or am I not standing up to someone I should?" In my clinical practice, I have found that in about 50 percent of panickers the initial, or a recurrent, panic occurs within the context of having "unacceptable" feelings or of not acting assertively. It may not be obvious. It would serve you well to examine your life closely and if things are not going well, ask why.

2. *I couldn't stop the panic.*

   Remember that you cannot always stop panics. Even if, like many people, you learn to curb your panic reactions right at the first sign of them, it does not always work.

3. *The symptoms were different and/or they were worse than ever.*

   You had a panic, but this time it was different or worse than ever. You give the panic a different meaning. Research has shown that actually very few people always have the same symptoms. Most people's symptoms vary over time. Look at the list of panic attack symptoms given in Chapter 3 and compare yours against them. Greater intensity of the symptoms does not mean greater danger. If you believe so, your conclusion is irrational, and you would benefit from doing some more work on your Automatic Thoughts, using Worksheet 6: "Challenging Automatic Thoughts."

4. *It happened at night. I never had night panics before.*

   Many people are terrified when awakened by an attack. This is very understandable, because you may feel even more vulnerable. However, it does not mean that the attacks are more dangerous. You may wish to reread the section on nocturnal panics in Chapter 7.

5. *It happened when I was on the freeway!* (This assumes you did not panic there before.)

   If panic or panic-like sensations occur in situations that are potentially more dangerous, such as on the freeway, you may become more frightened. As understandable as such a fear is, believe that you can still maintain control over your driving (and behavior in other potentially life-threatening situations). Numerous clients of mine and of other therapists have had panic attacks on the freeway without ever causing an accident. When asked to describe in detail what they actually did in the midst of their panic, they reported being extra cautious. It seems that their survival instinct took over.

6. *When the panic came, I couldn't think. I was beyond thinking rationally.*

   Even if you were completely taken by surprise, remember that you felt the same way during your initial panics. Yet you succeeded in slowing down the experience and gained control. Now it is likely to be easier the second or any other time around.

7. *I didn't think I needed the coping tools, like breathing, any longer.*

   If you look at the onset of panics as a wake-up call, that may mean that your previous habits and behaviors were unhelpful. You may have been subtly, chronically hyperventilating or you could have been acting submissively and nonassertively or you were under too much stress. If you learned new ways of thinking, breathing, and dealing with your life, keep up those skills! You may need to practice them for longer periods of time.

Setbacks: Taking a Fresh Look

Recovery never follows a straight line. For every two steps forward, you take one back; with four steps forward, you might take two or three back. The important question is, "Are you moving in a forward direction overall?" Being human means being imperfect. *This is normal.*

Being Human Means Being Imperfect.

If you want to heal yourself, setbacks actually provide you with an excellent measure of progress. If you don't have a panic for a long time, you have no way of knowing if you are just lucky or if you really have conquered the fear. How do you respond to a setback? Do you berate yourself as if you were at fault; do you lose hope and conclude that cognitive-behavioral methods don't work after all? Or can you remain compassionate toward yourself and get back to work? A setback means that you need to keep working more on the techniques. As strange as it sounds, a new panic is a new opportunity to practice what you have learned. You can learn more the second time around. The learning must go deeper and be more complete. *Don't give up!*

I have seen some clients take the learning more seriously after setbacks and then make more profound changes than the first time. Remember also that this book is packed with information and practices. Have you done the practices and exercises as instructed or have you rushed through segments? Go back and try to learn more.

For a Setback to Occur, You Must Have Had Some Success!

Circumstances That May Trigger Panics

- *Highly stressful times.*

  You cannot always prevent stress in your life. Yet, pay attention. Learn to notice when stress is building up. Are there things you can do to soften its impact? How are you reacting to it? Do you need to make changes to decrease your stress level? Do you have balance in your life, with time for exercise, fun, relaxation, and good eating habits?

- *Being overly tired, ill, or observing illness in a loved one.*

  Your defenses may be down. If you are dealing with illness, talk to people, seek out support groups in your community, go to church and pray if you are a believer.

- *You did not fully overcome your agoraphobic avoidance behavior.*

  If your avoidance behavior was incompletely overcome, the fear can creep up again much more easily than if you had fully overcome it. Even if you have conquered all of your phobias, keep confronting previously fearful situations, just in case. If you give in to the fear, you know that your anxiety will grow.

- *You started to taper off or totally stopped taking medications.*

  If this occurs, go through the entire program again. Very recent findings (Brown and Barlow, in press; Fava et al., 1994; Fava et al., 1995; and Marks et al., 1993) demonstrate that clients do *less well* in the long term with cognitive-behavioral treatment if they take benzodiazepine medications *concurrently* with the treatment. It appears that when anxiety levels are lowered with those medications, learning is less complete. Furthermore, the client does not fully trust his or her own resources and believes that the medications make the difference—not the cognitive-behavioral treatment. Thus, if you have difficulty getting off medications, go through the entire program again. Also, working through the book a second time will be a lot easier, whether you are doing it because you were previously on medications or not.

Look at Setbacks as Opportunities for New Growth— to Discover More About Yourself.

What You Can Do to Help Reduce Setbacks

1. Incorporate your coping skills into your normal life. Keep doing diaphragmatic breathing. Never give it up. Become an expert at discovering unhelpful Automatic Thoughts.

2. When confronting future stresses, be alert! Find ways, whatever it takes, to make the stress manageable.

3. Be assertive: Stand up for yourself!

4. Seek the support of your coach or another loved one as you continue in your recovery.

5. Reward yourself when overcoming fears.

6. Expose yourself to the situation where you had your first panic or your first reoccurrence of panic. Do it as soon as possible to regain your ground.

7. Do interoceptive exercises occasionally, at home as well as in other places. Do them to remind yourself how *you* can produce these physical sensations at will and that they are harmless. Remember the crucial goal is to overcome the fear of panic-induced sensations.

8. Exercise regularly to aid biological "toughening up."

9. Find ways to get rid of any "safety signals" and "safety behaviors."

10. Do not rest on your laurels as far as phobias are concerned. Keep exposing yourself to achieve full mastery in previously avoided places. If you still have some agoraphobia, set weekly goals and meet them; keep "polishing" your sense of mastery over situations.

11. Seek support from self-help groups. Consider becoming a member of the Anxiety Disorders Association of America, an organization for professionals and lay people suffering from anxiety disorders. That way you can be part of a larger network of people nationwide. Learn all you can about panic disorder and agoraphobia. The methods I have shared in this book are not the last word. The field is changing all the time.

12. If needed, seek professional help.

16

Living in the Here and Now

We move hurriedly through each day, scattered and fragmented, our minds occupied with what *will* happen, what *has* happened, or we are in the present but our minds are in a place *elsewhere than here.* We judge events as good or bad, and we judge our feelings, thoughts, and actions likewise. We often take these judgments very seriously. We may never be where we actually are, but always a step away, always running, always judging something in ourselves or in others.

Let's use this final chapter to stretch your mind's vision beyond the apparent boundaries. Question: What is there beyond the "What ifs?" and the "Whys?" Answer: Beyond is the *right now and right here*, this precious moment where I can be myself and live fully in the present, in my circumstance, whatever this might be. Who is this "I," this being so filled with skills and abilities, with intelligence, and with mysteries? Whether I feel happy, sad, joyous, anxious, angry, or disappointed, can I tolerate being with myself? Can I fully accept myself, whatever I am feeling, whoever I am? Even if I act a little "crazy" once in a while, can I trust that that does not detract from my basic sanity?

Always running, running. How can I recognize the mood I'm in when I am constantly running away from myself and judging myself? It is so much easier to project away from myself and to say, "He made me mad," or "This terrible thing happened." Can I take full responsibility for how I react to the events in my life? Can I allow myself to feel the difficult, painful, or unhappy times that are part of life and use them to create new opportunities? Can they be opportunities to learn even more about myself and how I relate to the world? Can I ever learn to fully attend to the here and now, to fully appreciate my aliveness and share some joy and affection with others while I still have this life? The answer to all of these questions is, "Of course you can." One way to learn how to live in the here and now is to practice meditation. One particularly effective form of meditation is called "Mindfulness Meditation." At the 1995 conference of the Anxiety Disorders Association of America I had the opportunity to hear Dr. Jon Kabat-Zinn talk about Mindfulness Meditation, which reinforced and gave further impetus to the ideas in this chapter.

Mindfulness Meditation is not just another relaxation technique that you can apply at certain stressful times. It is not even a way of living but rather a way of *being.* It is a way of learning to open oneself up to the actuality of the moment, learning to be aware and "awake" from moment to moment. It requires making a commitment to effecting profound changes in one's relationship to oneself and the outside world. By fully *being* in the here and now, open to the actuality of the moment, we have unique opportunities for self-understanding. When we are fully in the present, it prevents fragmentation of our "selves."

Mindfulness Meditation involves a number of steps. One is that of "calming breath." The exercise involves staying completely with your (diaphragmatic) breathing. You practice staying with it by becoming one with your breathing. You pay attention to your diaphragm, feeling it expand when breathing in and contract when breathing out. You try not to think in words but just to feel the gentle rhythm. This helps to "anchor" your awareness in the present. It calms your body and clears your mind. When your mind wanders off, you gently bring it back to your breathing. When I took the workshop led by Mrs. Marlene Schmitt (from Wheeling, West Virginia) and did the exercise, it was easy for me. As you may recall from Chapter 8, I have been using this technique for years to fall asleep, so it was relatively easy to "become one with my breathing."

Many of my clients found the diaphragmatic breathing the most useful tool for helping them combat their anxiety and achieve tranquility. Diapragmatic breathing lays the foundation for meditation. Consider practicing meditation on a regular basis.

Use Your Calming Breath to Stay in the Here and Now.

Another meditation process explained in the workshop was how to observe and then let go of your thoughts: How not to become attached to them. The incessant anxious thoughts of panickers are draining. You may be such a person. You may also place your panic thoughts on a pedestal, and give them tremendous importance. Yet, you do not have to attach much importance to them. You can learn to observe these short-lived events, thoughts, that come and go, without taking the bait. That is, see them pass by without judging them or fearing them. Watching thoughts come and go across your mind-screen can weaken their threatening nature. You can learn to passively observe the rise and fall and continuous flow of your thoughts without becoming attached to them. You simply observe and let go.

Hard to believe? Nevertheless, imagine having thoughts which previously made you intensely anxious and not being affected by them. A participant in the workshop said, "But I can't stop my thoughts from scaring me!" Although this was her reality then, she had the power to change that reality. So do you. You can learn not to respond fearfully to your frightening thoughts but to respond indifferently or even with mild interest, "Oh there's that old thought again," but it will no longer have the power to frighten you. What a tremendous sense of empowerment you would gain if you could realize that your thoughts do not have to control you!

You Cannot Fully Control the Present or Predict the Future, But You Do Have the Power to Find Peace of Mind NOW.

Consider studying and practicing Mindfulness Meditation or some other form of meditation as an entirely different alternative for learning to overcome anxiety and panic. This new way of being would provide one of the best deterrents to relapse.

Recommended Reading

Kabat-Zinn, J. 1990. *Full Catastrophe Living: Using the Wisdom of Your Body and Mind to Face Stress, Pain, and Illness.* New York: Dell Publishing.

Kabat-Zinn, J. 1994. *Wherever You Go, There You Are: Mindfulness Meditation in Everyday Life.* New York: Hyperion.

References

American Psychiatric Association. 1994. *Diagnostic and Statistical Manual of Mental Disorders, Fourth Edition.* Washington, D.C.: American Psychiatric Association.

Barlow, D.H. 1992. "Cognitive-Behavioral Approaches to Panic Disorder and Social Phobia." *Bulletin of the Menninger Clinic* 56: A14–A28.

Barlow, D.H. 1990. "Long-Term Outcome for Patients with Panic Disorder Treated with Cognitive-Behavioral Therapy." *Journal of Clinical Psychiatry* 51 (12, Suppl. A): 17–23.

Barlow, D.H. 1988. *Anxiety and Its Disorders: The Nature and Treatment of Anxiety and Panic.* New York: The Guilford Press.

Barlow, D.H., and Craske, M.G. 1994. *Mastery of Your Anxiety and Panic II.* Albany, NY: Graywind Publications Inc.

Beck, A.T., and Emery, G., with Greenberg, R.L. 1985. *Anxiety Disorders and Phobias: A Cognitive Perspective.* New York: Basic Books.

Beckfield, D.F. 1994. *Master Your Panic and Take Back Your Life!* San Luis Obispo, CA: Impact Publishers.

Bourne, E.J. 1990. *The Anxiety and Phobia Workbook.* Oakland, CA: New Harbinger Publications.

Brown, T.A., and Barlow, D.H. "Long-Term Outcome in Cognitive-Behavioral Treatment of Panic Disorder: Clinical Predictors and Alternative Strategies for Assessment." *Journal of Consulting and Clinical Psychology.* In press.

Burns, D.D. 1989. *The Feeling Good Handbook.* New York: William Morrow & Co.

Butler, P.E. 1981. *Self-Assertion for Women.* San Francisco: Harper & Row Publishers.

Clark, D.M. "Anxiety States: Panic and Generalized Anxiety." (Pages 53–96.) In: *Cognitive Behaviour Therapy for Psychiatric Problems: A Practical Guide.* eds. Hawton, K., Salkovskis, P.M., Kirk, J., and Clark, D.M. New York: Oxford University Press.

Craske, M.G., and Barlow, D.H. 1994. *Agoraphobia Supplement to the Mastery of Your Anxiety and Panic II.* Albany, NY: Graywind Publications, Inc.

Craske, M.G., and Rodriguez, B.I. 1994. "Behavioral Treatment of Panic Disorders and Agoraphobia." *Progress in Behavior Modification*. 29: 1–26.

Davis, M., Robbins-Eshelman, E., and McKay, M. 1988. *The Relaxation & Stress Reduction Workbook*. Oakland, CA: New Harbinger Publications.

Dienstbier, R.A. 1991. "Acquiring Physiological Stress Resistance: The Toughness Model." Presented as an invited address to the International Congress on Stress, Anxiety, and Emotional Disorders at the Universidade do Minho in Braga, Portugal.

Dienstbier, R.A., 1989. "Arousal and Physiological Toughness: Implications for Mental and Physical Health." *Psychological Review*. 96: 84–100.

Epstein, S. 1994. "Integration of the Cognitive and the Psychodynamic Unconscious." *American Psychologist*. 49 (8): 709–724.

Epstein, S. 1993. *You're Smarter Than You Think*. New York: Simon & Schuster.

Fava, G.A., Grandi, S., Belluardo, P., Savron, G., Raffi, A.R., Conti, S., and Saviotti, F.M. 1994. "Benzodiazepines and Anxiety Sensitivity in Panic Disorder." *Progress in Neuro-Psychopharmacological and Biological Psychiatry*. 18: 1163–1168.

Fava, G.A., Zielezny, M., Savron, G., and Grandi, S. 1995. "Long-Term Effects of Behavioural Treatment for Panic Disorder with Agoraphobia." *British Journal of Psychiatry*. 166: 87–92.

Freeman, A., Pretzer, J., Fleming. B., and Simon, K.M. 1990. *Clinical Applications of Cognitive Therapy*. New York: Plenum Press.

Hoffman, D.L., O'Leary, D.P., and Munjack, D.J. 1994. "Autorotation Test Abnormalities of the Horizontal and Vertical Vestibulo-Ocular Reflexes in Panic Disorder." *Otolaryngology-Head and Neck Surgery*. 110: 259–269.

Kabat-Zinn, J. 1994. *Wherever You Go, There You Are: Mindfulness Meditation in Everyday Life*. New York: Hyperion.

Kabat-Zinn, J. 1990. *Full Catastrophe Living: Using the Wisdom of Your Body and Mind to Face Stress, Pain, and Illness*. New York: Dell Publishing.

Ley, R., 1988 "Panic Attacks During Sleep: A Hyperventilation-Probability Model." *Journal of Behavior Therapy and Experimental Psychiatry*. 19: 181–192.

Ley, R. 1985. "Blood, Breath, and Fears: A Hyperventilation Theory of Panic Attacks and Agoraphobia." *Clinical Psychology Review*. 5: 271–285.

Margraf, J., Barlow, D.H., Clark, D.M., and Telch, M.J. 1993. "Psychological Treatment of Panic: Work in Progress on Outcome, Active Ingredients, and Follow-Up." *Behavior Research and Therapy*. 31: 1–8.

Marks, I.M., Swinson, R.P., Basoglu, M., Kuch, K., Noshirvani, H., O'Sullivan, G., Lelliott, P.T., Kirby, M., McNamee, G., Sengun, S., and Wickwire, K. 1993. "Alprazolam and Exposure Alone and Combined in Panic Disorder with Agoraphobia: A Controlled Study in London and Toronto." *British Journal of Psychiatry*. 162: 776–787.

McKay, M., Davis, M., and Fanning, P. 1981. *Thoughts and Feelings: The Art of Cognitive Stress Intervention*. Oakland, CA: New Harbinger Publications.

McNally, R.J. 1994. *Panic Disorder: A Critical Analysis*. New York: The Guilford Press.

Ornstein, R., and Sobel, D.S. 1994. "Treatment: Calming Anxiety, Phobias and Panic." *Mental Medicine Update*. III (3): 3–6.

Persons, J.B. 1989. *Cognitive Therapy in Practice: A Case Formulation Approach*. New York: W.W. Norton and Company.

Rodriguez, B.I., and Craske, M.G. 1993. "The Effects of Distraction During Exposure to Phobic Stimuli." *Behavior Research and Therapy.* 31 (6): 549–558.

Ross, J. 1994. *Triumph Over Fear.* New York: Bantam Books.

Smith, M.J. 1975. *When I Say No, I Feel Guilty.* New York: Bantam Books.

Timmons, B.H., and Ley, R., Eds. 1994. *Behavioral and Psychological Approaches to Breathing Disorders.* New York: Plenum Publishing Corp.

Williams, S.L. 1990. "Guided Mastery Treatment of Agoraphobia: Beyond Stimulus Exposure." *Progress in Behavior Modification.* 26: 89–121.

Williams, S.L., and Zane, G. 1989. "Guided Mastery and Stimulus Exposure Treatments for Severe Performance Anxiety in Agoraphobics." *Behavior Research and Therapy.* 27 (3): 237–245.

Resources

A.I.M. (Agoraphobics in Motion)
1729 Crooks Street
Royal Oak, MI 48067
(313) 547-0400

American Psychiatric Association (APA)
1400 K Street, NW
Washington, D.C. 20005
(202) 682-6000

American Psychological Association (APA)
750 First Street, NE
Washington, D.C. 20002
(202) 336-5500

Anxiety Disorders Association of America (ADAA)
6000 Executive Blvd., Suite 513
Rockville, MD 20852-3801
(301) 231-9350

Anxiety Disorders Behavioral Program
Department of Psychology
(Michelle G. Craske, Ph.D.)
University of California, Los Angeles
405 Hilgard Ave.
Los Angeles, CA 90024-1563
(310) 206-9191

Anxiety Disorders Center
(C. Alec Pollard, Ph.D.)
St. Louis University Health Sciences Center
1221 S. Grand Blvd.
St. Louis, MO 63104-1094
(314) 577-8718

Association for the Advancement of Behavior Therapy (AABT)
15 West 36th Street
New York, NY 10018
(212) 279-7970

Center for Stress and Anxiety Disorders
(David H. Barlow, Ph.D.)
State University of New York at Albany
1535 Western Avenue
Albany, NY 12203
(518) 456-4127

Freedom From Fear
308 Seaview Avenue
Staten Island, NY 10305
(718) 351-1717

National Alliance for the Mentally Ill
2101 Wilson Blvd. Suite 302
Arlington, VA 22201
(800) 950-NAMI

National Anxiety Foundation
3135 Custer Drive
Lexington, KY 40517

National Institute of Mental Health (NIMH)
Information Resources and Inquiry Branch, Room 15C-05
5600 Fishers Lane
Rockville, MD 20857
(301) 443-4513
1-800-64-PANIC

National Mental Health Association
1021 Prince Street
Alexandria, VA 22314-2971
(703) 684-7722

Phobics Anonymous
P.O. Box 1180
Palm Springs, CA 92263
(619) 322-COPE

Recovery, Inc.
802 North Dearborn Street
Chicago, IL 60610
(312) 337-5661

Other New Harbinger Self-Help Titles